Pluriversal Politics

A BOOK IN THE SERIES
Latin America in Translation / En Traducción / Em Tradução

Sponsored by the Duke–University of North Carolina
Program in Latin American Studies

Pluriversal Politics

The Real and the Possible

Arturo Escobar

TRANSLATED BY DAVID FRYE

Duke University Press   Durham and London   2020

Designed by Drew Sisk
Typeset in Portrait Text by Copperline Book Services

Library of Congress Cataloging-in-Publication Data
Names: Escobar, Arturo, [date] author.
Title: Pluriversal politics : the real and the possible /
Arturo Escobar ; translated by David Frye.
Description: Durham : Duke University Press, 2020. | Series:
Latin America in translation | Includes bibliographical
references and index.
Identifiers: LCCN 2019032508 (print) | LCCN 2019032509 (ebook)
ISBN 9781478007937 (hardcover)
ISBN 9781478008460 (paperback)
ISBN 9781478012108 (ebook)
Subjects: LCSH: Latin America—Politics and government— 21st
century. | Political culture—Latin America. | Indigenous peoples
—LatinAmerica —Politicsandgovernment. Classification: LCC
F1414.3 .E8413 2020 (print) |
LCC F 1414.3 (ebook) | DDC 980.04/1—dc23
LC record available at https://lccn.loc.gov/2019032508
LC ebook record available at https://lccn.loc.gov/2019032509

Cover art: Angie Vanessita, *Derechos de la Naturaleza*,
digital image, 2015.

To all those groups engaged in the defense of the pluriverse, particularly to Native peoples worldwide for their historical cosmologies of intimacy with the Earth; to all the women who resist masculinist modes of living, for nurturing relational worlds of care in everyday life; to the Palestinian people, for their tenacious struggle against occupation and their determined resistance against colonialist one-worldism; and to the Earth itself—soil, plant, animal, water, air, spirit—in reverence and trust.

CONTENTS

Most of these essays were written in the manner of the Latin American style of *ensayo*. Ensayos reflect salient intellectual-political debates of the moment. This does not mean that they deal with fleeting or inconsequential matters. On the contrary, at acute conjunctures such as the past two decades, often characterized in terms of a turn to the left from 1998 to 2015, followed by a vengeful return to the right in recent years, the essay form provides avenues to infuse the debates of the moment with new energy, orientation, or contents. These debates might refer to long-standing preoccupations, such as Latin American identities; the questions of development and modernity; the continent's insertion into global divisions of labor; or that always recurring question in intellectual-political debates, namely, the relation between theory and practice, or praxis. The ensayos might also help bring to light emerging concepts, such as pluriversality, autonomy, communality, and civilizational transitions, the main notions with which this volume deals. Essays of this sort are often free-flowing and as such are exempted from following rigorous academic convention, even if they might be implicitly or explicitly infused with scholarly considerations, as is the case with the chapters that follow. By presenting these texts to an academic audience in the English-speaking world, I ask readers to exercise a measure of epistemic pluralism.[1]

Taken as a whole, the essays convey the following proposition: that realities are plural and always in the making, and that this has profound political consequences. The very concept of world, as in the World Social Forum slogan "Another world is possible," has become more radically pluralized, none the less by social movements mobilizing against large-scale extractive operations in defense of their territories as veritable worlds where life is lived according to principles that differ significantly from those of the global juggernaut unleashed on them. If worlds are multiple, then the possible must also be multiple. This insight crystallized for me one day with the phrase that served as the title for the Spanish edition of this book, *another possible is possible*. Simply put, as I state in the introduction, another world is possible because another real and another possible are possible. That other world is a world where many worlds fit, or the pluriverse. By breaking with conventional premises of the real and the possible, the essays locate politics at this very level.

More than proscriptive, predictive, normative, or even diagnostic, the texts that follow are meant to provide a political horizon in the sense of offering tools for thinking about what to do in the face of the multipronged planetary crisis. They are meant to open paths for personal and collective action in this conjuncture. At the same time, it is important to clarify that the suggested paths are not the only conceivable ones regarding the ongoing devastation, seemingly without end in sight, brought about by predatory global capitalism and its generalized mode of expulsion (Sassen 2014). I specify the contours of such a political horizon only broadly, in terms of a set of axes and principles for personal and collective action (listed at the end of chapter 1), which are far from being a road map to follow. Even more, here and there I insist that each person, group, or community has to find its own way to engage with these axes, such as the relocalization of activities, the recommunalization of social life, and the depatriarchalization and decolonization of existence, in ways appropriate to their own location.

While the volume is indeed a collection of essays, it is also more than that. Its productivity should not be gauged primarily in terms of a more or less cogent theoretical framing, to be developed and expounded throughout the various chapters, as would be the case with a standard academic or modernist text (even if some theoretical coherence is present, especially in relation to the field of political ontology). Rather, the book should be assessed by the extent to which it succeeds in opening up the collective imagination to the idea that a certain kind of politics, an ontological politics toward the pluriverse, is indeed gaining ground in many world settings today. Its value and objective, then, are more prefigurative or annunciatory, if you wish. As the anthropologist Charles Hale put it, the book's main function "is not to analyze compelling problems, develop new theory, or offer a proscriptive program for what is to be done, but rather, to convince the reader to open his or her mind/emotion ontologically, to soak in the energy of so many others in distinct realms who have done so, and especially, to take inspiration from those who are putting those alternatives into practice."[2] Even if I am talking about a proposal to rethink politics for and from Latin America, grounded at its margins, the call *to imagine possibility differently* should resonate with all those who question the hegemonic possible, within which a world of many worlds is impossible. By reflecting on the tools and concepts being developed by social movements and activist-intellectuals south of the border, I hope to suggest other ways to think about the possible and the real and to resist the hegemonic operation positing one world, one real, and one possible, while making visible the myriad instances that this operation considers "nothing" or "impossible."

Multiple Reals and Possibles as a Description
of the Current Conjuncture

I am interested, in the spirit of cultural studies, in telling a better story in relation to the current conjuncture. As Stuart Hall and Lawrence Grossberg, the most adept practitioners of conjuncturalism, say, the articulation of the conjuncture requires a certain level of abstraction, aimed at making visible sites for effective political intervention. Such analyses are necessarily situated and contested, which explains why past conjunctural analyses, whether in the Marxist or non-Marxist traditions, have often been found to be wrong, flawed, or insufficient. The level of abstraction has to navigate between identifying the salient features of the moment (e.g., environmental crisis, skyrocketing inequality, heightened racism and xenophobia), on the one hand, and their relation to the *longue durée* of the epoch (e.g., heteropatriarchy, capitalism, coloniality, modernity, racism, Western civilization, or what have you), on the other. Given the complexity, contingency, and instability of any social context, the task is daunting. I do not pretend to have done any better in the pages that follow, beyond pointing at a set of concepts, arising from a number of social movements, on the one hand, and from academic trends around what has been called the ontological turn, on the other, that help us better to understand today's context. Grossberg refers to this feature of cultural analysis as "radical contextuality" (Grossberg, 2010, 2018, 2019).

The larger context for the essays is what in the tradition of Gramsci and Hall is called an organic crisis, a relatively rare occurrence. I refer to it as planetary crisis, civilizational crisis, or a crisis of climate, energy, poverty and inequality, and meaning. By adding meaning, I want to direct our attention to aspects of the crisis that have to deal with a host of formerly unaccented aspects, including ways of being, knowing, and doing (ontology); spirituality; identities; and culture, emotions, and desires. Conjunctural analysis would investigate the particular forces and sites of tension, antagonism, and contradictions at which this type of crisis manifests itself, and how they are, and might be, variously articulated by diverse political forces, whether of the Right, the Left, or emergent ones. It would also illuminate the spaces within which a counterhegemonic struggle might emerge. The most accomplished climate justice activists, such as Vandana Shiva, Naomi Klein, Patrick Bond, Nnimmo Bassey, and Joan Martínez-Alier, couch the climate crisis in similar ways, perhaps best exemplified by Klein's motto (2014) "This changes everything." In doing so, they articulate climate change as a crisis of global capitalism. Sometimes I extend Klein's title to imply that "everything needs to change," echoing a parallel, but somewhat distinct, collective effort at rearticulating global warming not only as a capitalist crisis but also as a crisis within modernity, that is, as related to a particular ontology or mode of being in the world.

I hope to have shown that, faced with a genuine crisis of our modes of existence in the world, we can credibly constitute the conjuncture as a struggle over a new reality, what might be called the pluriverse, and over the designs for the pluriverse (Escobar 2018). I situate my reading of the conjuncture within a set of dominant diagrams that go beyond capitalism and that in the parlance of Latin American critical theory today are referred to as the heteropatriarchal capitalist modern/colonial world system. This system structures our historical ontology as modern subjects. My main source of inspiration comes from activists of social movements who can be construed as problematizing such ontology as they mobilize in defense of their territories, worlds, and modes of existing. I draw chiefly from some Afro-Colombian and indigenous movements from the Colombian southwest. Their statements, and those by activists from similar movements, constitute the main archive of this volume's essays.

As in previous works, however (e.g., Escobar 2008, 2014b, 2018), I set this archive in conversation with academic trends focused on similar questions. I also show the limitations of contemporary social theory to advance our understanding of the crisis as a crisis of a particular civilizational model, coupled with recent attempts at moving beyond this impasse. The latter is the epistemic dimension of the argument, treated at some length in several of the chapters (e.g., chapters 3, 4, 5). Shifting the episteme of the modern social sciences, which I argue is deeply indebted to ontological dualisms, toward a post-Enlightenment configuration of knowledge forms should be one of the goals of academic cultural politics on a pluriversal register. Finally, I discuss how the active critical stance by movement activists summons us, personally and collectively, into a politics and ethics of interdependence and care as the paths for ushering in worlds and knowledges otherwise less shaped by axes of domination.

Some Tensions and Open Questions

In thinking about providing a context for English-speaking readers, I decided to focus on the relevance of pluriversal politics in Latin America from two vantage points: its relation to more established and well-known forms of politics, and the possibility of such politics taking place beyond Latin America, particularly in the United States.[3] I will explore these questions by thinking about the tensions between what, as a shorthand, I will call modernist and ontological politics, or universal and pluriversal politics. I should make clear from the outset that I side decidedly with the kinds of politics that defend a deeply relational understanding of life, particularly through the reweaving of the communal basis of social life, as opposed to the objectifying understanding of life, prevalent in patriarchal capitalist modern settings, as made up of separate, albeit interacting, entities and actions. While the former nondualist ontologies are at times resistant to heteropatriarchal and racist colonial capitalism, the latter have gone along, historically, with systems of domination based on hierarchy, control, violence, and war (e.g., Escobar 2018; Maturana and Verden-Zöller 1993, 2008; Segato 2016; von Werlhof 2011, 2015). In Latin America, the dominant strategies of doing away with, or at least neutralizing, difference (despite their violence) have not done away with the multiplicity of ways of worlding. This multiplicity finds expression today in the inability of established modern categories to define fully what is at stake in social struggles and conflicts. This is why the reemergence of multiple worlds in Latin America and the Caribbean makes the region a particularly fertile ground for articulating and advancing pluriversal proposals in both scholarly and activist worlds.

Let me introduce the notion of radical relationality. It refers to the fact that all entities that make up the world are so deeply interrelated that they have no intrinsic, separate existence by themselves. Modern epistemology grants entities a separate existence, thanks to the foundational premises of the separation between subject and object, mind and body, nature and humanity, reason and emotion, facts and values, us and them, and so forth. Ontological politics destabilize these dualisms. In both activist and scholarly domains, the challenge to the modernist separation between humans and nonhumans occupies an especially relevant place. The field of political ontology actually focuses on the analysis of environmental conflicts as ontological conflicts involving contrasting configurations of the human/nonhuman relation. As Marisol de la Cadena (2015) and Mario Blaser (2010, 2013; de la Cadena and Blaser 2018) have shown, much in indigenous worlds does not abide by the divide between humans and nonhumans, even if the divide is also present in many of their practices. The question thus arises of how to understand worlds that clearly live partly outside the separation between nature and humanity but also live with it, ignore it, are affected by it, use it strategically, and reject it—all at the same time. That they thus defend mountains or lakes against large-scale mining on the basis that they are "sentient beings" or "sacred entities" (our modern translation) calls for an ontological perspective that avoids translating them into "beliefs" concerning mere objects or independently existing things (see chapter 1; Escobar 2018).

For ease of exposition, allow me to distinguish between ontological politics proper, namely, those forms of politics that explicitly or implicitly draw on radical relationality, and modernist politics, which take for granted the ontology of separation. I should stress, however, that strictly speaking all forms of politics are ontological in that they all involve an ontological dimension: they have implications for what counts as real, for modes of existence, and for adjudicating ethical or nonethical action.[4] All forms of politics are relational, yet differently so. I sometimes use a heuristic to distinguish between "weak relationality" and "strong relationality." In the former, characteristic of modernist politics, entities are first assumed to be ontologically separate; then they are reunited through some sort of connection, such as a "network," but even when this is done, it is clear that the entities, now found to be related, preexist the connection. More importantly, modernist forms of politics stem from ontologies that are deeply embedded in the negation of the full humanity of multiple others and the nonhuman, and this has to be taken seriously into account when considering them as strategies for action. In radical ontological politics, by contrast, there are no intrinsically existing entities to be found, since nothing preexists the relations that constitute it; in other words, reality is relational through and through. Throughout the book, the reader will find ample instances of such nondualist ontologies and their corresponding pluriversal forms of politics.

I would like here first to examine the relations between pluriversal politics, on the one hand, and modernist forms of politics intended to effect progressive social change, on the other; following from that is a second issue, that of the relation between pluriversal politics and the Left. Together, these two issues raise a key question: do moderns have a role in ontological politics toward the pluriverse, on their own or alongside those explicitly advancing such politics? A third persistent question concerns the viability of ontological politics in actually existing communities. How prevalent and effective is this sort of relational and pluriversal politics, especially when compared with more established political strategies? Hereafter, I rehearse two contrasting answers to these questions. While the first set envisions the possibility of effective bridges between the various kinds of politics, the second, largely drawn from a trend in African American radical thought known as Afro-pessimism, is skeptical of such a possibility. My hope is that my comments will help readers to articulate their own sense of the relation between pluriversal and modernist politics.

On the Possibility of Articulating Ontological and Modernist Forms of Politics

Can modernist politics contribute to fostering a pluriversal politics? This seems to be a key issue related to ontological politics, and it takes several forms, all of them important. Can modernist forms of politics aimed at fostering radical social change (say, in relation to heteropatriarchy, white supremacy, and capitalism) be effective in resisting social injustices, potentially in tandem with pluriversal forms of politics? Or are they necessarily at odds? Do not the very people engaging in pluriversal ontological politics, such as those defending communal and autonomous worlds, also participate in modernist politics, for example, vis-à-vis the state? Can we moderns play a role in the politics of the pluriverse? While I do provide some partial answers to these questions in this volume, and in other recent books (2014b, 2018), given their recurrence, I would like to offer some brief additional comments. I do not think there is a way to settle this dispute once and for all; it will remain an open question.

Ontological Politics as Pluriversal Politics

Let me start with a straightforward statement: I believe multiple ways exist for those of us who operate on the basis of modernist politics to contribute to pluriversal politics even if not embracing ontological politics explicitly—for instance, modernist struggles for economic democratization, for depatriarchalization and the end of racism and homophobia, for environmental justice, and academic critiques. A substantial amount of resistance to injustices and inequities fits the bill. That said, it is also important to recognize that many modernist forms of politics are counterproductive in relation to pluriversal politics; they reproduce and strengthen, rather than undermine, the modernist ontology of separation from which they stem. This is especially the case with liberal forms.

Adapting a broad typology of forms of politics drawn from the field of international development (explained in chapter 6), I would propose a three-layered characterization to sort out and evaluate the field of political strategies.

The first layer comprises political strategies and designs conducted *in the name of progress and the improvement of people's conditions*; these are the standard biopolitical liberal forms of design and politics, such as those by most neoliberal governments, the World Bank, and mainstream NGOs. They take for granted the dominant world (in terms of markets, individual actions, productivity, competitiveness, the need for economic growth, etc.); taken as a whole, they can only reinforce the universals of modernity and their accompanying capitalist institutions with their strategies of domination, control, violence, and war; they are inimical to pluriversal politics.

The second layer comprises political strategies and designs *for social justice*: this is the kind of politics practiced with the intention of fostering greater social justice and environmental sustainability; it embraces human rights (including gender, sexual, and ethnic diversity), environmental justice, the reduction of inequality, direct alliances with social movements, and so forth. Some progressive development NGOs, such as Oxfam, and a number of social movements, might serve as a paradigm for this second trajectory. In principle, these forms of politics may contribute to pluriversal politics, especially if they are pushed toward the third trajectory.

The third option would be pluriversal politics proper, or political strategies and designs *for pluriversal transitions*. Those practicing this option would engage in ontological politics from the perspective of radical interdependence. In doing so, they would go beyond the binary of modernist and pluriversal politics, engaging all forms of politics in the same, though diverse, movement for civilizational transitions through meshworks of autonomous collectives and communities from both the Global North and the Global South.[5] No readily available models exist for this third kind of politics, although it is the subject of active experimentation by many social struggles at present. How these kinds of politics might initiate rhizomatic expansions from below, effectively relativizing modernity's universal ontology and the imaginary of one world that it actively produces, is an open question in contemporary social theory and activist debates.

Let me underscore that many activists and groups move in and out of the three types of politics just outlined. Even highly politicized social movements, such as those by ethnic, peasant, and urban marginal groups, engage in actions and critiques that can easily be qualified as modernist—for instance, in their critiques of inequality, corruption, and dispossession in the name of rights, culture, access to land and public services, and so forth. Readers will recognize such instances in the statements by some of the Afro-descendant and indigenous actors featured in the various chapters. In this way, their practice could be described as modernist, Left, and pluriversal at the same time. At their best, they engage in the interplay of politics from the perspective of their autonomy and through collective decision-making processes. I do not want to suggest, however, that all resistance by these groups is explicitly ontological or pluriversal.

Those committed to one or another form of leftist politics and alternative modernity can usefully consider the following questions, among others: What habitual forms of knowing, being, and doing does a given strategy contribute to challenge, destabilize, or transform? For instance, does the strategy or practice in question help us in the journey of deindividualization and toward recommunalization? Does it contribute to bringing about more local forms of economy that might, in turn, provide elements for designing the infrastructures needed for a responsible ethics of interexistence and the deep acceptance of radical difference? Does it make us more responsive to the notions of multiple reals and a world where many worlds fit? Does this shift encourage us to entertain other notions of the possible, significantly different from those on offer by capitalism, the state, the media, and most expert institutions? To what extent do our efforts to depatriarchalize and decolonize society move along the lines of liberating the Earth and weaving the pluriverse effectively with others, human and not?

The fact is that we all live within the Earth as pluriverse; we weave the pluriverse together with every existing being through our daily practices. We are all summoned to the task of repairing the Earth and the pluriverse, one stitch at a time, one design at a time, one loop at a time, so to speak (Escobar 2018). Some of our stitches and loops will likely contribute to the web of relations that sustain life, others less so or not at all. Our collective weaving of *a place*, including a form of habitation, is a major part of it. We are summoned by place into entanglements with each other and with nonhumans, whether in conflict or cooperation or both, as all of us, willy-nilly, live in coexistence with multiple others through intricate relations that define our very way of being, even if most often we imagine those relations as weak links from which we can easily disassociate ourselves. As the geographers Soren Larsen and Jay Johnson (2017) put it in their work on the contested nature of places and landscapes in which Native and non-Native peoples coexist, this confers on place a political and spiritual dimension, which I believe can and needs to be struggled over in urban territories as well (Escobar 2019).

This agency of place and the pluriverse—that they call us into coexistence with others—suggests that pluriversal politics itself involves an entanglement of forms, inhabiting a spectrum from the radically relational to the modernist liberal, and that we are all, ineluctably, part of it. Seen this way, the seemingly firm boundaries between the Global North and the Global South, and between what might be considered modern or not, weaken significantly and, eventually, begin to dissolve. Succinctly put, the struggle to reinhabit the pluriverse is everyone's. As we will learn from the Nasa indigenous movement in Colombia (chapter 3), we are all thrust into the liberation of Mother Earth from whichever place and position we happen to occupy, for as long as Earth is enslaved, as the Nasa argue, so are all living beings.

Pluriversal Politics and the Left

A second important question is that of the relation between ontological politics and the Left. The election of Hugo Chávez as president of Venezuela in December 1998 inaugurated a period of progressive governments in the continent that lasted until about 2015, when a turn to the right again manifested in Argentina, Brazil, and Chile, among others. According to the United Nations, the progressive governments accomplished noticeable reductions in poverty and modest reductions in inequality. However, their policies were based on utterly conventional development strategies, modernizing to their core, organized around the extraction of natural resources. For some observers, despite the reported accomplishments, these experiences demonstrated the limitations of achieving significant transformations within any modernizing Left framework (see Escobar 2010 for a review).

It might be the case, however, that taken as a whole, modernist-leftist policies create less inimical conditions for pluriversal politics than neoliberal right-wing regimes, which, in Latin America at least, are often bent on brutally crushing any form of dissent and resistance. Mexico and Colombia are, sadly, notorious cases in this regard. Pluriversal and leftist politics could be mutually enabling, though this convergence cannot be taken for granted, as exemplified by the repression of environmentalist and indigenous organizations in Ecuador and Bolivia under their respective Left governments. It is also the case that in their practice many social movements blur the boundaries between counterhegemonic and ontological politics. Drawing on Audre Lorde's (1984) well-known provocation ("The master's tools will never dismantle the master's house"), one might say that counterhegemonic politics use the master's tools to push radical demands forward, to the system's breaking point, if possible. This might involve modernist practices such as claiming rights, using legal instruments (such as the Indigenous and Tribal Peoples Convention, ILO 169, which has been used adroitly by indigenous peoples and ethnic minorities, albeit with mixed results), negotiating political rights with the state, and so on. Strategies of this sort make counterhegemonic use of hegemonic tools with varying degrees of effectiveness (Santos 2007).[6]

For these strategies to move along the lines of pluriversal politics, nevertheless, they must take on an explicitly political ontological character. In the spirit of Lorde's revolutionary imperative, this would imply, as maintained by some black and Latina/o scholars, broadening the parameters of change so as to articulate their anticapitalistic and antiracist stance with languages and strategies that push beyond the dominant ontologies. From this perspective, it should be clear that principles of struggle such as autonomy, territory, communality, and care cannot easily be accommodated within actually existing Left discourses; while much can be done to advance these causes through counter-hegemonic strategies, they also require an explicit ontological framing that advances the principles of interdependence and relationality.[7]

Pluriversal Politics in Actually Existing Communities

I deal in passing in these essays with the criticisms about the plausibility of pluriversal politics, particularly as compared with better-known Left strategies. These critiques are addressed to perspectives that are perceived as too localist and not infrequently take the form of charges of romanticism (see, e.g., Gibson-Graham 2002, for a countercritique). Emotions run high in these exchanges. I will not rehearse my responses here (see chapter 1; Escobar 2014a, 2018), but I would like to add some elements from the perspective of the previous discussion. Let me start by rearticulating the question, or rather questions: Is pluriversal politics a workable horizon for action? Is the construction of autonomous spaces from below sufficient to even make a dent in the global capitalist system of domination? We speak about recommunalization as essential to pluriversal politics, but are not communal logics central to the subordination of women and youth? Do the struggles in question really embody other principles of being, knowing, and doing, as ontological politics claims? Or, on the contrary, are they not mired in internal conflict and contradiction, thus too vulnerable to external threats and repression to have a chance of success? Are they not often reinscribed into modernist frameworks by their all-too-powerful adversaries, particularly the intolerant heteropatriarchal and economistic norms of capital and the state? Are not the territories of difference and the ZADs (*zones à défendre*, or zones to defend) liable to being reoccupied materially and ontologically by the powers that be?[8]

At the heart of these questions are the criteria for assessing the effectivity of diverse forms of politics and resistance. Thinking in terms of articulations, alliances, convergences, bridge building among systemic alternatives, and rhizomic and meshwork processes of connection among antisystemic movements is but a starting point. Positing the possibility of articulations among transformative alternatives, however, is essential for conveying the idea that, at times at least, they might be able to make a dent in the structures of devastation and oppression. This kind of thinking—along with a critical reassessment of well-known notions of rescaling, the nature of structural change, global/local binaries, and so forth—is crucial so that antisystemic alternatives are not dismissed as unviable, ineffective, place-specific, small, unrealistic, or noncredible alternatives to what exist. Ideas and movements aiming toward the convergence of alternatives endeavor to drive this point across.

The geographers Gibson-Graham have exposed the capitalocentric and globalocentric nature of a great deal of the critique of place-based alternatives. Most of these critics, whether Marxists or poststructuralists, they suggest, "do not see *themselves* as powerfully constituted by globalization. The realists see *the world* as taken over by global capitalism, the new Empire. The deconstructionists see *a dominant discourse* of globalization that is setting the political and policy agenda. In different ways, they both stand outside globalization, and see it 'as it is'—yet the power of globalization seems to have colonized their political imaginations" (2002, 34, 35). As I explain in chapter 1, this modernist and masculinist political thinking, which ineluctably disempowers the local and place based by locating the decisive power to change things in the global, depends on the ontological assumption of the existence of a one-world world, one real, and one possible. I am not saying that all those who adhere to modernist leftist politics fall into this globalocentric trap; very often, they also endorse progressive politics of place. I am suggesting, however, that the very question of the political effectiveness of a given movement or strategy is laden with discursive operations and emotional attachments that need to be made explicit as part of the process of making up our minds about it.

Moving toward the realization of multiple reals/possibles is the best antidote against globalocentric thinking; it enables us to consider the power of the place based and of local becoming in new forms, perhaps envisioning what Gibson-Graham imaginatively called a homeopathic politics, that of healing multiple locals through communal economies and logics connecting with each other into diffuse, constitutive, and sustaining forms of translocal meshworked power. Telling this story is perhaps not as thrilling as recounting the saga of the great capitalist machine and its potential overthrow, but it is one to which more and more groups seem committed. As Gibson-Graham put it, "The judgment that size and extensiveness are coincident with power is not simply a rational calculation in our view but also a discursive choice and emotional commitment. . . . Communities can be constituted around difference, across places, with openness to others as a central ethics. . . . New forms of community are to be constructed through cultivating the communal capacities of individuals and groups and, even more importantly, cultivating the self as a communal subject" (2002, 51, 52). In the last instance, it is a matter of cultivating ourselves as theorists and practitioners of multiple possibles, even as we alternate between diverse types of strategy. What practices of resubjectivation are needed for actively and effectively desiring nonpatriarchal, noncapitalist, and deeply relational modes of being, knowing, and doing? In other words, we need to disidentify ourselves actively with capitalism, masculinism, colonial, and racist practices and with the ontologies of separation that are an integral part of most, if not all, forms of oppression in the world today.

One might call this disidentification, following the Mexican feminist sociologist Raquel Gutiérrez Aguilar (2017), a *politics in the feminine*: one centered on the reproduction of life as a whole, along the care–conservation axis, in tandem with the social reappropriation of collectively produced goods (post-capitalism), and beyond the masculinist canons of the political linked to capital accumulation and the state. Or one might speak of it, with the Argentinean anthropologist Rita Segato (2016), as a politics that ends the "minoritization" of women that has accompanied the decommunalization (radical individuation) of modern worlds, in favor of a recommunalizing autonomous politics that reclaims the "ontological fullness" of women's worlds. For Segato, patriarchal masculinist ontologies, with their foundational binary matrix, not only represent "the first and permanent pedagogy of expropriation of value and its subsequent domination" (2016, 16) but continue to be at the basis of most forms of violence and predatory accumulation. They can only result in a "pedagogy of cruelty" functional to the deepening of dispossession. This ontological mandate has to be dismantled by building on the relational and communal practices that still inhabit, albeit in fragmentary and contradictory ways, many Afro-Latin American, indigenous, peasant, and urban marginal worlds. Let us listen to Segato's conclusion before broaching the notion of a radical rupture from the metaphysical structure of modernity (2016, 106):

> We need to remake our ways of living, to reconstruct the strong links existing in communities with the help of the "technologies of sociability" commanded by women in their domains; these locally rooted practices are embedded in the dense symbolic fabric of an alternative cosmos, dysfunctional to capital, and proper of the *pueblos* (peoples) in their political journey that have allowed them to survive throughout five hundred years of continued conquest. We need to advance this politics day by day, outside the state: to reweave the communal fabric as to restore the political character of domesticity proper of the communal. . . . *To choose the relational path is to opt for the historical project of being community.* . . . It means to endow relationality and the communal forms of happiness with a grammar of value and resistance capable of counteracting the powerful developmentalist, exploitative, and productivist rhetoric of things with its al-

leged meritocracy. *La estrategia a partir de ahora es femenina* [the strategy, from now on, is a feminine one] (my emphasis).

This is a feminist and radical relational politics I fully endorse.

On the Need for a Radical Rupture and Its Political Implications

We need to consider another position as we try to make up our minds about the strategies into which we might want to put our best energies and ideas. It can be stated in a number of forms. What do we do if we arrive at the conclusion that everything that surrounds us—institutions, governments, religions, academies, even the innermost aspects of our beings—has been so thoroughly colonized by modernity as to make any counterhegemonic use of modernist tools practically inoperative and counterproductive? If, confronted with the history of horrors visited on the pluriverse by the heteropatriarchal capitalist colonial/racist world system, one realizes that not much, perhaps nothing, of what the modern/colonial world has to offer is of value for the urgent task of reconstruction, repair, and resurgence of all, and particularly subaltern, worlds? Would these growing realizations—seriously entertained by some, albeit perhaps not too many, critics, in different parts of the world—not lead us to conclude that the time for a radical rupture and departure from those dominant worlds has arrived? This would seem to me a perfectly valid inference, even if it might make the question of praxis even more intractable. And it is the conclusion arrived at by a number of African American writers.

Before we go there, let me return to Bob Marley.[9] Let us listen to the following powerful statement on ontological politics from his 1979 song "Babylon System," which Marley sings in the perfect rhythm of Jamaican reggae:[10]

> We refuse to be
> What you wanted us to be
> We are what we are
> That's the way it's going to be.

One could find many layers of meaning in just this statement; it is indeed about identity, but not only; it is an unambiguous refusal of the ontological imperative to be in a particular way, a way that for black peoples all over the world involves at the least widespread misrecognition, oftentimes outright denial of their being, and not infrequently lethal forms of nonrelation, as in repeated police killings and mass incarceration. One can also read in these lyrics a call to everybody, black and nonblack, to refuse to be what "they" want us to be—*they* being the Babylon system, in Marley variously a synonym for Western civilization, capitalism, intractable racism, and unbridled globalization: "Babylon system is the vampire, yea! / Suckin' the children day by day, yeah! / Me say de Babylon system is the vampire, falling empire / Suckin' the blood of the sufferers, yeah!" It would not be far-fetched to suggest that it is also about whether one—we all—can join in the singing and feel a profound identification with those in dire need of disidentifying with "de system" as a matter of survival. For have all of us not, too, been "trodding in the winepress much too long"? Are we not part of the system he decries and condemns: "Building church and university, wooh, yeah! / Deceiving the people continually, yeah! / Me say them graduatin' thieves and murderers / Look out now they suckin' the blood of the sufferers, Yea! . . . Rebel, rebel!" Can we not be, too, part of the active forces compelled to "tell the children the truth," part of this truth being that "You can't educate I / For no equal opportunity / Talkin' 'bout my freedom / People freedom and liberty!"?

The Jamaican political theorist Anthony Bogues (2003) has written about Bob Marley in his book about black heretics and prophets as exemplary radical intellectuals who, operating in the interstices of modernity, have drawn not so much on the privileged critical resources offered by modern critical theory as on the "dread history" excavated from the practices of Caribbean subaltern resistance and worldviews (181). Such history contains "a profound radical ontological claim" that is critical, utopian, and redemptive. It constitutes grounds for a project of "becoming human, not white nor imitative of the colonial, but overturning white/European normativity" (13), precisely as in Marley's refusal to be "what you wanted us to be." For Bogues, heretics and prophets of this sort perform a crucial symbolic displacement; drawing on the Jamaican philosopher Sylvia Wynter, he argues that they contribute to "the creation of counterworld ideologies in the context where the black is a *nothing*" (176).[11] Needless to say, race is central to this politics, as Marley also reminds us: "Until the philosophy which holds one race superior and another inferior is finally and permanently discredited and abandoned, everywhere is war, me say war."[12]

The notion of the black person as nothing underlies the "metaphysical infrastructure" of Western modernity, as the influential black intellectual Nahum Chandler aptly calls it (2014). It discloses the impossibility for the black person of achieving ontological fullness as a human within any dominant onto-epistemic social and political order. It is inherent in the very declaration that "black lives matter." A common starting point is the virulent and seemingly endless violence against black peoples in general and young black males in particular. The writer Jesmyn Ward (2013) courageously describes the cultural and existential impact of such violence in a recent memoir, vividly speaking about the subsumed rage and accumulated grief caused by seeing so many close relatives and friends face violent deaths. How to speak about such a history of unending loss, she asks, a history that seemingly extends to any foreseeable future, so as to "write the narrative that remembers, write the narrative that says: *Hello. We are here. Listen*"? Not easy, she says (251).

Not easy for scholars, either, though the debates are intense and eloquent in ways I can hardly do any justice in a few paragraphs. "Theory of blackness is theory of the surreal presence," writes Fred Moten (2018, ix) concerning the regime of "epidermalization, criminalization, and genocidal regulation" underlying the stolen lives that accompany blackness, in the face of which only a reconstructive flight from imposition seems to make sense. The entire edifice of modern thought is involved in this predicament, as the Brazilian feminist scholar Denise Ferreira da Silva (2007) has argued in one of the most incisive treatments of the long-standing philosophical background of antiblackness. In her view, the deployment of racial difference anchors an onto-epistemic regime that for centuries until today's global times has prompted a kind of social subjection in which the most allegedly rational institutions of society, such as the law and the economy, provide the very tools of obliteration. This onto-epistemic context called globality, she argues, needs to be understood in these terms so as to undermine it.

Working within the archives of the Western critique of metaphysics, Calvin Warren (2018) develops this proposition, arriving at a political ontology of antiblackness as the most enduring constant in Western cultural history. For Warren, the prison-industrial complex as a form of reenslavement and the repeated police murdering of blacks should serve as testimony to the enduring force of this ontology at the social level. His argument, however, is primarily philosophical. From his perspective, all solutions on offer—whether couched in terms of black humanism, as in social and legal policies targeting antiblackness; or postmetaphysics, as in hermeneutic strategies proposing antiracist understandings of the human to contest racialized notions of being—are found wanting, if not counterproductive. The reason is that all these approaches overlook the fact that the black person fulfills the position of "nothing" in a world structured and ruled by metaphysical assumptions embedded in binary thinking, naturalized universals, liberal humanism, social rationalization, economism, and entrenched ideas of order, freedom, agency, and so forth. Only a politics of "improvement" is thinkable and practicable within this ontological order, and that will not suffice to redress the "metaphysical holocaust" (13) enacted by antiblackness as a systematic "accretion of practices, knowledge systems, and institutions *designed* to impose nothing onto blackness and the unending domination/eradication of black presence *as nothing incarnated*" (9; my emphasis).

For Warren, the corollary of this pervasive antiblackness is a kind of ontological terror that operates very differently for blacks (a perpetual falling, the source of violence and domination) than for whites (confronting the terror of the nothing that is blackness, and of the potential coming to an end of that nothing that, even if it were imaginable, could only be fathomed as a total upheaval of the existing metaphysical world, hence terror). From here follows a responsible black nihilism, with momentous implications:

> Part of the aim, then, is to dethrone the human from its metaphysical pedestal, reject the human, and explore different ways of existing that are not predicated on Being and its humanism. This is the *only* way black thinking can grapple with existence without Being. . . . Perhaps what I am suggesting is an *ontological revolution*, one that will destroy the world and its institutions (i.e., "the end of the world," as Fanon calls it). But these are our options, since the metaphysical holocaust will continue as long as the world *exists*. The nihilist revelation, however, is that such a revolution will destroy *all* life—far from the freedom dreams of the political idealists or the sobriety of the pragmatists. (23, 171)

The dire conclusion of an irredeemable antiblack world, from which no significant form of genuine coexistence can ever arise, has a redeeming end, for the abyss it sketches may lead into "something exceeding and preceding the metaphysical world" (171), namely, the spirit. It is thus that "black nihilism must rest in the crevice between the impossibility of transforming the world and the dynamic enduring power of spirit" (171).[13]

I find Warren's formulation compelling for the most part. His accomplished nihilism could be seen as a counterpoint to the notion of a responsible anthropocentrism posited by posthumanism and many transition narratives. I can see its major premises applying to Afro-Latin America, with the pertinent qualifications. There, too, a pervasive structure of antiblackness hangs over social life as a great onto-epistemic unconscious, along with anti-indigeneity. Looking at the black kids striving to clean the windows of passing cars at the main intersections in Cali, Colombia, or attempting to sell fruit or distribute a newspaper, most frequently encountering a deeply naturalized disrespect as a response, a dehumanizing gaze over which they have no control, one would have to conclude that an antiblack structure is inextricably entwined with the entire fabric of Latin American Euro-modernity. As another instantiation of antiblackness, I could cite what the brilliant Afro-Colombian activist Carlos Rosero once told me, explaining why his movement does not fight for inclusion: "Neither do we want to become citizens, since to do so would amount to returning to the times of slavery." As he put it elsewhere, "We are the descendants of the slave trade. Our papers say: 'Afro-descendants: descendants of the Africans brought to America with the transatlantic slave trade.' What do I personally think? If the slave trade is at the basis of capital accumulation, then inequality and racism are at the basis of the same process. I can make headway on the problem of territory, of ethno-education, up to a certain point, but if I do not solve the fundamental problem I do not solve anything" (cited in Escobar 2008, 69).

There are tensions between these Afro-Latin American statements and the African American radical thought so sketchily reviewed here. One source of tension is the emphasis on the political economy of antiblackness. It has always seemed to me much harder to articulate an anticapitalist critique in the United States as part of a critical race or gender discourse, whereas in Latin America an anticapitalist stance is most often taken as a given. But perhaps the most important source of tension stems from the agency that is often expressed by Afro-Latin American and other subaltern activists, committed as they are to fighting for lives of joy, meaning, and dignity, as among those struggling to keep the Colombian Pacific as a territory of life, peace, happiness, and freedom (see chapter 7). This agency, however, cannot be detected easily through philosophical and academic debates; it has to be experienced in place, as it happens; one would say, academically, that it has to be documented ethnographically, going well beyond the text. The valence of this agency is stressed in relational approaches to the city, focused on the everyday resourcefulness and survival tactics of popular groups in the poor neighborhoods of the Global South. In these works (e.g., Amin and Thrift 2017; Escobar 2019; Simone and Pieterse 2017), attention shifts to the play of affect, street intelligence, and network-like relational collective action—to the city's "ground-level hum," to use Amin and Thrift's vivid notion (2017, 5). There the ethnographic analysis focuses on the multiplicity of popular practices that often arise out of the sheer fact that the city—and, one may add, the metaphysical infrastructure that underlies it—does not work according to plan.

We also see the emphasis on the political economy of antiblackness in African thinkers such as Achille Mbembe (2017), who emphasizes the connection between antiblackness, modernity, and capitalism, from the time of the Atlantic slave trade—what the Cameroonian philosopher Fabien Eboussi Boulaga (2014) fittingly calls "the catastrophe"—to today's biodigital economy, finance capitalism, and neoliberal globalization. Do these various emphases pose challenges to the premises, conclusions, and politics of Afro-pessimism, even while sharing a great deal of its political ontology analysis? Only the question will be posed here, as I begin to move toward the conclusion. Let me quote from a contribution by Christina Sharpe to the Afro-pessimism debate to return to the initial question about the relation between modernist and pluriversal politics; in her view, Afro-pessimism is an attempt "to build a language that, despite the rewards and enticements to do otherwise, refuses to refuse blackness, that embraces 'without pathos' that which is constructed and defined as pathology. . . . It is work that insistently speaks what is being constituted as the unspeakable and enacts an ethical embrace of what is constituted as (affirmatively) unembraceable" (cited in Sexton 2016). This construes Afro-pessimism as an epistemological and an ethical project, which Jared Sexton also finds skillfully articulated in Wilderson's statement about being able to, finally, "think Blackness and agency together in an ethical manner" (cited in Sexton 2016).

The most eloquent statements about the need to consider simultaneously the everyday effects of racism and antiblackness and the agency of those most subject to it, it seems to me, come from black and Latina feminists, particularly in their insistence on an open-ended, reconstructive politics of difference, even if they are fully aware of how such politics risk becoming ineffectual or counterproductive. Equally significant in this regard is the emphasis on spirituality, love, healing, and the care for the nonhuman world, within a frame of radical social justice, espoused by some black and Latina feminists, such as bell hooks (2000), Fania and Angela Davis (2016), Gloria Anzaldúa, Chela Sandoval, and Cherríe Moraga (e.g., Anzaldúa and Keating 2002). I believe that in the works of these authors—diverse as they are—these constructive emphases and the political ontology of antiblackness are not mutually exclusive, yet their articulation needs to be discussed as they are tried out in practice.

Such articulations can most powerfully be gleaned, in my view, from the recent work of some black feminists in both the United States and Colombia. Let me start with *Wayward Lives, Beautiful Experiments*, Saidiya Hartman's (2019) incredibly original, powerful, and lucid reconstruction of the lives and deeds of young black women arriving from the South in New York (Harlem) and Philadelphia, between the 1880s and the 1930s, only to find an equally virulent, albeit different, form of racism in what they expected to be spaces of freedom in the urban North. The book's opening paragraph goes so much against the grain that it bears quoting in toto: "At the turn of the twentieth century, young black women were in open rebellion. They struggled to create autonomous and beautiful lives, to escape the new forms of servitude awaiting them, and to live as if they were free. This book recreates the radical imagination and wayward practices of these young women by describing the world through their eyes. It is a narrative written from nowhere, from the nowhere of the ghetto and the nowhere of utopia" (2019, xiii). As Hartman goes on to say, the book's aim is "to illuminate the radical imagination and everyday anarchy of ordinary colored girls, which has not only been overlooked, but is nearly unimaginable" (xiv). Upon arrival, what these girls find is "the plantation extended into the city" (4), the city as a new enclosure. This enclosure eventually became the "black ghetto," cemented by liberal social reformers and sociologists, the state, and the police, with their spatial, moral, and social strategies for improvement, as if saying "*Negro, don't even try to live*" (22). Women got the worst of it, owing to the entanglement of violence and sexuality that conditioned so much, if not everything, about them. Yet, Hartman tells us, the challenge is to see how they survived, and at times even thrived, in this context of brutality, deprivation, and poverty, how their beautiful experiments in living—in between the kitchen and the brothel, the street and the crowded tenements, the laundry work and their intimate lives in their bedrooms—yielded lives that were painful but at times also beautiful, fugitive moments of going about as if they were free, in the mist of "the insistent hunger of the slum" (84).

Hartman is surely painfully aware of the onto-epistemic grasp on black lives ("When would the colored female achieve her full status as a woman?" [177]), but she refuses to see only the horror and not the beauty, to linger on the tragedy without putting forward a compelling view of how young colored girls tried "to make a way out of no way, to not be defeated by defeat" (347). It was left to them to envision things otherwise, to dance within the enclosure, to set into motion "a fierce and expanded sense of what might be possible" (59). In so doing, they enacted another important moment in the long history of black radicalism and refusal. Hartman's creative, careful, and loving unearthing of the histories of these forgotten young women demonstrates why another possible is, must be, possible. It is an invitation to us all to reply positively to her question, "Who else would dare believe another world was possible . . . [and] be convinced that nothing could be said about the Negro problem, modernity, global capitalism, police brutality, state killings, and the Anthropocene if it did not take her into account?" (347). Who indeed?

That there is an entire archive of the "being-in-difference" embodied by black women has been superbly explored by Avery Gordon in her most recent book. But it is a question not just of enacting difference but of how such difference at time gets to constitute veritable moments of an "other utopianism" capable of creating spaces of autonomy, however fugitive and temporary. It is in these zones that one can glean the at-times sophisticated subaltern consciousness and understanding of what it would mean to live in a better world held by the black women living in many of the world's popular neighborhoods. Paying attention to them might help us see why the utopian is not an absolute impossibility, since "it is in us," too, in "all those things we are and we do that exceed or are just not expressions of what is dominant and dominating us" (2018, 64). "Running away," she says—an ancestral and paradigmatic Afro-diasporic practice, one might add—"is a process . . . of trying to find a way of living in different terms, whose outcome is unfortunately never given in advance. It's extremely difficult to let go of living on their terms, to let go of the bad and the good and find another way. It requires a certain degree of embodied indifference or organs for the alternative that conviction or rhetoric alone does not yield. It requires a certain practice or preparation in property relations with which we are often less familiar" (185).

To end, let us explore this theme of running away, and Hartman's "Who else . . ." question, by listening to the narratives of another group of black women in another "black city-within-the-city" (Hartman 2019, 17), the Distrito de Aguablanca, or DAB (Aguablanca District), in the city of Cali. Almost nonexistent in 1980, today the DAB reaches 700,000 inhabitants, a large percentage of them Afro-Colombians who have been forcefully displaced by armed conflict and land grabbing in other parts of the country's Southwest, particularly the Pacific rain forest region. There, *mujeresnegrasafrodescendientes de Cali* (black-Afrodescendant-women of Cali, or *munac*), a term introduced by Elba Palacios to convey the entangled forms of oppression faced by black women but also the multiple dimensions of their resistance and creativity, display enormous courage and creativity in constructing urban territories. Black feminist activist groups in the DAB—among them *Otras negras . . . y feministas!*, the Casa Cultural el Chontaduro, and the Colectivo Sentipensar Afrodiaspórico (Afro-diasporic Sentipensar Collective)—investigate the realities of the munac, construct autonomous networks of support, and develop frameworks for peaceful and dignified coexistence (see Campo et al. 2018; Lozano 2014, 2016, 2017; Machado 2017; Palacios 2019). Theirs can be said to be a practice of weaving urban worlds, where racialized and ethnicized women may find safer conditions for daily urban living. "Reexistence" is a major trope of these women's groups, a process of creating autonomous lives and constructing auspicious conditions for fostering life in general, building on historical memories of oppression and the manifold forms of negation of their being, but also on the recollection of their struggles for freedom, including the experience of *cimarronaje* (running away, maroon experiences), that always anchor their actions. This decolonial black radical feminism gets at the core of the centuries-old power relations in cities such as Cali. Of the munac, one could say, echoing Hartman (2019, 59), that they might be bringing about a "revolution in a minor key" (59), even if it is largely invisible to most inhabitants of the city, particularly its white and mestizo elite and middle classes.

In the last section, I tried to stage a dialogue between Latin American critical thought and black radical thought and politics, highlighting the debates introduced by black feminists. At the academic level, one can muse over the possibility of sustained conversations among what, in my view, are some of the most vibrant academic debates at present, particularly the following strands: first, black radical thought and black and Latina feminist thought in the United States; second, Latin American decolonial feminisms (Espinosa, Gómez, and Ochoa 2014; Segato 2015, 2016), black feminist thought, and decolonial thinking (see, e.g., Mignolo and Walsh 2018 for recent statement); and third, the critical thinking emerging from indigenous intellectuals across the Americas.

The importance of the question of blackness and agency is paramount, if we are to heed Mbembe's argument that, with the intensification of the global economy of dispossession, we are attending to a generalized blackness, a veritable *becoming black of the world* (2017, 6). Here again we find an array of positions in tension, including, among others, Mbembe's appeal to a notion of a universal community, even if an open one—a common world in which all of us can be full human beings (182), on the heels of onto-epistemic restitution and reparation.

A Final Note on Political Ontology and Radical Relationality

Earlier I made the case that we all weave the pluriverse together through our designs and daily practices; thus the struggle to reinhabit the pluriverse in an Earth-wise manner is not just for indigenous peoples or people in the Global South but for everyone. The Native Canadian author Leanne Simpson has driven this point home vehemently, as far as indigenous peoples are concerned (2017, 246):

> We must continuously build and rebuild indigenous worlds. This work starts in motion, in decolonial love, in flight, in relationship, in biiskabi-yang, in generosity, humility, and kindness, and this is where it also ends. I cannot be prescriptive here because these processes are profoundly intimate and emergent and are ultimately the collective responsibilities of

those who belong to unique and diverse indigenous nations. I don't want to imagine or dream futures. I want a better present.

I would like to suggest that this statement—an active lesson from indigenous movements to all who wish to struggle for the pluriverse—applies to all worlds, with certain caveats. First, it is crucial to acknowledge that not all resistance is ontological in the relational sense that Simpson's Radical Resurgence Project so powerfully envisions. We need to push all strategies and forms of politics ontologically and decolonially. What I mean by this is the following: First, we all need to actively unlearn the ontologies of separation and a single real that shape our bodies and worlds; for instance, can we unlearn the liberal individual—that antirelational Trojan horse that inhabits each of us in modern worlds—in a similar way that we endeavor to unlearn patriarchy, racism, and heterosexism? Second, we all need to be mindful of the multiple ways in which our actions depend on, and often reinforce, the metaphysical infrastructure of the current dominant systems, including its universal constructs and objectifying relations, its anthropocentrism, secularism, and Eurocentrism, and its colonialist hierarchical classifications in terms of race, gender, and sexuality.

As the essays in this volume contend, most worlds live under ontological occupation. Such occupation is effected through the categories and hierarchical classifications historically deployed by governments, corporations, organized religions, and the academy as the main purveyors of a dominant onto-epistemic structure. Environmental conflicts in Latin America and elsewhere make this assertion patently clear. At stake, for instance, with the expansion of oil palm cultivation, large-scale hydroelectric dams, mining for gold and strategic minerals, and many mega development projects is not only the forced displacement, if not outright destruction, of particular territories and worlds but their active occupation by the modernist ontologies serving as scaffolding for relentless growth and hyperaccumulation at the top. This type of environmental-cum-ontological conflict is precisely the focus of political ontology, a nascent field that provides the architecture for this volume. The various essays contribute to constructing this emergent field as a space for exploring the politics of the pluriverse, building on the notion of multiple realities and possibles implicit in the agenda of many social movements. While the chapters can be read as self-contained units, they build toward this understanding through different registers. Many of the essays will provide readers with a synoptic view of Latin American social theory at present.

In locating these essays between the present moment (the brutality of neoliberal globalization) and the epoch (capitalist Euro-modernity), I have suggested that we might feasibly construe the current conjuncture in terms of a civilizational crisis. Whether one articulates the conjuncture as the struggle over modernity, going beyond Euro-modernity toward multiple modernities, as Grossberg (2010, 2019) has cogently done, or in terms of the crisis of civilizational models pointing to transitions beyond modernity as a key possibility space, and perhaps attractor, for a multiplicity of struggles, I side with scholars for whom the forging of new connections and transformative orientations is a central practice. Political ontology is part of this effort. As Blaser (2013) puts it, political ontology is not a new approach for another realist claim on the real; in fact, the forms of ontological politics discussed in this book are but a manner of foregrounding the array of ways of conceiving what exists so as to make tangible the claim of multiple ontologies or worlds. In this vein, political ontology is a way of telling the stories of world making differently, in the hope that other spaces for the enactment of the pluriverse might open up.

To conclude, let us listen to the straightforward and powerful rendition of articulatory politics by the women gathered at the International Forum on Feminicides of Racialized and Ethnicized Peoples, held in the predominantly black port city of Buenaventura, on the Colombian Pacific, not far from Cali, in April 2016. The forum denounced the systemic connection between the genocide of women, and black women in particular, and global capital accumulation. It brought together many of the lines of argumentation discussed in this preface, ending with a commitment to the radical relationality and pluriversal politics embedded in the notions of Ubuntu and Buen Vivir as civilizational alternatives. Radical relationality emerges in this kind of political space as the best possible antidote to the metaphysics of separation and isolation and the ontologies of antiblackness, coloniality, heteropatriarchal social orders, and the devastation of the Earth. Radical relationality is an answer to the imperative that "to reweave community out of the existing fragments should thus be our banner" (Segato 2016, 27). The forum's final declaration partially states:

> We analyzed together the current upsurge in diverse forms of violence against women and their relation with global capital accumulation and its racist and colonialist expression in Latin America. We concluded that feminicides are functional to territorial dispossession and the extermination of indigenous, black, and popular rural and urban communities and peoples. We also examined the forms of resistance and autonomous organizing by women from the space of their communities.... We experienced with joy women's ability to create and re-create common existence, their

active sharing and capacity to repair their grief and pain, transforming them into knowledge and struggles for justice.

We demand from the state, governments, transnational corporations, and [societies] in general to stop the war against women, their communities and peoples, to respect their territories and guarantee their lives. . . . We exhort social movement organizations to assume a deep commitment toward dismantling colonial capitalist patriarchy, so that we can journey in line with our desires and aspirations toward Ubuntu and Buen Vivir.[14]

These essays deal with the politics of the possible, with the way our notions of what is real and what is possible determine both our political practice, from the personal to the collective, and our sense of hope. I am asking readers to reflect on whether it is possible to have a different way of thinking, or rather a different way of *sentipensar*, about what is possible. I emphasize sentipensar (and its correlative noun, *sentipensamiento*), as currently used by activists in various parts of Latin America, to suggest a way of knowing that does not separate thinking from feeling, reason from emotion, knowledge from caring. This activist epistemology lies at the very heart of this book.[1]

By a different way of sentipensar about the possible, I mean more than a clever variation on the well-known formulation that emerged from the World Social Forum, which first met in Porto Alegre, Brazil, in 2001: "Another world is possible." Though I am partly inspired by the reformulation of possible worlds that was so intelligently and passionately set forth at that forum, in this book I seek a different sort of effect, one derived from the idea that to reach those possible worlds, we first have to go back to an even more basic level, the level of what we call "the real," and consider this other formulation: another world is possible because another reality is possible. In other words, conventional thinking about the real and the possible will never get us to those other worlds. This sentipensamiento is emerging powerfully among subaltern groups and movements, as well as in critical spaces within the academy; it's in the air, and many people and social groups are starting to think it explicitly. It's what is behind the essays that follow.

These essays were written between 2014 and 2017, in contexts ranging from academic presentations to activist events—vague as the line between those two domains often is, especially in Latin America. All but chapters 4 and 6 were originally written in Spanish, and all have been slightly revised, except for the introduction and chapter 1, which were written in the main for this book, and chapter 8, which incorporates new material.

I am aware of the abstract nature of the proposition that *another possible is possible*. In the first chapter, I present some of the theoretical underpinnings behind this proposition. Readers who wish can skip that chapter and go straight to the rest, perhaps returning to the theoretical discussion later on.

Though each chapter can be read independently of the others (so that it would be no problem to start by reading the last chapter first, for example), in a way they are all in dialogue with one another, creating synergies in the exposition of the main ideas.

I should note that these chapters were written before the remarkable events in Colombia during the first half of 2017, including the mass civic strikes in the predominantly black cities of Quibdó and Buenaventura; the granting of legal rights to the Atrato River by the Constitutional Court of Colombia; and especially the successful referendums against large-scale mining and hydrocarbon exploration and drilling in a number of communities, such as when more than 97 percent of the population of the town of Cajamarca, Tolima, voted against what would have been one of the largest gold mines in the world (La Colosa, belonging to the South African corporation AngloGold Ashanti), a case with enormous international repercussions. These cases, coming about despite intensive efforts on the part of the state to undermine them, suggest a possible scenario that is perhaps a bit daring and undoubtedly provisional: In Colombia (and perhaps in Mexico as well), conditions may soon be ripe for meaningful social transformation, given the crisis and the extreme dysfunction that have gripped the institutions in both countries and the discourse about them, as well as the increasingly brutal repression of the people.

I don't think this proposal is completely unreasonable. Might we be talking about a possible *pachakuti*, a world reversal, in these countries, perhaps in the short to medium term? Perhaps one like the pachakuti that shook Bolivia with huge indigenous and working-class insurrections between 2000 and 2006, leading to the election of Evo Morales as president of that country, though his regime has since failed to establish a regulatory system outside of, against, and beyond the established capitalist social order?

Exploring this hypothesis would take a lot of collective research and debate. The work would have to be based on the premise that "there are historical moments in which a society's internal conflicts, hostilities, and rifts overflow all the structures designed to administer and channel them," as the Mexican sociologist Raquel Gutiérrez Aguilar (2008, 19) suggests in her excellent investigation of the events that led to the Bolivian pachakuti. Thinking about Colombia and Mexico from this perspective would also be a productive exercise. Are conditions being established for a pachakuti in those countries? Might their current social dynamics be helping to "permanently reconfigure the instituted order on several levels and through contrasting tempos" and doing so "in an expansive and permanent yet discontinuous way; that is: laying down rhythms, generating cadences" (21)? Are they perhaps generating "the potential to alter social reality in a profound way so as to preserve, through transformation, long-standing and collective living worlds and to produce new and fertile forms of governance, connection, and self-regulation" (351)? The perspective of this book is that we cannot imaginatively approach these questions using the conventional lenses of the real and the possible.[2]

ACKNOWLEDGMENTS

I have always insisted that all intellectual production is collective, even more so if we consider it from the perspective of interrelationships and interdependence, the central focus of this book. What we usually consider "influences" can often be seen as coauthorships, or at least as "conversations with." The thoughts and ideas of others appear here and there in what one writes, and those are what these acknowledgments refer to, with special affection. Marisol de la Cadena, Mario Blaser, Cristina Rojas, and Michal Osterweil have been my traveling companions on the road to understanding relationality and its importance in the struggle to defend and rebuild territories and worlds, and they read drafts of the introduction and chapter 1 with a critical eye. Members of the Process of Black Communities (Proceso de Comunidades Negras, PCN) remain important in my writing. My special thanks on this occasion go to Marilyn Machado, Charo Mina Rojas, Carlos Rosero, Francia Márquez, Yellen Aguilar, and Danelly Estupiñán.

I would like to mention some of the people I have been in more direct contact with over the two or three years when I was writing these texts, and whose works and influence I see most clearly in them: Eduardo Gudynas, Patricia Botero, Betty Ruth Lozano, Gustavo Esteva, Xochitl Leyva, Vilma Almendra, Manuel Rozental, Enrique Leff, Diana Gómez, Laura Gutiérrez, Verónica Gago, Maristella Svampa, Rita Segato, Claudia von Werlhof, Raquel Gutiérrez Aguilar, Alberto Acosta, Álvaro Pedrosa, Olver Quijano, Javier Tobar, Adolfo Albán Achinte, Catherine Walsh, Janet Conway, Boaventura de Sousa Santos, Astrid Ulloa, María Mercedes Campo, Elba Mercedes Palacios, David López Matta, Anthony Dest, Sheila Grunner, Catalina Toro, Gabriela Merlinsky, Viviane Weitzner, Tatiana Roa, Joan Martínez Alier, Federico Demaria, Giorgos Kallis, Mario Pérez, Eduardo Restrepo, Natalia Quiroga, Lina Álvarez Villarreal, Eloísa Berman, Iván Vargas, Alfredo Martínez, Andrea Botero, Ulrich Oslender, Carlos Walter Porto Gonçalves, and the team of researchers from Scandinavia and the Andes gathered by Esben Leifsen for the project "Extracting Justice: Exploring the Role of Prior Consultation in the Resolution of Socio-Environmental Conflicts in Latin America," funded by the Norwegian Research Council (2013–17).

Thanks to the team at my Colombian publisher, Ediciones Desde Abajo, for embracing this book, and for the wonderful job they do of disseminating critical and emancipatory perspectives and meaningful reflections from the very heart of popular and subaltern experiences.

This English version has benefited hugely from extensive comments by reviewers for Duke University Press and from friends Charles R. Hale, Orin Starn, and Marisol de la Cadena. Their thoughtful comments are reflected throughout the book, but especially in the preface to the English edition. A two-week stay at the University of California in Santa Barbara (March 2019), at Charlie R. Hale's invitation, was likewise extremely significant in terms of conversations about the preface. I am particularly indebted to Avery Gordon, Paul Amar, and Elizabeth Robinson for enlightening conversations on Afro-pessimism, the politics of transitions, and pluriversality.

This English version originated in a conversation with Gisela Fosado, my editor at Duke University Press. When she asked me one day what I was work-ing on, I mentioned that I had just finished a book of essays explicitly written in Spanish, even if, as I hastened to add, I knew very well that what doesn't ex-ist in English doesn't exist for the Anglo-American academy. "Let's see if we can do something about that," she replied. Soon after, she proposed the book to the Latin America in Translation Series that UNC Press and Duke Univer-sity Press have maintained for a good number of years. My thanks to the series committee for welcoming the book among its titles in translation, and very especially to Gisela for her steady encouragement, support, friendship, and active feedback and insights into what I happen to be writing about. Finally, I am very grateful to David Frye for his willingness to undertake the translation and for the excellent job he did on all aspects of the text.

Another Possible Is Possible

These are bold perspectives, but in the short term we can't afford the luxury of working to reproduce mechanical scenarios. If possible, the experience of collective global coexistence in recent years, the practice of sociocultural diversity, of political ecology, and of a humanizing environmental history will allow us to design new though imprecise civilizational horizons.

—HÉCTOR ALIMONDA (1949–2017), IN MEMORIAM

(Voz de mujer)
Tú no puedes comprar el viento
Tú no puedes comprar el sol
Tú no puedes comprar la lluvia
Tú no puedes comprar el calor
Tú no puedes comprar las nubes
Tú no puedes comprar los colores
Tú no puedes comprar mi alegría
Tú no puedes comprar mis dolores. . . .

(Woman's voice)
You can't buy the wind
You can't buy the sun
You can't buy the rain
You can't buy the heat
You can't buy the clouds
You can't buy the colors
You can't buy my joy
You can't buy my sorrows. . . .

(Coro: voces de mujeres)
Vamos caminando
Vamos dibujando el camino
Aquí se respira lucha

(Vamos caminando)
Yo canto porque se escucha
(Vamos caminando)
Aquí estamos de pie
¡Que viva la América!

(Chorus: women's voices)
Let's keep walking
Let's trace the path
Here we breathe the struggle
(Let's keep walking)
I sing to be heard
(Let's keep walking)
Here we're standing up
Viva América!

—CALLE 13, "LATINOAMÉRICA"

Reality is a proposition that we use as an explanatory notion to explain our experiences. Moreover, we use it in different ways according to our emotions. This is why there are different notions of reality in different cultures or in different moments of history. . . . We live the "real" as the presence of our experience. I saw it, I heard it, I touched it.

—HUMBERTO MATURANA, "METADESIGN: PART II" (1997), 3

This is a series of essays about the politics of the possible, about our ideas about the real and the possible and how they determine our political practice, from the personal to the collective, as well as our sense of hope. We could have turned to any number of theories, from quantum physics or complexity theory to anthropological analysis, to show how we live with a fairly naive concept of the real, but in the end, as Maturana suggests in the epigraph, we make decisions with our emotions, or at least not entirely with our reason. This is why I suggest we must sentipensar (feel-think) new notions about what is real and thus what is possible.

To put it as succinctly as possible, I would say that we base our conventional notions of what is real on a belief that we interact with the world as individuals separate from that world; the world seems external, outside of us, a predictable context within which we move about freely. The scientific principles we learn in our formal schooling (and that the media rely on) teach us that we can understand this world by gazing on it as neutral and objective observers. The conventional scientific approach thus instills in us a cosmovision that divides the world into subjects and objects, a world we can understand and manipulate at will. The entire edifice of modern Western civilization (with its particular forms of patriarchy, racism, and capitalist exploitation) is based on this objectivizing operation—on this dualist ontology, as we will call it—because it is based on a strict separation between subject and object, reason and emotion, and many other dualisms that we will uncover in this book, and yet more dualisms that readers will go on to discover on their own.

Now, although this dualist ontology of self-contained subjects and objects has already raised a wide range of critiques and inquiries, as I explain in the first chapter, it is still hard to understand its serious implications for the way in which we live our lives, construct our worlds, and conduct our politics. Questioning these notions is not easy, because we grow up and live with them; we bring them to life with our actions. What could be more solid than the world on which we are standing? What could be more real than the world surrounding us, in which our minds seemingly wake up every morning? It is hard to deny. Whenever we leave the house, whenever we walk about the world, we have to take for granted that doors, streets, offices, computers, people, and so on exist. These are no illusions.

At the same time, as we will see, all these things, including ourselves, do not exist quite so independently of one another as we suppose. The question is how this basic fact of experience has become a belief in an "objective reality" about an "external world" consisting of "entities" distributed through space, each of them independent of the multiplicity of interactions that produce them. This objectivizing stance leads to the ethos of human dominion over nature that forms the basis for patriarchal culture and capitalist societies. It prevents and disempowers us from coexisting with the full range of human and nonhuman beings in a collaborative manner that is wiser in its relationship with the Earth and with the flow of life. It creates a single reality from which all other realities and senses of the real are excluded, thus profoundly limiting the scope of the political.

Questioning this belief in a single reality means developing another, entirely different understanding of what change and transformation are, and thus of what politics can be. The real, the possible, and the political are all joined at the hip. It is precisely because other possibles have been turned into "impossibles" that we find it so difficult to imagine other realities. Speaking of other possibles and other realities forces us to rethink many of our everyday practices and politics.[1]

Reflecting critically on politics from this perspective is crucial if we are going to have a horizon from which we can move toward open-ended civilizational (nontotalitarian) transitions. If all we have is a political practice based on the conventional understanding of the real/possible, it will be extremely difficult for us to extract ourselves from the current global politics of war that underlies capital accumulation. Our current understandings are inadequate to confronting the capitalist hydra. We would end up in a struggle for mere survival, functioning on behalf of a system that has been constantly expanding for five hundred years, at war with the planet and with all of life.[2] We can see that the capitalist system depends on this objectivizing and dualist conception of the real in so many of its dimensions: the idea of self-contained spheres ("economics," "society," "politics," "culture," and so on), as if the ceaseless flow of matter/life could be squeezed into these neatly organized pigeonholes; the construct of the autonomous "individual" who maximizes his "utility" through market decisions; the idea of a self-regulating market, as if it were not linked by multiple strands to the whole meshwork of the real; the concept of nature as a "resource" rather than as life itself; and the mode of understanding that it relies on, the so-called science of economics, a veritable Cartesian castle in the sky founded on these same presuppositions. These premises, and many more, form the ontological basis of capital and its practice of plunder and destruction.

The questions posed in this book are based on two interrelated points. The first concerns the rise in recent decades of so many realities that hegemonic discourses about the real had previously deemed inexistent or else implausible alternatives to what exists (Santos 2014), including most social groups located on the oppressed side of colonial binaries: black and indigenous people, women, peasants, marginalized urban dwellers of all sorts. From many of these subaltern realities, we now get a wide variety of proposals for "worlding" life on new premises; in other words, for constructing other worlds. For instance, the proposal of the indigenous Nasa people of southwestern Colombia (see chapters 2 and 3), which they base on their statement on the liberation of Mother Earth, arises from an utterly different notion of the real/possible and other practices of world making.

The second underlying point is the awareness that all existence is radically interdependent. Everything exists in relation, arising and developing in meshworks of relations. Perhaps to make it manageable, we modern humans have invented the powerful fictions of the individual (the ego), the economy, free markets, nature, and many more, each of them as an irrefutable reality that exists intrinsically on its own. These beliefs work quite effectively, for they end up producing us as such. But are we really the autonomous individuals we imagine ourselves to be? Can we really separate something called "the economy" from the endless, ceaseless flow of life? Aren't we humans also "nature," so that all the things we have invented as "nonhuman" (food, air, water, minerals, microorganisms) also constitute us? When we appeal to reason, when we call for "thinking with a cool head," aren't we paradoxically making an emotional and selective decision? Asking ourselves these questions marks the beginning of a long journey toward a life consonant with other ontologies, a journey toward a profound consciousness of the relationality and interdependence of all that exists, which is in turn indispensable for imagining other possible worlds.

A main objective in gathering these texts under the rubric of *Another Possible Is Possible* (the title of the Spanish-language edition) is to provide political-theoretical tools to counter a powerful tendency of experts, politicians of the Right, and many intellectuals of the Left, to delegitimize all arguments favoring local struggles to transform the world and to exclude proposals by subaltern groups from serious consideration, because—they argue—such proposals will never suffice to change the situation substantially. In the case of the Right, only the "major players," such as science and technology, corporations, states, and institutions like the World Bank, are capable of dealing with the serious problems of poverty and environmental degradation. For the traditional Left, local alternatives will never be powerful enough to overthrow the "monsters" of capitalism, imperialism, or globalization. From their perspective (often enough shared by the average person in the street), the alternatives proposed by these groups are too local, small, partial, utopian, and unrealistic, or else they think that the groups proposing them "are trying to make us go backward." But perhaps the most common and devastating label that they plaster on them is *romantic*. In the final analysis, both Right and Left use their respective premises of what is real and possible to arrive at the same place: they reproduce the world as we know it. At this level, they are all the same. Talking about "another possible" offers an antidote to these accusations of romanticism.

I would also suggest that, given the gravity of the multiple crises the planet is now dealing with (crises of the environment, the climate, society, and meaning), subaltern pluriversal proposals are proving that we have a more urgent need today than ever for new thinking about the real/possible. At a time like this, we can apply the well-known principle (often attributed to Einstein) that "we cannot resolve the problems of one era using the same mental frame that created them," or the formulation of the Portuguese sociologist Boaventura de Sousa Santos, "we have modern problems for which there are no modern solutions"—such as climate change. We might also decide to accept, in the words of a young Afro-Colombian activist from the Pacific rain forest on the border between Colombia and Ecuador that is currently being ravaged by "development," that "we cannot think about our world in the same way; either we take a step forward, or we'll fall twenty years behind."[3] It is, in the final analysis, a matter of making the unthinkable thinkable, and the thinkable believable and possible. This is an essential principle for the civilizational transitions that so many groups and activists are now calling for.

The following chapters are an invitation to stop thinking about our worlds with the dominant categories that created these crises, and instead to move forward in a process of relearning the real/possible, beyond the certitudes of modernity and the conventional categories that, it is worth underlining, are the very ones used by the institutions perpetuating the crisis: the World Bank, the great corporations, most states, organized religions, and also to a large extent the academy. Their categories replicate the conception of the world held by the powerful. The nightly news shows repeat them day after day in their reports on "the way things are," *as if the world really were that way*. We cannot reconstruct the world and create genuinely new worlds using the same categories by which we are destroying it! I hope these texts may help us to develop antidotes to the accusation of romanticism, or at least to radically invert it. Aren't the true romantics the people who insist that more of the same (more corporate solutions, more World Bank–style development, more "green economies") will lead to lasting improvements? We should arrive at the conclusion that we can't expect anything good—for life, for land, for people—to come out of such institutions.[4]

In everyday language, believing in a single notion of the real/possible usually translates into "being realistic." Maybe we can now add a question mark or two to this expression. What does "being realistic" mean? It means believing that in the final analysis there is a single correct way to see and understand things (based on rationality and science); believing that these (our) universal truths must prevail against all others, which in our view are less correct, or false; being convinced that we live in a world made of a single world, and being shocked by the opposite possibility; and being sure that the truth of this single (usually Western) reality—which obviously we all share, as we should!—is the space from which we ought to promote our projects (whether they be for becoming very rich or for resisting capitalism). Often, it also means we believe that the knowledge of men, of whites, of Euro-Americans and Euro-Latin

Americans (whether or not we belong to these groups), is superior to that of all other social groups and that their lives are more desirable. It means thinking that those who insist, in their obstinacy, on defending principles other than these are hopeless romantics who really don't have to be listened to. It means, finally, giving up the right to dream. How small this "reality" shrinks by the time we have filtered it through our questions. The world of the *incurable realists* is reduced to a CNN version of life, to the realpolitik of nation-states, and to self-help schemes that serve the big corporations.

Finally, a word on the subtitle of the Spanish edition of the book, *Abya Yala/Afro/Latino América*. In the prologue, I referred straightforwardly to Latin America. As we will see in chapter 2, that name conceals the colonial histories of conquest and enslavement that constitute it. Renaming this continent is a first step toward participating in a politics of the real and of the possible. From that point forward, we should dig more deeply into the pluralization of the worlds that inhabit it, and begin to think from the viewpoints of those cosmovisions that have always conceptualized and constructed their existence from below and with the Earth.

Guide to the Book

Allow me to present briefly each of the chapters that follow, including the context in which each was produced.

Chapter 1, "Theory and the Un/Real: Tools for Rethinking 'Reality' and the Possible," uses a theoretical reflection to draw links between a series of domains—some theoretical, others not—within which we may investigate other concepts of the real and the possible. We find a first series of spaces in many ancestral traditions, from the cosmovisions of indigenous peoples, animism, and matriarchal societies to Buddhism and Earth-based spiritualities. The second series derives more directly from the academy; it includes cybernetics and the sciences of complexity, self-organization, and emergence; the attention that is once more being given to ontology in social theory, in what is known as the ontological turn; and finally the notion of a pluriverse. Far from being mere holdovers from a bygone time, the first series of spaces still drives the construction of contemporary worlds. The second evinces noteworthy attempts to think beyond the idea of a single world, a single reality, a single form of the possible. These trends will help us to derealize the realist that each of us carries within ourselves, and to think-live with a more complex and effective awareness of the inexhaustible *tejido* (weave) of interdependence that sustains life and allows it to flourish, which is to say, the pluriverse.

Chapter 2, "From Below, on the Left, and with the Earth," was first prepared for the Seventh Latin American and Caribbean Conference on Social Sciences organized by CLACSO (Consejo Latinoamericano de Ciencias Sociales), which took place in Medellín, November 9-13, 2015. Held every four years, this is the most prominent event in the social sciences in Latin America, attracting a huge number of participants, especially young scholars. I was interested in showing that Latin American critical thought is not in crisis, as some have argued based on the apparent end of the progressive cycle in Latin America, but rather that it is in fact more vibrant and dynamic than ever. The theoretical contributions to a rethinking of the region resonate all across the continent—in meetings among native peoples; in *mingas de pensamiento* (collective thought activities); in debates among urban and rural movements and collectives; in assemblies of communities in resistance; in mobilizations of young people, women, peasants, and environmentalists; and undoubtedly in some of the sectors that have traditionally been considered the quintessential spaces for thought, such as the academy and the arts. Here I use the Zapatista expression for thinking about alternatives, "from below and on the Left," but I explicitly add the dimension of Earth as essential to any critical thought in the present. Thinking from below brings me back to reflecting on the current bumper crop of writing on the notions of territory, autonomy, and communality, to which I pay special attention. Finally, for useful ideas about how to think with the Earth, I turn not to the thought of ecologists (important as it is) but to the cosmovisions or relational ontologies of territory-peoples (indigenous peoples and Afro-descendants, in particular), for they are closely in tune with the Earth.

Chapter 3, "The Earth~Form of Life: Nasa Thought and the Limits to the Episteme of Modernity," continues exploring thought about the Earth, though in a somewhat more academic register. The essay was originally prepared for the opening address in honor of the new doctorate in the cultural history of Colombia at the Universidad del Valle in Cali on November 1, 2016. I first presented it a few days earlier at the International Colloquium of Multiple Knowledges and Social and Political Sciences (Universidad Nacional, Bogotá, October 18-21, 2016). In it I outline a potential line of research based on Michel Foucault's archaeological analysis of discourse. But my basic motivation for writing this text was something else: to construct an argument based on a statement that the Nasa people of the northern Cauca region in Colombia proposed more than a decade ago, the Liberation of Mother Earth, which I bring up at the end of chapter 2. Taking off from this Nasa statement, the chapter sets up a conversation between the Nasa proposal and discourse analysis. A detailed reading of the Nasa archive allows me to propose the adoption of the notion of the Liberation of Mother Earth (a genuine concept-movement) as a potent principle for all political action and design work. This principle will show us a path toward undertaking, from wherever we happen to be, the task of "weaving life in freedom." The lucid knowledge of this indigenous people from northern Cauca imbues us with the idea of a civilizational change, from the Man-form (that of anthropocentric modernity) to the Earth~form of life (relationality and biocentrism).

Chapter 4, "*Sentipensar* with the Earth," prepared for the International Colloquium on Epistemologies of the South, held at Coimbra, Portugal, July 10–12, 2014, reflects on how the concept of the epistemologies of the South proposed by Boaventura de Sousa Santos can serve as a framework for recognizing the diversity of ways of understanding the world and giving meaning to existence. It aims at highlighting the ontological dimension of the epistemologies of the South. Working on this framework, the chapter describes the concept of "relational ontologies," illustrating other sorts of theoretical tools for those who wish no longer to be complicit in the silencing of popular knowledges and experiences on the part of Eurocentric globalization. Up against the hegemonic idea of "One World made from one world"—the capitalist, patriarchal, and colonial globalized world—the text suggests a transition to "a world in which many worlds fit," the pluriverse. It offers examples of popular resistance against extractive mining, which involve not only physical occupation but also what I term the "ontological occupation" of territories. The text then suggests that the knowledges derived from subaltern groups are more appropriate to the profound social transformations needed to face the planetary crisis than many forms of knowledge produced in the academy.

Chapter 5, "Notes on Intellectual Colonialism and the Dilemmas of Latin American Social Theory," was written at the invitation of Maristella Svampa for a special issue of the sociology journal of the Universidad Nacional de La Plata in Argentina. Maristella asked authors to address two issues: first, how we should think about intellectual or epistemic dependence with respect to the theoretical currents of the central countries; and second, questioning the conditions for producing a more independent social science. I respond in the first part of the chapter by questioning whether it is possible to think outside the modern episteme, which I describe based on Foucault's concept of episteme. In the second part I briefly discuss some areas of emerging research in Latin America that, in a variety of ways, are all poking around the boundaries of the episteme, so to speak: relationality, Buen Vivir (Good Living), nature rights, decolonial feminisms, and civilizational transitions, among others. In the final section I present at greater length a few examples of autonomous social theory production with which I am somewhat familiar, from Mexico, Colombia, Ecuador, and Argentina. These experiences involve the explicit creation of interepistemic spaces in which the primacy of academic understandings is subverted in favor of a determined stance for the "knowledges otherwise" of subaltern groups.

Chapter 6, "Postdevelopment @ 25: On 'Being Stuck' and Moving Forward, Sideways, Backward, and Otherwise," is a conversation with Gustavo Esteva, perhaps the most perceptive and persistent critic of development, originally prepared for a special issue of *Third World Quarterly* on the occasion of the twenty-fifth anniversary of the publication of the English translation of *The Development Dictionary*, edited by Wolfgang Sachs. In our discussion of postdevelopment, we reassess the critiques of the concept and openly discuss what "living beyond development" means today. The topics we cover include how development discourse continues to shape mentalities and practices; the tensions and contradictions in the institutional world, which remains trapped in its compulsion for development and particularly with the so-called sustainable development goals, established by the UN for the 2015–2030 period; the new forms and manifestations of resistance to development; and the relevant experiences that give us a glimpse of worlds that exist beyond development and are heading toward the pluriverse, worlds that are at work creatively constructing a contemporary art of living. Along the way, we propose a few ideas about rethinking "development cooperation" in terms of effective acts of solidarity for civilizational transitions, both in the Global South and in the Global North, perhaps ultimately dissolving that border.

Chapter 7, "Cosmo/Visions of the Colombian Pacific Coast Region and Their Socioenvironmental Implications," was prepared for the forum "Pacific Vision: Sustainable Territory," organized by *Revista Semana* of Bogotá (the most important weekly in Colombia), the World Wildlife Fund (WWF), and the United Nations Development Program (UNDP), which took place in Bogotá on May 18, 2016, with participants from the government, major economic interests, the academy, and a handful of activists. The economic and social crisis assailing the planet has put the Pacific region of Colombia—and other regions with similarly high levels of biological and cultural diversity—in a particularly vital position. As I argue in this text, however, realizing this planetary vocation will require us to collectively establish a novel way of looking at things that is quite unlike the so-called development strategies currently prevailing throughout the region. By accepting this historical challenge, the Pacific would be signing up for an ambitious transition strategy in which territorial sustainability equates to the sustainability of life as a whole—a view far from the economistic concepts of productivity, competitiveness, and efficiency. As I try to show, many of the ideas necessary for this transition toward Otro Pazí-fico Posible, "Another Possible Peacific"—the motto of an international campaign defending the region—already exist in the proposals and practices of some territorial-ethnic communities and organizations in the region, and in some academic approaches. Promoting a transition vision for the Pacific with any resoluteness, however, will require a true codesign strategy in which many people committed to genuine intercultural dialogue would have to participate. In such a strategy, we will find a different form of conceptualizing social action for the so-called postconflict period.

Finally, chapter 8, "Beyond 'Regional Development,'" explores the potential of codesign, as conceived by and for the autonomy of local subaltern communities. It centers on the generation of a transitional imaginary for a particular region in the Southwest of Colombia, the geographical valley of the Río Cauca, whose largest urban center is the city of Cali. For more than a century, this region has been subjected to a capitalist model based on sugarcane plantations in the flatlands and extensive cattle ranching in the foothills. The ecological devastation caused by this model is already evident in the hills, aquifers, rivers, forests, farmland, and wetlands, as is the massive, profoundly unjust, and painful social and territorial dislocation of the peasants and communities of African descent in the region. This region can be reimagined as a true bastion of agricultural production of organic fruits, vegetables, grains, and tropical plants, and as a genuinely multicultural region of small and midsize agricultural producers, and a functional, decentralized network of towns and midsize cities. Imagining an end to sugarcane and to the upper-class and middle-class ways of life supported by the agroindustrial model, however, is still unthinkable for the elites and governing officials, and also for most of the people. In this chapter, I use an ontological design perspective to work out the rudiments of an autonomous design proposal, as a collective exercise in codesign toward a new socionatural configuration that will be quite unlike what we have now, including in the cities. To imagine this beautiful, fertile, and now utterly devastated valley from both the historical perspective of the self-organization and relationality of life and that of the cosmovisions and desires of subaltern groups and other interested groups, we have to go far beyond all known schemes of regional development and prevailing notions of urban planning. In terms of theory, this chapter tries to show that "another design is possible," for it is based on a different reading of reality. It behooves us to take seriously the hypothesis that another possible is possible.

Taken as a whole, these chapters may be considered essays in political on-tology and pluriverse studies. They form part of the collective project to move beyond (or behind or sideways of) the modern onto-epistemic formation. How-ever, and perhaps more relevantly, they are also an effort to contribute to re-alizing the communal and pro-autonomy worlds that keep popping up, with more and more insolence, and perhaps more forcefully as well, in some regions of Abya Yala/Afro/Latino América, come hell or high water, and glimpses of which can already be seen in the most unexpected corners of the planet, in-cluding the Global North. Out of all these dissident imaginations and epis-temic insurrections, with all the doubts, obstacles, and contradictions of their concrete practices, we may be witnessing the slow rebirth of the pluriverse.

I

Theory and the Un/Real

Tools for Rethinking "Reality"
and the Possible

Daily life is the experiential setting in which we experience reality as real. But it is a fairly odd real. Though recognizing this involves a process that is as much intellectual as it is existential, there are a few theoretical tools that we will find helpful to pick up and use along the way. They are undoubtedly not the only tools, and perhaps they are not even the most effective ones, but at this historical moment they are the ones that a number of people and some social groups have collectively been discovering to be important and useful for imagining new pathways of resistance against the capitalist hydra and for imagining and reconstructing different worlds. In this chapter, I aim to develop some of these tools, based on research in two areas: certain ancestral philosophies and practices, and several trends in academic fields. In these two areas, we will identify some sources for another way of understanding the real and the possible.

To fully research the proposition of other possible reals, we would have to move with an open mind through two dimensions. First, we have to approach the spaces that might reveal the existence of other worlds—other forms of knowing~doing~being, with no separation among these—in which the real and the possible are conceived differently.[1] Second, we must reflect deeply on the practices that have constituted us, the people of modernity, as the sort of subjects we are, but particularly as subjects who believe in "the real" (and thus in scientific truth, economics, the individual, and markets as self-constituted entities). This double research is beyond the scope of the present work, and to some extent I have already tackled it in a recent book (Escobar 2018). This chapter has a much more modest aim: to suggest, with a nod to both the conceptual and the intuitive, the abstract and the emotional, that this is a hypothesis worthy of consideration, even if considering it thoroughly might lead us into territories where we would often have to question some of our deepest certainties.

If we look at the field of social life today, we can discern several major sources for rethinking the real/possible. First, the great ancestral civilizations and the teachings of many spiritual and cultural traditions whose cosmovisions have been determined more by radical interdependence than by ontologies of separation. Second, the matriarchal or matriztic ontologies that prevailed among many social groups before the consolidation of patriarchy, and some of which practices still inform our lives. Third, Buddhism and other Earth spiritualities, for their frontal critique of the self and the real. Finally, a series of academic trends focusing on the role of the nonhuman in the production of the worlds we live in, which also contain important clues for understanding the real/possible in a different way. These sources often overlap. Let us look at some of the features of each.

The difference between "reality" and "the real" is worth clarifying. This is not an easy point. The British sociologist of science John Law speaks of the process by which "an unformed but generative flux of forces and relations that work to produce particular realities" and multiple worlds (Law 2004, 7) is reduced by moderns to "a specific external reality," a "reality" (as Maturana said in the epigraph to the introduction) that then becomes the material of our experience. How does such a thing occur? For Law, the key lies in the prevailing Western idea of a single world composed of an underlying reality (a nature, or a real) and many cultures. The notion of a "One-World World" (oww) is predicated on the West's ability to arrogate to itself the right to be "the world" and to relegate all other worlds to its rules, to a state of subordination, or to nonexistence. It is thus an imperialist, colonial notion. It is, however, an extremely seductive idea; the best way to dispel it may be ethnographic and decolonial, as Law suggests:

> So here's the difference: in a European or a Northern way of thinking the world carries on by itself. People don't *perform* it. It's *outside* us and we're *contained* by it. But that's not true for Aboriginal people. The idea of a reified reality out there, detached from the work and the rituals that constantly re-enact it, makes no sense. Land doesn't *belong* to people. Perhaps it would be better to say that people belong to the land. Or, perhaps even better still, we might say that processes of continuous creation redo land, people, life and the spiritual world altogether, and in specific locations. (Law 2011, 1)

As Law is quick to point out, "The differences are *not* simply matters of belief. They are also a *matter of reals*" (Law 2011, 2, his emphasis). The Western realist episteme translates non-Western reals into beliefs, so that only the reality validated by science is real. We have science (and thus the true perception of the real); "they" can only have "beliefs" (myths, ideologies, legends, superstitions, local but never universal knowledges, and so on). When the OWW is enacted, this Euro-American metaphysics (Law 2004, 15) effectively hides multiple realities through complex processes involving power. By showing ethnographically how a variety of realities are canceled based on the assumption of a single "external reality," we can begin to counter this ontological politics with a different politics based on multiple reals—that is, on radical ontological difference and pluriversality. Social movements have shown that this assumption of a single world with a single truth (a true legacy of colonialism) is one of the foundations of neoliberal globalization (e.g., Esteva 2005). This is why these movements aim to counter it with a vision of a world in which many worlds fit.

My partial solution to this problem is as follows: If we can speak of a real that is shared by all of us living beings, it is the "unformed but generative flux of forces and relations" that Law writes about (in scientific terms: the complex self-organizing dynamics of matter and energy, and Earth itself), from which all the forms of the planet and the universe emerge. Many ancestral cosmovisions include similar notions, such as the perpetual circulation of life, which I discuss later. This position is validated by common sense, and it is all we can assume as a shared reality. This flux of life gives rise to many reals and different worlds. By externalizing the real—in other words, by seeing it as external and different from us humans—we urban-moderns reduce it to a single real and invent the concept of "reality" to explain it. This concept of a singular reality is in turn firmly anchored in objectivizing Cartesian epistemologies, in a dualist ontology of self-contained subjects and objects, and in a whole set of mechanisms and practices that constitute us as "autonomous individuals."

Ancestral Sources, Still Alive

Perhaps the most important sources of inspiration for learning about possible nondualist ways of living are the cosmovisions of the original peoples in many parts of the world (Aboriginal Australians, indigenous peoples in the Americas, the Muntu cosmology of Africa, animist cosmologies, and shamanic traditions, among many others). In the West we mainly know about them through anthropology and geography. We have learned many interesting things from these fields about lifeways based on radical interdependence. These lifeways are embodied in practices centered on territory, kinship, spirituality, ritual, the arts, and relationships with the environment.

There is, to give one example, the well-known case of the Kogui, Arhuaco, Wiwa, and Kankuamo groups in the Sierra Nevada de Santa Marta in northwestern Colombia, among whom we find a relational ontology based on the idea that territories are living beings with memories, spaces in which the sacred and the everyday are lived experiences, possessing their own rights, which embody their relationships with other beings and the ways they interrelate with them. Recognition of these territories takes place through a reading of the ancestral markings that were inscribed on sacred sites in the earliest times, which indicate the present course of action. These territorialities are experienced and constructed on a profoundly relational ontology, in sharp contrast to the OWW ontology held by the state, economic interests, and armed actors. The ultimate purpose is to ensure *the circulation of life* through a series of practices involving knowledges, sacred sites, seeds, and rituals. For the Colombian anthropologist Astrid Ulloa, this ontology of the circulation of life, which truly forms an alternative framework for sustainability, is the basis on which these groups build their project for autonomy under the harsh conditions caused by external pressure on their territories (Ulloa 2010, 2011, 2012).[2]

Among the most interesting conclusions of these studies for our purposes are these: In many nonmodern collectives ("societies"), the individual-community dichotomy does not exist, and as such "the individual" does not exist; persons exist in relation to their ancestors, their kin, their communities, the natural world. Likewise, there is no notion of nature as separate from the human realm; instead, life is thought of as a complex web of human and nonhuman. And there is no such category as "economics," separate from social life. Life in these groups evinces an attachment to place and to territory, in addition to a communal foundation that we urban-moderns have cast aside as archaic, inefficient, or restricting to individual liberty. In the present day, however, we are witnessing renewed interest in place and in the recommunalization of social life as key elements in a strategy for transitioning to life models that will allow us to coexist without destroying ourselves or the Earth.

Some of these groups are fighting, in their difficult but dynamic encounter with globalization, to persevere as the living worlds that they are, and not as "cultures" of anthropological or folkloric interest contained within the regulated spaces of neoliberal multiculturalism. As we will see in some of the essays in this book, novel social forms and *worlds in movement* are emerging today from these relational ontologies when groups mobilize to defend their territories against the developmentalist and extractivist avalanche of capital. Though none of these groups has all the answers, any more than moderns do, when it comes to standing up to the crisis and the needed transitions, we still have a lot to learn from them. They are rightly articulating, perhaps more clearly than anyone, the concepts of civilizational crisis and of changing the civilizational model.

Matriarchal Societies and Matriztic Ontologies

If we asked people in the street to name the main causes of the current global crisis, few of them would mention patriarchy. But the crisis of Western civilization is unquestionably rooted in the long development, over the past six thousand years, of patriarchal cultures at the expense of matriarchal ones.[3] Contrary to what people widely believe, matriarchy is defined not by the dominance of women over men but rather by an entirely different concept of life, one based not on domination and hierarchies but on the relational web of life. The Chilean biologist Humberto Maturana and the German psychologist Gerda Verden-Zöller (1993, 2008) draw a distinction between "European patriarchal culture" and the "matristic cultures" that predominated in eastern Europe until the developing patriarchy gradually displaced them, beginning about five or six thousand years ago. Like the feminist writers, Maturana and Verden-Zöller adopt an ontological perspective: "Matristic and patriarchal cultures are different ways of living, different forms of relating, different forms of emotioning; that is, different closed networks of conversation that are realized in each case by both men and women" (2008, 92).[4] Patriarchal culture is characterized by actions and emotions that value competition, war, hierarchies, power, growth, procreation, domination of others, and claiming ownership, and that rationalize these things in the name of truth and individual freedom. In this culture, which encompasses most modern humans, we live lives filled with distrust while seeking certainty by means of control, including the control of the natural world. The objectivizing notion of the real is well suited to this demand for control.

Matriztic cultures arise and prosper "in the awareness of the interconnectivity of all existence, and therefore, it can only be lived continuously in the implicit understanding that all human actions always have consequences for the totality of existence" (Maturana and Verden-Zöller 1993, 47). They were historically characterized by conversations emphasizing inclusion, participation, collaboration, coinspiration, respect and mutual acceptance, sacredness, and the recurrent, cyclical renewal of life. Some matriztic practices persist in contemporary modern cultures (even more so among native peoples)—for example, contradictory though these may be, in relationships between mothers and children, in loving relationships, and in the principles of democracy. The ethical and political implications are clear:

> If we wish to act differently, if we wish to live in a different world, we must transform our desires; to do so we must first change our conversations.... This can only be done by recovering matristic life.... The matristic way of life intrinsically opens a space for coexistence by accepting both the legitimacy of all ways of life and the possibility of coming to an agreement and consensus about generating a common project of living in harmony . . . by allowing us to see and experience the interactions and coparticipation of all live things in the living of all live things. The patriarchal way of life [on the contrary] restricts our understanding of life and of nature, by making us seek to manipulate everything unidirectionally in the desire to control living. (Maturana and Verden-Zöller 1993, 105)

Here we can begin to sense the importance of transforming our understanding of the real and the possible, because our conventional understandings have come down to us through this long history of heteropatriarchy and denial of interdependence, which has led to an entire ethos of control, domination, and the denial of what the Argentine feminist anthropologist Rita Segato (2015) calls *el mundo-aldea* ("the village-world," the communal worlds organized around reciprocal relationships) by what she calls *el mundo-Estado* ("the state-world," with its ontology of domination and control). For Segato, patriarchy constitutes the foundation of all other forms of subordination, imposing a true "pedagogy of cruelty" on most societies. Such a pedagogy of cruelty and control could only arise from an ontology of one world, one real, and only one appropriate form of the possible: the patriarchal way.

This view of the long history of patriarchy and Western modernity as the background of our contemporary crisis lies in the fact that these processes remain *an active historical force today*. Heteropatriarchal ways of being are fundamental to the historicity of our modern being-in-the-world. This is why we say that another possible must be possible: a notion of the possible that refuses to accept the patriarchal (and, we might add, wrongheaded) understanding of the real as something external that should be dominated.

Buddhism as Nondualistic Philosophy and as Critique of Self and the Real

Buddhism is particularly useful for illuminating the shortcomings of our everyday understanding of "the real" in modern worlds. I often point out that

Buddhists have spent the past twenty-five hundred years researching some-thing as fundamental as the nature of the mind, which we in the West have only studied for a scant century or two (with the development of the philoso-phy of language, the philosophy of mind, and in recent years the cognitive sciences). More than a religion, Buddhism is a philosophy of life based on a so-phisticated understanding of the mind. One of the foundations of Buddhism is the principle of interdependence. Buddhism has one of the most powerful notions in this regard: nothing exists by itself; we interexist with everything on Earth; everything in life is the result of processes of *dependent coarising*. This principle of "interbeing" has been amply developed in Buddhist thought, but it characterizes many other cultural groups as well. In short, for Buddhism, *nothing exists intrinsically; everything is mutually constituted*. The mind is thus com-pletely devoid of subject-object dualism. Arriving at this realization—at a form of experience beyond the subject-object division and at a form of perception free of conceptual elaborations—is called perfect wisdom, or "emptiness." Liv-ing with such divisions, on the contrary, is the cause of all suffering.[5]

This leads to another of the most radical elements of Buddhism, which is the absence of what we call the "self" or individual being; for Buddhism, in-deed, being attached to self and fixated on an objectivizing notion of "the real" brings about suffering, not freedom. I sometimes ask my students, a bit in jest, if they've ever seen the "self"; it's hard to say for sure, isn't it? The assertion that every phenomenon is naturally devoid of "real" or genuine existence, even the self, is fairly counterintuitive, since in daily life we see everything as really existing. But this "reality" is relative. Within Buddhism, the belief that things have a real existence is a form of ignorance. Mindfulness meditation, a form of meditation centered on full attention or awareness, is the practice that pre-pares us to destroy this conviction that we have always lived with; it allows us to train our minds to overcome such "obfuscation." As the great Tibetan Bud-dhist teacher Nagarjuna taught nearly two thousand years ago:

First be rid of evil,
Then be rid of self,
Finally be rid of thoughts.
Wise is the one who knows this.
—(DALAI LAMA 1994, 20)

We read something similar in another classic tract: "The root [of all trouble] is that the world is not real, but we take whatever is there as being real. . . . Because of this we will encounter many difficulties and sufferings" (Thrangu

Rinpoche 2003, 270). Similarly, "the root of all problems is the idea of the individual self" (271).[6]

Buddhist practice thus aims to develop the spiritual qualities necessary for seeing the nature of phenomena clearly, which is precisely that these phenomena (including the personal self) have no reality in themselves. The ego dissolves in the infinite flow of life, beyond the notions of life and death, of individual will and permanent realities. The result of these realizations can only be an infinite compassion, desire for the happiness and the cessation of suffering for all living beings, without exception. The radical interdependence of everything in existence, absolute impermanence, and compassion are therefore the three major areas of Buddhist meditation.

Similarly, we find a range of "new spiritualities" centered on the Earth. Some of them are influenced by Buddhism. All embrace sacredness and the active agency of nature, including nonhuman beings. Many of them are inspired by ancestral indigenous, pantheistic, or animist cosmovisions and are critical of mechanistic and reductionist scientific cosmovisions. By contrast, they recognize the intelligence of the universe. In their opposition to the destruction of the natural world by capitalism and development, they are allies of postdevelopment. They insist on the inherent value of all living things, beyond any questions of utility, and thus they often work with movements for nature rights (Eisenstein 2018). In the words of Thomas Berry, a founder of the spiritual ecology movement, "The universe is a communion of subjects, not a collection of objects" (1988, 96). In their new manifestations, these forms of Earth spirituality are perhaps more common in the Global North, but they are beginning to appear in the Global South, especially among ecologists, ecofeminists, and ecovillages. They have always been a part of many indigenous movements all across the Americas.

We know very little about the renewed emphasis on African spiritualities in movements within the diaspora, and in black, indigenous, and shamanic spiritualities in a number of environmentalist urban movements. Some of these forms of spirituality have existed in long-established daily practices, as shown by Betty Ruth Lozano (2017) in relation to the work of black midwives in the Pacific region of Colombia and Ecuador. For Lozano, in addition to being practitioners of reexistence and spiritual leaders, traditional midwives are also insurgent imaginations who fight to maintain the relationality of their worlds, even in the face of the fiercest attacks. In Abya Yala/Afro/Latino América, it would thus seem that we are witnessing a rebirth of the spiritual as an integral dimension of the real and of struggles by many people, social movements, and NGOs that seek to transform the destructive and alienating lifeways of capitalist societies, which have become the norm, especially for the urban middle classes, trapped as they are in consumerism.

I am not suggesting that we should all convert to Buddhism (in actuality, Buddhism does not practice "conversion," unlike almost all religions, nation-states, and academic institutions in the world, which never tire of evangelizing) or embrace this or that spiritual practice. We can pick up this age-old wisdom to suit our abilities and interests, based on an assiduous reading of some texts. We have more and more resources in the West for deindividualizing ourselves and once again enjoying living more in tune with the incessant flow of life, with an awareness of interdependence, impermanence, and the ethics of compassion and care. The truth is that we Western-moderns have gotten used to living profoundly bifurcated lives, splitting mind from body when we know, because we can feel it, that they are ineluctably united with each other and with the universe; dividing reason from emotion, thinking from being, individual from community (as if we could exist in total solitude); firmly believing in the existence of an all-powerful ego (as in the US Army recruiting slogan "Be All You Can Be" or that capitalist archetype "the self-made man"), when we have the existential certainty that every act by the so-called self involves profound and complex collective histories.

After this rapid review of these three sources, we might assert that they all encourage us to "derealize" ourselves; and though it could seem contrary to common sense, derealization means recommunalizing, reconnecting, relocalizing, deindividualizing (perhaps we should say rerealizing ourselves in a different way). And this, in turn, leads us to attempt to leave, to the extent we can, the worlds that program us to live according to the dictates of a belief in one reality, one world, one truth, and ultimately one very blinkered vision of the possible. We have a few guidelines for finding paths in this direction, such as leaving behind the control-form of life in favor of the cooperation-form and interrelationships, following the inspiration of matriarchal thought and Earth spiritualities; venturing into the territories of interbeing, as so many poets and wise women and men of numerous cultures have been telling us to do for centuries; and perhaps learning to walk with the peoples whose major cosmovisions are still nourished by the sources of interexistence, leading them to rise up in defense of their life territories.

A Few Theoretical and Academic Sources

I said earlier that we have more and more resources in our intellectual and existential contexts for meaningfully reorienting our ways of thinking~living.[7]

I am referring to sources from within the West itself, including the academy. Scholars today are rediscovering a series of thinkers whose works on the immanent ability of matter to create life and on life's radically processual nature constitute a clear statement in favor of nonduality, such as Spinoza, Bergson, the North American pragmatists (James, Dewey), the mathematician and philosopher Alfred North Whitehead, and, closer to our own era, the two great proponents of "rhizomatic" thought, Deleuze and Guattari. We can learn much from these authors' works; they help us to unlearn others.

Cybernetics, or the Impossibility of Objective Observation

In the contemporary period, one of the earliest efforts at developing a non-dualist, non-Cartesian epistemology came with cybernetics, continuing today with complexity and living system theories. Beginning in the 1960s, cybernetics demonstrated conclusively that it was impossible to separate the observer from the observed (with the development of "second-order cybernetics"). In a retrospective essay, Heinz von Foerster (1991), one of the founders of the field, referred to its development as a historic leap from viewing things as if they existed "out there" (with the pretense that we are independent observers watching the world pass by, as if through a peephole) to "observing the observation." He concluded that an observer is in fact "a participant actor in the drama of mutual interaction of the give and take in the circularity of human relations," and thus "objectivity . . . is a popular device for avoiding responsibility" (1991, 2, 5). Before poststructuralism, these systems theorists launched a radical critique of the great principle of scientific objectivity, that is, the separation between the observer and the observed. This conclusion still remains at the center of debates about the real: to know is to transform yourself and the unfolding universe.

Drawing on this legacy, the Chilean neurobiologist Francisco Varela (1999, 8) declared that "the world is not something that is given to us but something we engage in by moving, touching, breathing, eating." For Maturana and Varela, an uninterrupted coincidence exists between our being, our doing, and our knowing; the corollary is that "we confront the problem of understanding how our experience—the praxis of our living—is coupled to a surrounding world which appears filled with regularities that are at every instant the result of our biological and social histories" (1987, 241). We should note that, in this conception, reality is constructed minute by minute through our participation in the world. There is no "real" to which we can appeal as the final arbiter of the truth, or from which we can be entirely separated. Mind, body, and world are inextricably united. We may conclude that the world is a codesign in which we all—and all beings, like it or not—participate, not as the outside, objective, "free," and distanced observers we imagine ourselves to be, but because we are ineluctably "thrown" existentially into this task. The final conclusion that Maturana and Varela (1987, 248) come to is no less surprising and equally foreign to Western rationalism: "*We have only the world that we bring forth with others, and only love helps us bring it forth*" (their italics).[8]

Closely related to cybernetics are the theoretical frameworks of complexity, self-organization, and emergence. The social and human sciences have been slow in reacting to revelatory teachings of these developments. The key question in complexity theory is how order arises from the complex dynamics of materiality—its dynamic unfolding—through unusual processes that cannot be grasped based on an understanding of the properties of the elements that make up the entity or system in question. Complexity is the science of emergent forms, of how they attain coherence and consistency despite everything, of the dance between order and disorder. The emergence of the living and the social involves both linear processes (relationships of cause and effect) and nonlinear processes, leading to situations where there is no predictability or control but there is intelligibility, to an alternation between convergence (around an attractor) and divergence. An important corollary of this focus is that the control of natural phenomena that was the aim of reductionist science slips through our fingers, given the unpredictability of processes and consequently the fact that we cannot know "the real" in any absolute sense. The biologists Ricard Solé and Brian Goodwin derive an important conclusion from this realization: "There are other options, such as participating rather than controlling, that is, recognizing that we can influence complex systems and proceeding cautiously with such influence because of the fundamental unpredictability of our actions and their consequences. . . . Complexity shows us that we live in a fascinating but counterintuitive universe. . . . The study of complexity and emergent phenomena is opening the door of a library never before explored, full of amazing books with unexpected insights" (2000, 28, 303). These "counterintuitive" forms of reading the books of the pluriverse lead us to another understanding of the real/possible.

The Ontological Turn, or the Return of the Repressed Terms in the Dualisms of Modernity

Let us move on to another interesting academic development, sometimes known as the "ontological turn" in social theory, which is especially prominent in anthropology, geography, and political philosophy but also affects other disciplines. For many decades, social theory was primarily concerned with epistemological questions, besides social questions, properly speaking: the meaning of understanding, the conditions for understanding, and the consequences of different ways of understanding or of producing expert discourses on reality. It set aside ontological concerns, by which I mean (in the context of these essays, though we will shortly see a special definition of ontology) the diverse ways of being, existing, inhabiting, and building worlds. For the past couple of decades, the latter concerns have been emerging once more, largely as an effort to recover everything that classic and contemporary social theory (including poststructuralism) left out, precisely because of its stark dualisms. Thus theorists are again thinking about the nonhuman, the inert (things, objects, the nonorganic), the body, and infrastructures, on the one hand; but also, on the other hand, about the emotions, affect, and spirituality as vital forces that contribute to building the worlds in which we live.

In other words, these thinkers are bringing back into social theory all the elements that had been set aside because of the exclusively anthropocentric concern with "the social," including social structures and classes, identities, the individual, political economy, discourse, the state, institutions, and power. It is interesting to note that the new questions center on the repressed side of many of the dualisms of modernity. It is now legitimate to conceptualize reality as composed of networks, assemblages, and meshworked socionatural complexes in which the human and the nonhuman are implicated with each other in complicated and ever-changing ways, instead of well-defined and more or less permanent structures. In these new concepts, we find an attempt to make interdependence and relationality visible—to put the human and the nonhuman once more in dynamic relation to each other—with various degrees of success.

The most openly political approach among these developments is developing in the growing field of political ontology. The term "political ontology" was coined by the anthropologist Mario Blaser (2009, 2010, 2013) and is still being developed by Blaser along with Marisol de la Cadena and myself (de la Cadena 2010, 2015; Escobar 2014b, 2018), though it has begun to make headway in the academy and with a number of students, intellectuals, and activists. Blaser proposes a three-layered definition of ontology. On the first level, ontology refers to the assumptions that each social group makes about the kinds of beings that exist in the world and the conditions under which they exist—a sort of inventory of beings and their relationships. The second layer refers to the ways that these premises give rise to particular socionatural configurations: the ways in which they are realized, so to speak, in their worlds. In other words, ontologies do not precede our everyday practices; our worlds are enacted through concrete practices. Finally, ontologies often manifest themselves as narratives, which provide us with clues for understanding the assumptions that underlie them. This third level is amply substantiated in the ethnographic literature on myths and rituals (creation myths, for example). It also exists in the narratives that we moderns tell ourselves about ourselves, that our politicians repeat over and over again in their speeches, and that invariably reverberate in the interpretations that the nightly news gives about what is happening in the world.

Political ontology refers in the first instance to the practices involved in creating a particular world or ontology; it also provides a space for studying the relationships between worlds, including the conflicts that result when different ontologies or worlds strive to preserve their existence in their interactions with other worlds, under asymmetric conditions of power. Political ontology exists in the space between critical currents in the academy and the ongoing struggles to defend territories and worlds. It reveals the ontological dimension of accumulation through dispossession that is taking place in many parts of the world under extractivist development models, especially in large-scale mining, biofuel production, and the appropriation of land linked to commercial agriculture. It lets us see why environmental conflicts are often at the same time ontological conflicts—that is, conflicts over contrasting ways of existing and making worlds. Finally, political ontology seeks to highlight and promote the pluriverse while resisting the tendency to represent the world as if it were only one. It records the rise and political mobilization of relationality as a space for struggle and life force. It bears witness to the urge to rebel among many communities faced with the ravages caused by a world that has arrogated to itself the right to be "the world."

The historicity of political ontology is shown by the absolute need, as indicated by the large number of protests and demonstrations by indigenous people, Afro-descendants, and peasants in Latin America, to defend their relational territories~worlds from the ravages of large-scale extractive operations (see, e.g., Gudynas 2015). It emphasizes, in opposition to the ontological occupation of the territories and lives of these communities and the destruction of worlds carried out by the capitalist globalization project, the importance of thinking from the viewpoint of these life configurations, which, even if partially connected to the globalized worlds, are not yet entirely determined by them (de la Cadena 2015).

The Pluriverse: A World Where Many Worlds Fit

Finally, we come to a notion that is crucial to many of the developments I have briefly outlined: the pluriverse. This concept questions the concept of universality, one of the pillars of Western modernity. Modernity created the idea that we live in a world that has room for only one world, the OWW, now globalized. Up against this premise, the Zapatistas proposed the concept of *a world in which many worlds might fit*; this is, in fact, the most succinct and eloquent definition of the pluriverse. Put another way, whereas the West has managed to universalize its own idea of the world, which only modern science can know and thoroughly study, the notion of the pluriverse inverts this seductive formula, suggesting pluriversality as a shared project based on a multiplicity of worlds and ways of worlding life.

The pluriverse refers to the idea of multiple worlds but also to the idea of life as limitless flow, which I mentioned in the introduction to this chapter. If this is the case, all attempts at fragmenting and classifying that profoundly open and undecidable world are bound to be partial at best, and to reproduce dichotomous, dualist thinking in damaging ways. For the British anthropologist Tim Ingold (2000, 2011), the world is anything but a static, inanimate, or inert container. The world is, to the contrary, a web formed of interwoven lines and threads, always in motion. We humans are, like all other living creatures, immersed in this web. In studying animist cultures and philosophies, Ingold came to the idea of a sentient universe, in which all beings continuously and reciprocally produce their existence. *In this view of the world, it is practically impossible to delimit a single, stable "real."* To do so, one would have to imagine entire sections of the web as inanimate and static. This is why we urban-moderns imagine the world as an inanimate surface to be *occupied*; for many relational cultures, to the contrary, human beings and other beings *inhabit* a world that is alive. While moderns *occupy* space, nonmoderns *inhabit* places, moving along the threads that the place produces. As Ingold says (2011, 129):

> Rather than thinking of ourselves only as observers, picking our way around the objects lying about on the ground of a ready-formed world, we must imagine ourselves in the first place as participants, each immersed with the whole of our being in the currents of a world-in-formation: in the sunlight we see in, the rain we hear in and the wind we feel in. Participation is not opposed to observation but is a condition for it, just as light is a condition for seeing things, sound for hearing them, and feeling for touching them.[9]

I should emphasize that the pluriverse does not assume that worlds are completely separate, interacting with and bumping into one another like so many billiard balls. On the contrary, worlds are completely interlinked, though under unequal conditions of power. We can have no doubt that the dominant modern worlds have globalized themselves and today partially occupy all other worlds on the planet. However, the fact that worlds are interlinked through partial connections does not turn them all into the same thing. Furthermore, worlds may be part of one another (certainly subaltern worlds harbor the modern worlds inside themselves) but at the same time be radically different. For example, many indigenous worlds have learned to live with the separation between humans and nonhumans (and thus have begun to speak of nonhumans as "natural resources"), but they also resist this separation when they mobilize in defense of mountains, lakes, rivers, and lagoons by arguing that they are living, sentient beings, not mere objects to which we give the insipid and apparently benign name of "natural resources" (de la Cadena 2015; Blaser 2010).

Talking about the pluriverse entails making visible the existence of multiple worlds. Indeed, the spread of protests arising in these worlds is what has made the politics of the pluriverse and the very field of political ontology possible. By the same token, it is clear that conventional solutions to our social and environmental crisis, having come out of the categories of the One-World World (with its single vision of the real and of the possible, which is to say, its form of deciding things based on the principle known colloquially as "more of the same"), can at best mitigate our unsustainability and inequality, but it will not be able to give us any guidance for the essential task of making the pluriverse sustainable. We cannot emerge from the crisis with the categories of the world that created the crisis (development, growth, markets, competitiveness, the individual, and so on).

It must be stressed that the pluriverse is not just a trendy concept; it is a whole practice. Living in accordance with the idea that there are multiple worlds, partially connected but radically different, entails an entire different ethics of life, of being~doing~knowing. It means attenuating the capacity of modern certainties about the real and the possible (and their most important correlates, such as the individual, economics, and science) to mold our personal and collective lives. Ultimately, pluriversal politics aim to create conditions favorable to the flourishing of the pluriverse, other ways of world making. Many groups currently rebelling against developmentalist extractivism are resisting this One-World World; they are instances of the pluriverse rising up. Throughout these essays, readers will find ideas and approaches for a politics of the pluriverse. The most important of these include the liberation of Mother Earth (put forward by the indigenous Nasa people of Colombia), the recommunalization of social life, and the relocalization of productive activities such as food, energy, and the economy.

So where does this leave the question of the real? Though this question will never be completely resolved, we can suggest a few criteria from a perspective of strong relationality; that is, from the viewpoint of an epistemology and an ontology without subjects, objects, and acts conceived as self-sufficient and intrinsically independent—what the North American biologist Kriti Sharma (2015) calls radical contingency. First, we can state that the dominant epistemologies and ontologies are indeed what "sustain both the sense of *separateness* of objects from subjects and the sense of *interaction* of objects with subjects" (Sharma 2015, 100, italics in original). Subjects, objects, actions, structures, properties and identities, and so on, depend on these assumptions. Second, we see how this "commonsense essentialism" is stronger among those of us who continue to live in the "Cartesian theater" where mind and body, knowledge and being, are experienced as separate. Third, as I have suggested, in spiritual traditions such as Buddhism and animism, as well as in many traditional cosmologies, we find ways of blurring these essentialisms or of keeping them at bay through special practices and rituals, but often also through daily practices that allow us to actively cultivate interexisting. Finally, we conclude that the way to a relational ontology is necessarily through challenging this objectivizing notion of the real.

I am not suggesting that this will be easy to achieve. As Sharma points out:

> Sometimes when we come across a spider's web, it can be difficult to find where it's anchored; yet the assumption is that it is anchored somewhere. Similarly, it is easy to assume that the dense net of experiences is anchored somewhere—in a world of objects, or in a body, brain, or soul. We often believe that the regularities we experience must be grounded in some kind of substance *beyond* them—material, spiritual, or mental. However, it is entirely possible that the net is aloft, that it is not tethered to anything outside of it, in fact, as far as anyone can tell, the net is *all there is*, so there can be nothing outside of it that could serve as a tether. (2015, 100–101)

The peoples we call "traditional" have no problem living with this uncertainty. It now falls to us urban-moderns to relearn how to live in full awareness of the pluriverse. And as some of the texts we have consulted insist, we cannot restrict our learning process to the intellectual plane; important as that aspect is, it is even more important for us to develop a practice (which could be meditation, mindfulness, collective political practice, ontologically oriented design, or a combination of these things, and doubtless many other practices that every group and person may come up with). In this regard, let us cite a well-known Buddhist text from the eighth century, the *Bodhicharyavatara*, or *A Guide to the Bodhisattva's Way of Life* (quoted in Dalai Lama 1994, 51):

> To keep a guard again and yet again
> Upon the state and actions of our minds and bodies—
> This alone and only this defines
> The sense of mental watchfulness.
>
> All this I must express in action;
> What is to be gained by mouthing syllables?
> What invalid was ever helped
> By mere reading of the doctor's treatises?

I find a lot of harmony between this idea (which could be applied to a revolutionary and pro-autonomy ethics) and the words of Subcomandante Galeano, who spoke of the dilemma confronting the Zapatista movement after the uprising of January 1, 1994, when he asked himself, "What next? . . . Kill or die as the only destiny? Or should we reconstruct the path of life, that which those from above had broken and continue breaking?" To which he answered, in part: "Whoever noticed then that this early dilemma was not an individual one would have perhaps better understood what has occurred in the Zapatista reality over the last twenty years. But I was telling you that we came across this question and this dilemma. And we chose. . . . Instead of fighting for a place in the Parthenon of individualized deaths of those from below, we chose to construct life."[10] As Manuel Rozental wrote in his commentary on this text (2017b, 36), these words express what you hear in social struggles. "The problem isn't about Indians, or about [farmers]; it's about living or dying. It's deciding to live without excluding others' perspectives, from the perspective of all women and men, and once we've made that decision, it's: all right, already!"

Some Axes and Principles for Thinking about the Transitions

To conclude, I would like to propose a series of axes and principles for thinking about strategies for transitions, to be developed throughout the book. Transitions will be more transformative and effective to the extent that they contribute to the following processes (these axes and principles will often overlap, and they might be in tension with one another; a strategy will be more transformative if it attempts to follow several of these principles at once):

Three design and redesign principles:

The recommunalization of social life, as a counter to the dominant individualizing imperative and as the foundation for human action from the perspective of the interdependence of everything that exists.

The relocalization of activities, in the domains of economy, food, health, energy, transportation, education, building, and so forth, to resist the delocalizing tendencies of capitalist globalization, strengthen local and regional economies, and foster convivial modes of living.

The strengthening of collective local autonomies and direct forms of democracy, as a means to lessen the dependence on norms established by experts and the state; critically revalorize local knowledges and values; and promote horizontal political strategies based on people's self-organization, potentially linking up with other similar transformative experiments and autonomous movements elsewhere.

Three broad theoretico-political principles for transition strategies:

The simultaneous depatriarchalization and decolonization of societies, as a way to move decidedly toward nonpatriarchal, nonracist, and postcapitalist social practices and organizations.

The liberation of Mother Earth, as an ethical-political principle to create novel forms of existing as living beings and to rethink the relations between humans and nonhumans in mutually enhancing manners.

The flourishing of the pluriverse, to weave multiple paths toward a world of many worlds, countering the power of the current model of a single globalized world and the capitalist hydra that anchors it.

2

From Below, on the Left, and with the Earth

The Difference That Abya Yala/Afro/ Latino América Makes

Salgo a caminar
por la cintura cósmica del sur
piso en la región
más vegetal del tiempo y de la luz
siento al caminar
toda la piel de América en mi piel
y anda en mi sangre un río
que libera en mi voz su caudal.

I head out to walk
along the cosmic waist of the South.
I tread through the greenest region
of time and of light.
As I walk I feel
all of América's skin against my skin
and in my blood a river flows,
setting its full force free through my voice.

—ARMANDO TEJADA GÓMEZ, "CANCIÓN CON TODOS"
(SONG POPULARIZED BY MERCEDES SOSA)

In a recent post on the América Latina en Movimiento website, titled "The Crisis of Latin American Critical Thought,"[1] the well-known leftist intellectual Emir Sader decries "the relative absence of a critical intelligentsia" in

Latin America, particularly at a time of renewed attacks by the Right against progressive governments. "There is no lack of ideas for critical thinkers," Sader continues; "there is a need to fight for spaces for the debate, but what is really lacking is participation; we lack organizations that could call for critical intellectuals to participate actively in confronting the theoretical and political problems that the progressive processes face in Latin America. . . . Today it is essential that we recover the link between critical thought and the struggle to overcome neoliberalism, between theory and practice, between intellectuals and concrete political engagement."

Professor Sader's plea contains a lot to unpack. In particular, we should all think seriously about the epistemic, economic, political, and military rearticulation of the processes of domination at the national, continental, and global levels in place after 2015, and we should always be ready to respond to an appeal for taking up the question of praxis again, including questioning the relevance of the intellectual in public life in our societies. However, certain key questions are also in play that any analysis of Latin American critical thought (LACT) is bound to consider: What constitutes LACT today? Can we confine it within progressive or Left thought? What exactly is in crisis here? The thinking of progressive governments? Of the Lefts? Do these categories exhaust the field—which in my opinion is much larger, perhaps inexhaustible—of critical thought among communities, movements, and peoples? Moreover, what is the role of critical thought in social transformations?

As the subtitle of this chapter suggests, we are looking not merely at a continent unified by its history and culture, "Latin America," but at a pluriverse, a world made of many worlds. The indigenous and Afro-descendant worlds in particular have become especially important in redefining a supposedly shared identity and reality, hence the new term I am suggesting: Abya Yala/Afro/Latino América. It is not the best possible designation, given the internal diversity of each of its three dimensions, and it hides other key dimensions (rural-urban, class, gender, generation, sexuality, religion and spirituality), but it gives us an initial way of problematizing and at least making us hesitate when we invoke Latin America so casually.[2]

Two Hypotheses about Critical Thought in Abya Yala/Afro/Latino América

The argument I want to lay out here is that LACT is not in crisis; indeed, it could be said to be more vibrant and dynamic than ever. The political-theoretical contributions to rethinking the region resonate all across the continent—in meetings among native peoples, in *mingas* (collective work parties) for thinking, in debates among urban and rural movements and collectives, in assemblies of communities in resistance, in mobilizations of young people, women, peasants, and environmentalists, and undoubtedly in some of the sectors that have traditionally been considered the quintessential spaces for thought, such as the academy and the arts.[3]

A list of the most important currents in LACT would have to include, among others, the critiques of modernity and decolonial theory; the various feminisms (autonomous, decolonial, communitarian, and indigenous and Afrodescendant); the wide range of debates on ecology and alternative economies, including political ecology, social and solidarity economies, communal economies, and the commons; pro-autonomy positions; other and new spiritualities; and the various proposals for civilizational transitions, interculturality, postdevelopment, Buen Vivir (Good Living), and postextractivism.[4] Even more important, *every genealogy and every catalog of LACT today must include the categories, knowledges, and understandings of the communities themselves and their organizations as one of the most powerful expressions of critical thought.* This last proposition constitutes the greatest challenge to LACT, given that the epistemic structure of modernity (whether liberal, rightist, or leftist) has largely been erected atop the effective erasure of this crucial level of thought, and it is precisely this level that is emerging most clearly and substantially today, as we will see.

An analysis of the current state of play in the region and around the globe and how it is reflected in Latin American political-theoretical debates leads us to put forward the following hypotheses: First, that LACT is not gravely ill but flourishing. Second, that the understandings of *pueblos en movimiento* (peoples in movement), of communities in resistance, and of many social movements are at the forefront of thinking for the transitions, and they take on special relevance for reconstructing worlds in the face of the serious ecological and social crises we face—often more relevant than the understandings of the experts, the institutions, and the academy. (To be clear: I am not saying that the latter are useless, just that they are obviously insufficient to the job of generating questions and guidelines for confronting the crisis.)

To see this, however, we must broaden the epistemic and social space beyond what has traditionally been considered LACT and include, alongside the thinking of the Left, at least two major currents that have been emerging over the past twenty years as important sources of critical work: the currents arising in struggles and thinking "from below," and the currents attuned to the dynamics of the Earth. I will call these currents *pensamiento autonómico*, or "pro-autonomy thought," and *pensamiento de la Tierra*, or "Earth thought," respectively.

By "pro-autonomy thought," I am referring to the thinking, more and more articulated and debated, that has emerged from the pro-autonomy processes that were crystallized in Zapatismo but also include a wide variety of experiences and projects from all over the continent, from the south of Mexico to the southwest of Colombia, and from there to the Mapuche struggles in the southern part of the continent. All these movements emphasize rebuilding the communal as the mainstay of autonomy. Autonomy, communality, and territoriality are the three key concepts in this current.

By "Earth thought," I refer not to the environmentalist movement or the field of ecology but rather to the dimension that every community that genuinely inhabits a territory knows is vital to its existence: the indissoluble connection with the Earth and with all living beings. This dimension is eloquently expressed not through theoretical understandings but through art (weavings), myths, place-centric economic and cultural practices, and struggles for territory and in defense of Pachamama, Mother Earth. This form of expression makes it not less important but perhaps even more so for taking on the crucial job of all critical thinking in the present moment, which I will refer to as "the reconstituting of worlds."

I will not be able to situate this argument within the long and illustrious history of LACT. Let us just say that, from certain points of view (such as that of decolonial thought), the genealogy of a *pensamiento otro* ("another way of thinking") stretches back to colonial times, with roots in the works of indigenous intellectuals and freedom-seeking Maroons. Also, several critical debates from nineteenth-century Latin America remain relevant today, from posing the dichotomy between civilization and barbarism to the early debate about Latin American modernity at the end of that century, giving rise to tensions between conservative but antiliberal visions (Arielismo) and anti-imperialist "Our America" visions (José Martí), which likewise remain relevant. Marxism and anarchism had begun to play important roles by the early years of the twentieth century, and the second half of the century saw the famous debate between the philosophers Leopoldo Zea and Augusto Salazar Bondy over the question of whether "a philosophy of Our America exists."

Note, however, that these debates all took place within Eurocentric circles and never concerned themselves deeply with their relevance for communities or for "the masses."[5] It was only after Orlando Fals Borda published his radical critique *Ciencia propia y colonialismo intelectual* (A Science of Our Own and Intellectual Colonialism) in 1970 and Paulo Freire came out with his influential book *Pedagogy of the Oppressed* in 1968 (with English and Spanish translations published in 1970) that the epistemic edifice of the academies, both critical and Left, was shaken and what we now would call "the other ways of knowing" of subaltern worlds began to be taken seriously.

This is doubtless an inadequate and perhaps overly neat account of the rich tradition of LACT, but I include it for the sake of the two hypotheses outlined earlier. The popular education and communication movements inspired by Fals Borda (with his "participatory action research" program) and Freire (with his "consciousness-raising" pedagogy) led to innumerable transformative protests and demonstrations in the 1970s and 1980s, often on the part of revolutionary struggles fueled by Marxism and the whole range of the Left, but always emphasizing the need to take people's ways of knowing seriously. Today we find echoes of this precious legacy in the pro-autonomy and Earth thought currents, though they are epistemically more radicalized than the projects of earlier decades.

I would like to define LACT for the purposes of this essay as the intermeshing of three great currents: Left thought, pro-autonomy thought, and Earth thought. These are not separate and preconstituted spheres; they overlap, sometimes feeding into one another, sometimes in open conflict. My argument is that today we must cultivate all three currents, keeping them in tension and in continual dialogue, abandoning all pretense of universalizing them and possessing the truth. In other words, we should take the Zapatista slogan "From below and on the Left" and add a third fundamental basis: "with the Earth" (which is to a degree implicit in Zapatismo). In the following section, I begin by making a few short observations on the crucial importance of "thinking from the Left" and then offer an outline, necessarily provisional, of the other two currents.[6]

I. Thought on the Left

The Left is so many things: theory, strategy, practice, history of struggle, humanism, images, emotions, song, art, sorrows, victories and defeats, revolutions, moments of beauty and of horror, and many more. How can we help but feel inspired, even now, by the most beautiful moments of the socialist, anarchist, and communist revolutions, through their powerful history? At least for my generation, how can we not get emotional, contradictory though our emotions may be, when we see the charismatic figure of Che, or Camilo Torres holding the gun that he never fired while waiting for death to find him—icons that still adorn the walls of public universities in Colombia and all over the continent and may still make us smile when we see them? How can we not recall the deep red of the flags in peasant and proletarian protest marches of yore, or peasants reading Chairman Mao's ubiquitous *Little Red Book* while waiting to march to defend their right to the land?[7] How can we not incorporate the revolutionary Left's principles of social justice, the imaginaries of equality, and the ideals of liberty and emancipation into every struggle and every theory?

At the level of theory, it is vital to remember the many contributions of dialectical materialism and historical materialism, and its rethinking in the encounter with developmentalism (dependency theory), environmentalism (ecological Marxism), feminism, liberation theology, poststructuralism (e.g., Laclau and Mouffe), culture (e.g., Stuart Hall, Latin American cultural studies, interculturality), and postcolonial and decolonial theory. However, though this broad array of theories remains clearly relevant, today we can easily recognize the inevitable bits of modernism clinging to historical materialism (such as its aspiration to universality, totality, teleology, and truth, which filter through even the sharp analytical lens of the dialectic). Furthermore, we cannot ignore that we are learning new forms of thinking about materiality from ecological economics, from theories of complexity, emergence, autopoiesis and self-organization, and from the new ways of thinking about the contributions of everything that was left out by the modernist explanation of the real, ranging from objects and things, with their "vibrant materiality," to the whole gamut of the nonhuman (microorganisms, animals, numerous species, minerals), which are as determinant of the configurations of the real as the social relations of production. These new "materialist ontologies" even have room for emotions, feelings, and the spiritual as active forces that produce reality.

I want to stress two points in this brief recap. First, the break that the new materialisms have made with the anthropocentrism of the materialisms of modernity. Second, and as a corollary, the epistemic opening that the currents we associate with the Left necessarily need to undergo. By "epistemic opening," I refer to the need to abandon all pretense of universality and truth and to actively embrace those other ways of thinking, of struggling, and of existing that are emerging—sometimes clearly and forcefully stated, sometimes nebulously and haltingly, but always in an affirmative way that points to other models for living—in so many places all across a continent that seems to be reaching its boiling point.[8] This opening might lead intellectuals on the Left to think beyond the episteme of modernity, to dare abandon once and for all their most treasured categories, including development, economic growth, progress, even the very category of "man." It challenges them to feel-think with the Earth and with communities in resistance so as to rearticulate and enrich their thought.

I should make clear that I have not focused here on analyzing the difference between "progressivism" and "the Left," or on the well-informed critiques of the neoextractivism practiced by progressive governments, or on the apparent exhaustion of the progressive neoextractivist and developmentalist model. Nor have I joined the important debates over the crisis and the potential rethinking of the Left that are now taking place in countries such as Brazil, Venezuela, Ecuador, Argentina, and Bolivia. Finally, I have not attempted to analyze the appropriation by some progressive governments of potentially radical concepts such as Buen Vivir (Good Living) or the rights of nature.[9] I must note, however, that from the perspective I have expressed here, any politics of the Left based on excluding other points of view, suppressing criticism, and repressing grassroots organizations for going against the official line can only represent a narrow and questionable view of thinking on the Left. That is how officialist Lefts appropriate and undermine the experiences and categories of peoples and movements. The debate about this sort of progressivism is heating up across the continent—and for good reason. I hope that the two currents I explore next will contribute new aspects to the debate.

II. Thought of or from Below

The earth is in charge, the people give the orders, and the government obeys. Building Autonomy.

A specter is haunting the continent—the specter of autonomism.[10] And we might add: "All the powers of old [Latin America] have entered into a holy alliance to exorcize this specter. . . . It is high time that [autonomists] should openly, in the face of the whole world, publish their views, their aims, their tendencies, and meet this nursery tale of the specter of [autonomism] with a manifesto of the party itself." In this case, of course, it will not be one manifesto for a single party or movement but a multiplicity of manifestos for the multiplicity of worlds that our Zapatista comrades tell us about, a world of many worlds. These will be the multiple visions of the people "who just got tired of not existing and started blazing a trail" (Rozental 2017b), the subjects of dignified rage, the women and men who are fighting to win a dignified place for the peoples of the color of the Earth.

This second trend we are proposing, "autonomism," is undeniably a political-theoretical force that has begun to travel steadily across Abya Yala/Afro/Latino América, against all odds and despite its many vicissitudes. It has arisen from the political mobilization of the collective and relational existence of a wide variety of subaltern groups—indigenous and Afro-descendant peoples, peasants, residents of urban working-class territories, young people, women in solidarity. It is the wave made by the wretched of the earth to defend their territories against the onslaught of neoliberal global capital and individualist and consumerist modernity. It can be seen in action in many of the protest movements over the past two decades, in interepistemic encounters, in mingas for thinking, in peoples' summits, and in all sorts of confluences where the central protagonists are the understandings of the communities and peoples that base their resistance on the logics of life in their own worlds. It involves all those who defend themselves against extractivist development because they know perfectly well that "for development to come in, people have to leave," in the words frequently expressed by Afro-Colombian leaders, men and women, who have experienced being forced from their territories under pressure from so-called progress.

At the level of theory, autonomism is related to a broad range of tendencies, from decolonial thought and subaltern and postcolonial studies to the epistemologies of the South and political ecology, among others. It is clearly akin to notions such as the decolonization of knowledge, cognitive justice, and interculturality. But its political-theoretical anchor is composed of three main concepts: autonomy, communality, and territoriality, only the first of which has any sort of genealogy among the Lefts, especially within anarchism. New notions of community are reappearing in several political-epistemic spaces, including indigenous, Afro-descendant, and peasant protest movements, especially in Mexico, Bolivia, Colombia, Ecuador, and Peru. The notion of community is used in various senses: communality, communal groups and practices, the struggle for the commons, communitism (communitary activism). Communality (the condition of being communal) thus constitutes both the horizon of what is intelligible in the culture of deep América and also the new struggles, even in urban contexts; it is a central category in the lives of many peoples, and it continues to be their most basic lived experience. Any concept of community in this sense should be taken in a nonessentialist way, considering "the community" in all its heterogeneity and historicity, as inhabiting the same place as heteropatriarchal capitalism, but at the same time always partaking of ancestral sources (the relational web of communal existence) while resolutely open to the future in its autonomy.[11]

Autonomism finds its raison d'être in the deepening ontological occupation of the territories and the life~worlds of the territory~peoples by every sort of extractivism and by neoliberal globalization. This occupation is being carried out by a One-World World (capitalist, patriarchal, white, secular, modern, liberal) that arrogates to itself the right to be "the world" and refuses to interact with all these other worlds that are mobilizing with greater and greater conceptual clarity and political power to defend their different models for living. Autonomism speaks to us of societies in movement, rather than of social movements, as Raúl Zibechi has suggested in reference to the wave of popularindigenous insurrections that brought Evo Morales to power. We might refer even more appropriately to "worlds in movement," because what emerges are genuine *relational worlds* in which the communal has priority over the individual, the connection with the Earth over the separation between humans and nonhumans, and Buen Vivir (Good Living) over economics.

In the language of political ontology, we could say that many territorialethnic struggles can be seen as ontological struggles—to defend other models of living. They interrupt the globalizing project of creating a One-World World. Such struggles are crucial for making ecological and cultural transitions to the pluriverse. They are the cutting edge in the search for alternative models of life, economics, and society. They are struggles that set "communitarian meshworks" against "coalitions of transnational corporations," in search of a society reorganized on the basis of local and regional autonomies (Gutiérrez Aguilar 2013); an economy self-managed on communal principles, even if connected to the market; and a relationship with the state, but only to contain the rationality of the state as far as possible. In short, they are struggles seeking to organize themselves as the powers of a different, other, nonliberal, nonstate, and noncapitalist society. Though this defense arises from (partly) communitarian and noncapitalist roots, it entails a whole history of relationships with capitalist modernity. "It is a matter of recovering, reconstructing, and revitalizing place and territory, this time in order to reproduce life," say the Nasa comrades, men and women, from southwestern Colombia, "and so give rein to forms opposed to the totalizing and homogenizing goal of capitalism" (Quijano 2012, 210).

Autonomy is therefore a political-theoretical practice of territorial-ethnic movements—thinking things through "from the inside out," as some Afrodescendant women leaders in Colombia put it, or "changing our traditions traditionally," and changing the form of change, as they say in Oaxaca (Esteva 2005). "In fact, the key to autonomy is that a living system finds its way into the next moment by acting appropriately out of its own resources," Francisco Varela (1999, 11) tells us, giving a definition that applies as well to communities. It entails defending some practices, transforming others, and inventing new practices. We could say that, at its finest, autonomy is a theory and practice of interexistence, a design tool for the pluriverse (see Escobar 2018 for an exhaustive explanation of this concept).

The aim of autonomy is the realization of the communal, understood as laying down the conditions for the continuous self-creation of communities (their autopoiesis) and for their successful structural coupling with their ever more globalized surroundings. As the indigenous Misak community members from Northern Cauca in Colombia say, they must "reclaim the land in order to reclaim everything . . . which is why we must think with our own heads, speaking our own language and studying our own history, analyzing and passing on our own experiences, as the other pueblos do" (Cabildo Indígena de Guambía 2007, quoted in Quijano 2012, 257). Or as the Nasa put it in their movement, the Social and Communitarian Minga, "Words without actions are empty. Actions without words are blind. Actions and words without the spirit of the community are death itself." Autonomy, communality, territory, and relationality appear intimately linked here, constituting an entire original political-theoretical framework inside this second critical current of Abya Yala/Afro/Latino América.

III. Earth Thought

Relationality—the relational way of being, knowing, and doing, defined as the socionatural configurations that arise from the recognition of the radical interdependence of all living things, where nothing preexists the relationships that constitute it—is the great correlate of autonomy and communality. This can be seen in the cosmovisions of many peoples, such as the African philosophy of Muntu, or concepts of Mother Earth such as Pachamama, *Ñuke mapu*, Uma Kiwe, and many others. It is also implicit in the concept of civilizational crisis—assuming that the current crisis was caused by a particular model of the world (an ontology), the modern civilization of separation and disconnection that sees humans and nonhumans, mind and body, individual and community, reason and emotion, and so on, as separate, self-constituted entities.

Relational ontologies or worlds are based on the notion that all living beings are expressions of the creative force of the earth, of its self-organizing and its constant emergence. Nothing exists unless everything exists ("I am because you are," because everything else exists, says the southern African principle of Ubuntu). In the words of the North American ecologist and theologian Thomas Berry, the Earth is "a communion of subjects, not a collection of objects." The mandate of the Earth of which many activists speak therefore urges us to live in such a way that all can live. The territory~peoples find it easiest to comply with this mandate: "We are the continuation of the Earth; let's look out from the heart of the Earth" (Marcos Yule, Nasa governor). There is a good reason why the relationship with the Earth is central to the indigenous, Afro-, and peasant struggles in the present context.

From this perspective, the great challenge for the Left and to autonomism is learning how to sentipensar with the Earth, how to listen deeply to both the cries of the poor and the cries of the Earth (Leonardo Boff; *Laudato Si'*). It is refreshing to think that of the three currents discussed here, the third is by far the oldest. It has always been around, ever since peoples first learned that they are Earth and relations, expressions of the creative force of the universe; that every being is an Earth-being. It exists in the cosmocentric thought undergirding the webs and meshworks that form life; the thought that knows, through feeling, that everything in the universe is alive and that consciousness is not a human prerogative but a property spread across the whole spectrum of life. It is the thought of the men and women who defend a mountain against mining because it is a living being, an *apu* (de la Cadena 2015); who defend the high plateaus and natural springs because they are the source of life, often sacred places where the human, the natural, and the spiritual join to become a living, intermeshed complex. It also lies at the base of the recommunalization of life, the relocalization of economics and production, the defense of seeds, the rejection of GMOs and free trade agreements, and the defense of agroecology and food sovereignty (Gutiérrez Escobar 2017).

We can say without the slightest anachronism that the "cosmogonies" of many cultures around the world are the original Earth thought. This also was, and to a degree still is, the thought of matriarchal communities, as Claudia von Werlhof (2015) has spent more than two decades explaining in her critical theory of patriarchy; matriarchal not in the sense of women's domination, but in the sense of cultures that put the highest value on cooperation, recognizing the other, horizontality, participation, and sacredness, rather than on the aggression, domination, war, control, and appropriation found in patriarchal societies, which over their five thousand years of history have gradually taken over all the societies on the planet. The Chilean biologist Humberto Maturana and his colleague Gerda Verden-Zöller (1993, 2008) have a similar take in their idea of "matriztic cultures" and "the biology of love," referring to cultures that live in profound awareness of the interconnection of everything in existence and resist a life course based on appropriation and control because their "emotioning" tells them, precisely, to live in mutual respect and convivially (see chapter 1).[12]

Earth thought underlies concepts of territory. "Anyone can have land, but territory is another matter," say some Afro-descendant elders on the Pacific coast of Colombia, that country's great black region. Territory is the space for enacting relational worlds. It is the place for the women and men who care for the land, as the women of the small black community of La Toma in Northern Cauca perceptively put it as they mobilized to combat illegal gold mining: "To the women who care for their territories. To the women and men who take care of the Life of Dignity, Simplicity, and Solidarity. Everything we have gone through and experienced, we did it for the love that we've known in our territories. . . . Our land is our place for dreaming our future in dignity. . . . Maybe that is why they persecute us, because we want a life of autonomy and not dependence, a life where we don't have to beg or be the victims."[13] Hence the slogan of their march, "Territory is life and life is not for sale, it is to be loved and defended."

We also find Earth thought in many indigenous peoples' cosmoaction, which centers on defense of territory and on their *Planes de Vida* (Life Plans). Territory is "the vital space that ensures survival as a people, as a culture in peaceful coexistence with nature and the spirits. Territory is our genuine historical text, which keeps the tradition of those of us who inhabit it alive. It represents and describes the principles and practices of our culture. It means effective authority over the physical and spiritual space. As a collective space of existence, it makes the harmonious coexistence of peoples possible. It grounds the indigenous cosmovision as the reason for our survival."[14] Thus their strategy is aimed at *"recovering the land in order to recover everything*—authority, justice, work; which is why we must think with our own heads, speaking our own language and studying our own history, analyzing and passing on our own experiences, as the other peoples do."[15] Likewise, the Misak people explain their Life Plan as a project for "constructing and reconstructing a vital space for being born, growing up, remaining in, and flowing. The plan is a narrative of life and survival, it is the construction of a path to facilitate the journey through life, and not merely the construction of a planning methodology."[16]

This is why many indigenous peoples describe their political struggle in terms close to the Nasa principle of "the liberation of Mother Earth." The key question for these movements is: how can the conditions for existence and reexistence be maintained in the face of the onslaught of developmentalism, extractivism, and modernity? This question and the idea of Mother Earth liberation are potent concepts for any political practice right now: for the Left and for pro-autonomy processes as much as for environmental struggles and fights for other ways of living. They link environmental justice, cognitive justice, autonomy, and the defense of worlds. Under the same rubric, we will also find the movement for the rights of nature, among the genuinely biocentric ideas (ones that go beyond speeches or superficial references to sustainability or Pachamama).

For us, the urban-moderns living in the spaces most strongly marked by the liberal model of life (the ontology of the individual, the market), relationality presents a major challenge, given how much personal inner work it takes to unlearn the civilization of disconnection, economism, science, and the individual. Perhaps it means abandoning the individual idea that we have of radical political practice. How can we take the inspiration of relationality seriously? How can we relearn interexisting with all humans and nonhumans? Should we regain some familiarity with the Earth to relearn the art of sentipensar with it? How can we do so in urban, decommunalized contexts? Unfortunately progressivism, and perhaps a good portion of the Left, is far from understanding this mandate. As Gudynas puts it, neither Right nor Left "understands nature."[17]

Final Note: Exiting Modernity?

The epistemic opening of the Left means daring to question development, the poorly named notion of progress, and modernity. Only in this way can Left thought participate in thinking about and constructing the civilizational transitions coming out of pro-autonomy and Earth thought and struggles. As is well known, the progressivism of the past two decades has been profoundly modernizing, and its economic model is based on a hard core of modernity premises, including those of economic growth and extractivism.

In both the Global North and the Global South, the thinking about these transitions has been very clear that the transitions have to go beyond the model of life imposed in almost every corner of the world by a certain dominating vision of modernity.[18] We will manage to get out of modernity only by holding on to all three currents for support. Healing human life and the Earth will take a true transition "from a period of human devastation of the Earth to a period when humans would be present to the planet in a mutually enhancing manner," as the Earth liberation theologians Thomas Berry and Leonardo Boff express it.[19] It will mean moving decisively toward a new era that these ecologists call the Ecozoic, the era of the house of life. Climate change is only one of the most blatant manifestations of the systematic devastation of life by racist, patriarchal capitalist modernity.

The Liberation of Mother Earth, a concept based on the cosmocentrism and cosmoaction of many territory~peoples, calls on us to "dreamagine" (*disoñar*) how to re/design all worlds. This act of "dreamagination" (*disoñación*) aims to reconstitute the fabric of life, of territories, and of communalized economies. As one Misak youth said, it's a matter of turning the grief of centuries of oppression into hope and turning hope into a basis for autonomy.[20] For the Afro-Colombian activists of the Pacific coast who have been so hard-hit by developmentalism, their region is a Territory of Life, Joy, Hope, and Freedom. There is a wise principle for the political practice of all the Lefts in the notion of "weaving life in freedom."

The three currents I have discussed constitute not an additive model but rather one of multiple interconnections. These are not paradigms that can neatly replace one another. It is clear, however, that the Left and autonomism (and humanity) must turn to the Earth. The "posthuman" human—the "human" that emerges from the end of anthropocentrism—will have to learn all over again how to live in human and nonhuman communities, in the only world that we truly share, which is the planet. The recommunalization of life and the relocalization of our economies and food production insofar as possible— key principles of the activisms and designs for the transition—become principles appropriate to our political-theoretical practice in the present. Indeed, we can already find powerful intermeshings of Left, autonomy, and Earth thought in interepistemic encounters such as the Networks and Mingas para el Buen Vivir ("Work Parties for Good Living") in Popayán, Colombia, and in events such as the Symposium on Critical Thought Facing the Capitalist Hydra, convened by the Zapatistas (EZLN) and held at CIDECI-UniTierra in San Cristóbal de las Casas, Chiapas, Mexico, in May 2015.[21]

Many, if not most, of these communalitarian and autonomous experiences in defense of the Earth are inevitably weakened by the antagonistic circumstances under which they occur, in spite of their commitment to the transformations. It is worth mentioning that, in their quest for autonomy, some fall back into developmentalism, others are subverted from within by their own leaders, still others reinscribe old forms of oppression or create new ones, and it is not uncommon for mobilizations to falter under the incredible weight of the pressures of the moment or because of overt repression. Antagonisms are inherent to all social practice. This hardly disqualifies the actions of "actually existing communities," nor should it condemn them to the residual category of being unrealistic, too local, or romantic. Here lies the hope: after all, as Esteva says (2009), hope is not the conviction that something will happen, but that something makes sense, whatever happens.

Those who still insist on the path of development and modernity are either suicidal or, at the least, ecocidal, and without question they are historical anachronisms. By contrast, those who defend place, territory, and the

Earth are neither romantics nor "infantile." They represent the cutting edge of thought, for they are attuned to the Earth and to justice, and they understand the central issue of our historical moment: the transitions to other models for living, toward a pluriverse of worlds. We cannot imagine and construct postcapitalism (and the postconflict era) using the categories and experiences that created the conflict (particularly development and economic growth). Jumping straight to Buen Vivir without completing the industrialization and modernization phase is less romantic than it would be to complete that phase, whether in a Left or a Right fashion. As indigenous, peasant, and Afrodescendant activists often put it in their meetings, "We cannot construct our world with more of the same. . . . What's possible has already been done; now let's go for the impossible."

Do we dare affirm that, with the complexity of the critical thinking on the three currents so schematically outlined here, Abya Yala/Afro/Latino América today presents the world with a different model for thinking about the world and about life? In this—despite all the tensions and contradictions between the currents and within each of them—we find the "Latin American difference" for the first half of the twenty-first century. One thing that we can confidently say, together with the great Mercedes Sosa, is that peoples, collectives, movements, artists, and intellectuals walk their words "along the cosmic waist of the South," in "the greenest region of time and of light," which is the beautiful continent where we live.

Thanks be to life, for giving us so much. . . .

3

The Earth~Form of Life

*Nasa Thought and the Limits
to the Episteme of Modernity*

Our struggle will continue until the sun stops shining.
—NASA PROTEST BANNER, MAY 10, 2017

(Andean rhythm)
Out with war and destruction
Out with power and exploitation
Out with corrupt politicians
Out with injustice and ambition
Out already with globalization
Out with death and invasion
Out with the businessman and his vision . . .
Long live the mountains and their colors
I'll sing to the plateau and the wind
May a new forest ease our sorrows
I went in search of water and found none
The river fairies lament the madness
Of man, who has finished off the forest . . .
Beloved mountains of mine, light of my valley
May the world help in your regeneration
May you never lack water in the future
May the air be as pure as our love for you.

—LONG LIVE THE MOUNTAINS!, BY THE NASA MUSICAL YOUTH GROUP FXIW

I. A New Statement

A new statement travels the world: *The Liberation of Mother Earth*.[1] Recently put forth by indigenous Nasa women and men, this statement proclaims the possibility of another world to come.[2] This is why they say, "From this sacred corner of the planet, as ancestral peoples rooted in these Cauca lands, we do our part for the earth and for life, we fight for the earth and for life." But they warn, "This struggle comes out of Northern Cauca, but it is not Northern Cauca's struggle. It comes from the Nasa people, but it is not the Nasa people's. Because life itself is at risk when the earth is exploited in the capitalist way, which throws the climate, the ecosystems, everything out of balance. From Northern Cauca we say: enough, it's time to liberate her." And they add: "These words explain and challenge; that is why they must be read from the heart, and the anger, the sorrow, the love for life, and the commitment must be shared. Now we designate our acts for feeling and claiming the company of all peoples who deserve to inhabit this home, Mother Earth, in freedom."

How should we understand this statement, particularly without making a narrow appeal to an ahistorical founding subject ("the indigenous peoples"), concepts new or old (community, ancestrality, territory), the persistent themes ("environmental devastation," "sustainability"), or new declarative modes (communication discourse), though of course it might involve all of these? What historical vectors inspire and energize it? How can we go beyond the surface details of the phrases and clauses that it comprises, some of which I will repeat in this chapter? Might the Nasa statement constitute the foundation for a novel discourse formation? Even be the harbinger of a coming new episteme? Could the statement thus become "words that explain and challenge" for all the people, and all the peoples, who respect life and love the Earth? This is the proposal—apparently simple, but complicated to demonstrate— that I try to develop in this chapter.

The release of the Mother Earth liberation statement in 2004 took place against a tightly packed historical background of struggles, including, in recent decades, the Consejo Regional Indígena del Cauca (CRIC, Cauca Region Indigenous Council) program for recovering land and enlarging the *resguardos* (indigenous communal lands) beginning in the 1970s; the founding of the Organización Nacional Indígena de Colombia (ONIC, National Indigenous Organization of Colombia) in 1985 and the Asociación de Cabildos Indígenas del Norte del Cauca (ACIN, Association of Northern Cauca Indigenous Assemblies) in 1994; the important national movement of the Minga Social y Comunitaria (Social and Communitarian Work Party) beginning in 2008; and the rise of communitarian projects and local economies (the Planes de Vida, or Life Plans) and strategies for defending indigenous territories and autonomy—all of this in the midst of hideous violence, massacres, displacement by landowners and armed actors, and the perpetual breaking of treaties signed by the state: in short, the death project of capitalist globalization. The mandate was updated in December 2014 with a new round of reclaiming land, this time from the ranches of the largest landowners in Colombia, such as Carlos Arturo Ardila Lülle, on the part of the indigenous communities of Corinto. This also took place in the context of the co-optation of indigenous leaders by the state and, undoubtedly, of profound contradictions and internal tensions.[3]

But let us listen to a bit more of the statement:

> But we say that so long as we are indigenous people—that is, children of the earth—our mother is not free to live, as she will be after she becomes once more the collective hearth and homeland of the peoples who care for her, respect her, and live with her; and until such a time, neither will we her children be free. We peoples are all slaves, along with the animals and living beings, until we can help our mother regain her freedom.
>
> And as we said in 2005 and now reaffirm, *la desalambrada de Uma Kiwe* (debarbedwiring Uma Kiwe) means debarbedwiring the heart. Debarbedwiring the heart means debarbedwiring Mother Earth. Who would have believed it: heart and earth are one and the same being. This is what we know and feel at this moment. This being so, should we get on board the progress train? As errand boys, as bosses?

We could easily use the rest of the essay to discuss the profound sentiments that shimmer in these paragraphs. On the anthropological side, for example, we could delve into the treasure trove of cultural-historic practices that provide the fertile ground from which the statement emerged. Going in this direction, ecological anthropology would speak to us of the particular understanding of nature that characterizes the Nasa world; as they put it:

> We spring from the earth, we rejoice in her, and we return again to her womb when we die. The earth has always been our joy, we tie ourselves up with her from our first moment—*nos ombligamos* (we feel ourselves *umbilicated*)—we respect her and we take care of her between us all, men and women. . . . For us, the earth . . . is the great house where we live with all other beings, the mother who gives us everything.

We could analyze this same thought through political economy, political ecology, and political ontology, seeking to understand how the concept is based on an ontology that does not strictly divide the human from the nonhuman, as modern worlds do, but instead reveals a cosmovision in which the universe is one continuous whole where everything is alive, and how this cosmovision is under assault by the death project of capital and development, generating environmental conflicts—illegal mining, biofuels, illegal crops—that devastate ecosystems and worlds. These would all be important and pertinent analyses.

But for this occasion, I have another sort of analysis in mind, as I have already suggested in my initial questions. Let us move on to it, then.

II. On Statements, Discursive Formations, and Epistemes: Modernity as Onto-Epistemic Configuration

The prominence I have given to the Nasa statement will tell anyone familiar with the works of Michel Foucault that I am referring to his archaeology and discourse perspective. We know that Foucault was one of the great anthropologists of modernity; his critical works on asylums, hospitals, prisons, factories, schools, military barracks, and sexualities are genuine historical ethnographies of the discourses and practices that have constituted us as moderns. We know that he diagnosed better than anyone the forms by which power functioned in these societies, and he discovered that the design of apparently benign institutions brought an entire series of tools into use that systematically linked ways of knowing and forms of power, so as to produce the normalized and disciplinary societies in which we must live today. We know, finally, that in the final analysis the aim of these tools and institutions is to contain and administer life itself. Thus we recall key concepts such as the microphysics of power, biopolitics, governmentality, genealogy, problematizations, and discourse analysis—the latter being ubiquitous in Foucault's work.

But it seems to me that nowadays we know much less about the "archaeological" phase of Foucault's writing, as it is sometimes called (in contradistinction to the "genealogical" phase that began with *Discipline and Punish*, first published in 1975), which includes his works from *Madness and Civilization* (1961) to *The Archaeology of Knowledge* (1969). My purpose here is not to summarize the main contributions of this phase but rather to highlight a few notions that will help us see what is historically innovative about the Nasa statement. I refer to the concepts of statement, archive, discursive formation, and episteme. (I would also have to explain briefly the notions of nondiscursive formation; the role of object, concept, strategies, and enunciative modalities in discourse; interpositivities; and the transformation of discourse—but these explanations can only be passingly brief.)

Let us begin with the statement. Foucault, according to Deleuze, is "a new archivist," because "henceforth he will deal only with statements. He will not concern himself with what previous archivists have treated in a thousand different ways: propositions and phrases" (Deleuze 1988, 1). The statement does not point us toward a transcendental subject, meaning, or truth, nor does it convey a logic of chains of inference, derivations, or contradictions, as phrases and propositions do. In the first instance, the statement can be thought of as an "atom of discourse," as Foucault tells us in *The Archaeology of Knowledge* (1972, 80). But it is much more than this. "Any statement . . . does not have as its *correlate* an individual or a particular object that is designated by this or that word in the sentence. . . . What might be defined as the *correlate* of the statement is a group of domains in which such objects may appear and to which such relations may be assigned. . . . [The statement] is linked rather to a 'referential' that is made up not of 'things,' 'facts,' 'realities,' or 'beings,' but of laws of possibility, rules of existence for the objects that are named, designated, or described within it, and for the relations that are affirmed or denied in it" (91). The statement is thus a paradoxical object. "Instead of being something said once and for all . . . the statement, as it emerges in its materiality, appears with a status, enters into various networks and various fields of use, . . . circulates, is used, disappears, allows or prevents the realization of a desire, serves or resists various interests, participates in challenge and struggle, and becomes a theme of appropriation or rivalry" (105).

Here we approach the notion of discourse, which refers to the "group of statements that belong to a single system of formation," such as the discourses of the clinic, economics, sexuality, or, as we will see shortly, the discourse of development (107). Discourse analysis describes the relationship between statements. This description can be roughly phrased in terms of the formation of objects, concepts, strategies, and themes that are developed in it, but the key point is to investigate the system of relationships that ties all of them together—that is, the discursive practice that determines that only certain things can be said, even if the discourse creates the impression of a wide variety of forms and truths. This is what Foucault calls "regularity in dispersion"— the fact that what can be said in a statement is vigorously regulated, even if the phrases and propositions that fill it—objects, concepts, themes, and so on— seem to proliferate ad infinitum. In the final analysis, and to our surprise, within any given discourse, few things can be said. This is why Foucault says that statements are "rare," but it is this rarity that becomes the basis for discursive formations, including those of the social sciences, which thus acquire their status as "positivities."

Think about the discourse of development, articulated around key statements such as "the Third World is underdeveloped," "the key to development is economic growth, which depends on capital expenditures and technology," or "modernization is the path to progress for all societies." It is well known that this discourse arose at the end of World War II as a result of a complex historical conjuncture that led to the problematization of poverty. What does it mean to assert that development began to function as a discourse; that is, that it created a space in which only certain things could be said or even imagined? Undoubtedly it means describing the objects, concepts, and strategies that go along with it (capital, technology, population, poverty, modernization, agriculture, urbanization, cultural orientations, and so many more); referring to the nondiscursive formations with which this discourse was articulated (economic conditions, institutions such as the World Bank, the formal end of colonialism and the Cold War, and so on); and, finally, mapping the knowledges that gave form to it. But the crucial thing in the archaeological analysis of the discursive formation called development is to research the system of relationships among these elements, objects, concepts, strategies, and institutions, which combined in such a way that this discourse was able to create systematically the objects of which it spoke, group them, arrange them in a certain way, and confer on them a certain unity. This discursive practice laid down, and still lays down, the rules of the game: who may speak, with what authority, what can be said, how one may act. The vast area over which this discourse ranged freely covered practically the entire cultural, economic, and political geography of the so-called Third World. Assembling the archive of this discourse means elucidating the system of statement formation and transformation and questioning the possibilities of a rupture of this system so that someday we might enter an episteme "beyond development," which some people call a postdevelopment era.

At the most basic level, discourses are diagrams, abstract machines, mechanisms of knowledge-power. Deleuze was seemingly struggling to explain the novelty of the Foucauldian notion of discourse when he resorted to calling on these other concepts. Discourse articulates the visible and the enunciable or articulable—visible materialities and articulable functions. "Every mechanism is a mushy mixture of the visible and the articulable" (Deleuze 1988, 38). "The *diagram*," Deleuze says, "is no longer an auditory or visual archive but a map, a cartography that is coextensive with the whole social field. . . . It is a machine that is almost blind and mute, even though it makes others see and speak" (34). This is why Foucault says that he is not only a new archivist but also a new cartographer, as his influence on geography attests. But what, then, is the archive?

If the realm of statements constitutes, so to speak, a topological space (as Deleuze says, turning to mathematics for support), "a complex volume," as Foucault explains (1972, 128), then "the archive is first the law of what can be said, the system that governs the appearance of statements as unique events. . . . It is that which, at the very root of the statement-event . . . defines at the outset *the system of its enunciability*" and of its functioning (129). The archive, in short, is *"the general system of the formation and transformation of statements"* (130). The archive, in this way, is not a mere compilation of statements.

It should be clear that nothing in the foregoing discussion suggests that discourses cannot change, as as some readers of Foucault have concluded. The task of archaeology is to describe the contradictions, additions, extensions, oppositions, and reorganizations that take place within a discourse; in other words, its "many irregularities" (156) and *"spaces of dissension"* (152). In the case of development, it is to show the multiplicity of approaches, strategies, and qualifiers that to some extent have modified it (sustainable, participatory, with a gender perspective, local, millennium goals, and so on). But the most important inspiration of archaeological analysis is to show how, under all this seeming and incessant learning, innovation, and change, the same basic system of relations continues, making discursive practice a constant. Foucault refers poetically to this fact when he says that "discourse is snatched from the law of development and established in a discontinuous atemporality. It is immobilized in fragments: precarious splinters of eternity" (166). In the case of development discourse, our precarious eternity has lasted seven decades, an irritating and destructive splinter in the lives of peoples.

We have now reached the last concept I would like to discuss: the episteme (see, e.g., Foucault 1970, 5–7; 1972, 191–92; and the foreword and preface to the English edition, 1972, x–xxiv). Foucault defines the episteme as an intermediate level of knowledge, situated between the underlying domain where the phenomenon of life takes place ("the fundamental codes of a culture"), on the one hand, and the space of science explicitly constituted as such ("the scientific theories or the philosophical interpretations"), on the other (1972, xx). This "middle region" (xxi) determines the conditions that make knowledge possible for a given era and culture. Thus, in *The Order of Things*, he analyzes three epistemes (corresponding to the Renaissance, the Classical Age, and the Modern Age), the rules that regulated each of them, and the discontinuities between them. He traces the vicissitudes of knowledge within each era in relation to the forms of thinking about life, work, and language. He finds that the episteme acts as a sort of *"positive unconscious* of knowledge" or as a "historical *a priori*" (1972, xi, xxii) that molds, for each era, what can be known and said,

Epistemological ("Secondary order")	**Science** (General theories about the order of things; reflexive knowledge)
Epistemic (Archaeological, "primary order")	**Episteme** (Pure experience of order; "positive unconscious of knowledge"; historical *a priori*)
Phenomenal (Life in movement)	**Background of understanding** (Fundamental codes of a culture; "the encoded eye"; life-worlds)

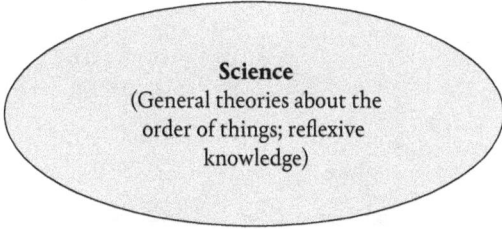

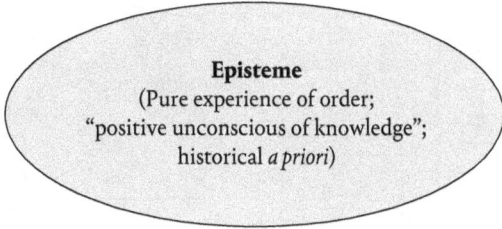

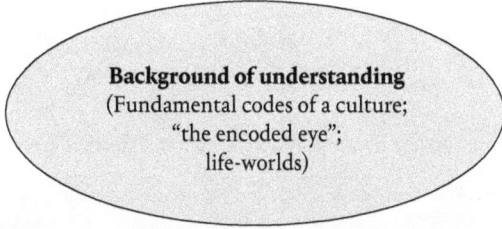

Figure 3.1. Three levels in the structures of thought

regardless of whether the knowledgeable people or experts are conscious of the fact. The fields that were known in the classical period (from the middle of the seventeenth century to the end of the eighteenth) as "natural history," "analysis of wealth," and "general grammar" cease to exist as such after the break that inaugurates the modern period, giving way then to "biology," "political economy," and "linguistics," with all the positivity that we still endow those fields with today. Finally, he discovers that the episteme of modernity, which crystallized around the end of the eighteenth century, is determined by the figure of "Man," which has been set up ever since as the subject, basis, and object of all knowledge—the foundational anthropocentrism of modernity (figure 3.1).

Let us look at another visualization of the episteme of modernity (figure 3.2). It is well known that the episteme of modernity is built on two great dualisms: the split between culture and nature and the colonial division between

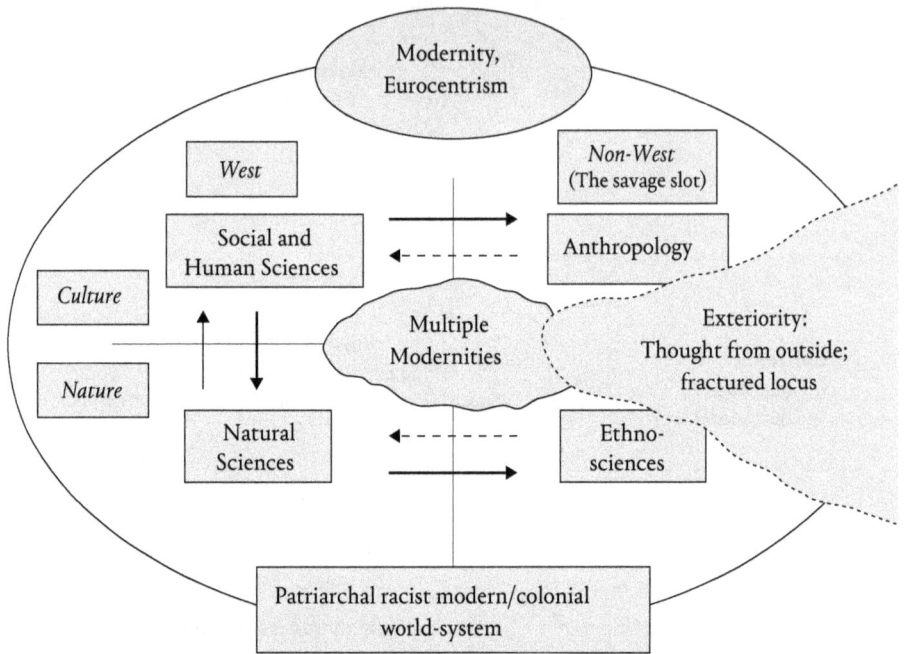

Figure 3.2. The episteme of modernity and the modern/colonial world-system

West and non-West. The last chapter of *The Order of Things*, "The Human Sciences," outlines what we might call the division of labor of modernity. Thus Western societies are the only ones equipped to have knowledge of man and nature. Anthropology was tasked with studying "the savage slot"—a dubious task, but one with the potential for destabilizing the entire episteme.

At the center of the diagram, we see what questions the West from inside the episteme, producing alternative modernities, or other modernities (nondominant ones, or non-Westernizing ones)—the very multiplicity that is "modernity," but still from within the onto-epistemic modern configuration. A more definitive subversion can only come from outside—or, in fact, from the encounter between outside and inside, from the "fractured locus" generated by colonial difference, according to María Lugones's lucid concept (2010a, 2010b)—from where we might perceive at last the pending end of this configuration. But before we come back to this register, let us consider how Foucault explains this possibility.

The last paragraph of *The Order of Things* is often cited as the clearest statement ever made on "the death of man." Let us listen:

If those arrangements were to disappear as they appeared, if some event of which we can at the moment do no more than sense the possibility—without knowing either what its form will be or what it promises—were to cause them to crumble, as the ground of Classical thought did, at the end of the eighteenth century, then one can certainly wager that man would be erased, like a face drawn in sand at the edge of the sea. (1972, 387)

This end of man is what the Nasa statement aims at (together with many other demonstrations, from many other perspectives). But we are getting ahead of ourselves again, for two interrelated aspects are relevant to our task of rethinking the possible end of the onto-epistemic formation of modernity.

First, how can one discursive formation be replaced by another? How do positivities disappear, not to mention the region of interpositivity that constitutes an episteme (see, e.g., Foucault 1972, 159, 173)? Moreover, what constitutes change at the level of the episteme? This is one of the most important questions raised by the archaeology of knowledge. Transformation does not imply that an entire series of concepts, objects, themes, and so on, is replaced by another, though there often is a substantial makeover in this regard; nor is it a homogeneous process that develops in exactly the same way in every area, beginning with a major rupture. Examining the disappearance of one positivity and the emergence of others means analyzing various types of transformation: of the elements that constitute the system of formation; of the relations among them; of the relations between the rules of formation; and of the transformation of relations among diverse positivities (sciences and knowledges). It is a matter of identifying discontinuities at the level of practical discourse. In this sense, the Foucauldian criterion of the disappearance of a discursive formation is somewhat isomorphic with Maturana and Varela's (1980, 1987) criterion for the conservation of the autopoiesis of living beings: the conservation of the system of relations between the elements and the basic processes that define the living being as the unity that it is. As for discourses, as well as epistemes, we might say with Maturana and Varela that they maintain "operational closure": they are "closed" systems—insofar as they must preserve the system of relations that constitute them—but ones that have "structural coupling" with their environments, that is, with nondiscursive formations and with other discourses.

Second, what does the episteme of the era of Man have to do with death and life? The figure of Man that emerged with the new episteme, "in his ambiguous position as an object of knowledge and as a subject that knows" (Foucault 1972, 312), has as its condition of possibility the discovery of his finitude; whether because it was incontrovertibly discovered by nineteenth-century clinical science, with its brand-new method of pathological anatomy, or because the political economy of Ricardo or Malthus discovered the iron law of having to work to avoid death, under the imperative of the law of diminishing returns, the ineluctable pressure of population growth, the modern onto-epistemic configuration inaugurated a hitherto-unknown analytic of finitude. Foucault lucidly expresses this idea in the opening and closing pages of *The Birth of the Clinic*, his second great book. "This book is about space, about language, and about death; it is about the act of seeing, the gaze," the first statement announces (1973, ix). And toward the end, after explaining in detail the development of a whole new body of empirical knowledge under the mandate "open a few corpses," he concludes:

> It will no doubt remain a decisive fact about our culture that its first scientific discourse . . . had to pass through this stage of death. . . . It is understandable, then, that medicine should have had such importance in the constitution of the sciences of man—an importance that is not only methodological, but ontological, in that it concerns man's being as object of positive knowledge. . . . [Ever since,] medical thought is fully engaged in the philosophical status of man. (243–45)

We rarely reflect on the foundational role of death in the creation of the modern ontology—the fact that "modern man . . . is possible only as a figuration of finitude" (1973, 318); that to know and maximize life, modernity had to invent death, not as a "natural" but as a "violent" fact as the eighteenth-century French pathologist Bichat argued, in Foucault's analysis, which is to say, not as simply another aspect of the flow of life. With their transversal effect, the dualisms of modernity affect everything: human-nonhuman, modern-nonmodern, mind-body, secular-sacred, reason-emotion, and life-death; these binaries all constitute an ontology of separation established by the political technologies of modernity on top of the incessant flow of life, against which the relational worlds of the territory~peoples are rebelling, as we will see shortly. Let us change tempos, then.

III. Toward an Ecological Episteme, or the Earth~Form of Life

The growing trend of questioning the dualisms that constitute modernity comes from two major sources. First is the Earth herself, Pachamama, giving ever clearer proofs of how she is severely affected by human activities (anthropogenic changes). Then there is the development of a great movement to defend Earth, especially the demonstrations and protests carried out by a wide spectrum of subaltern groups and territory~peoples whose very survival as worlds depends on the continuity and healing of Mother Earth.

If the problematization of life that gave rise to the modern episteme had to pass through death, might we hazard the idea that we are now witnessing a new problematizing of life, triggered by the devastation of the living produced by that same form of modernity? From this perspective, "the living" (*lo vivo*) is, we must emphasize, *everything that exists*, challenging the living-nonliving and organic-inert binaries that are foundational to modern sciences. We must imagine that the universe is not an inert space to be occupied but rather a living whole that we may inhabit.

Let us try putting this another way. If the forces of humanity ceased to produce the *God-form* with the close of the classical era and began enacting the *Man-form*, then we should dare to think that, with the political activation of the nondualist (relational) onto-epistemic that we are witnessing today, the most powerful statements of which are the thinking of the Nasa and other territory~peoples, we have begun our journey toward the era of the "Earth~form," the Pacha~form, the Gaia~form, the Ecozoic, or the era of the house of life. We would no longer be speaking of *incipit Homo*, "here Man begins" (Deleuze 1988, 127), as in modernity, but rather of *incipit Terra*, as befits the Ecozoic onto-epistemic formation: the era of the Earth would at last begin. The forces of humanity would be entering into a relation with forces from the outside, which could be none other than the forces of the liberated Earth. They would be yielding to a new dimension of finitude, but from the vantage point of relationality and life, not from a finitude defined by the modern conceptions of history and economy, with their notion of accumulation and their ingrained teleology. I will devote the rest of this chapter to this proposition.

For clues about the direction to take, let us look in two spaces related to territoriality: communality and autonomy, already introduced in the previous chapter. First we will look in statements of Nasa thought (we might well turn to notions and declarations from indigenous, Afro-descendant, peasant, ecologist, and women's organizations, but for reasons of space and of constructing the "archive" consistently, I will limit myself to the Nasa, with perhaps a couple of exceptions). Then we will turn to certain critical intellectual trends, both inside the academy and outside of it. Let us take a look.

A. Territory as History Book

One key comes to us from the Consejo Regional Indígena del Cauca (CRIC). For this organization, territory means "the vital space that ensures their survival as a people, as a culture living together in harmony with nature and the spirits. *Territory is our true history book, keeping alive the tradition of we who live in it.* . . . As a collective space of existence, it makes living together in harmony between peoples possible. It underlies the indigenous cosmovision as the reason for our survival" (CRIC 2008, quoted in Quijano 2012). What does the phrase "territory is our true history book" mean? I think it refers to much more than orality, knowledge about nature, or so-called traditional practices. How can we construct the archive of this "history book," bearing in mind the full spectrum of beings—human and nonhuman—who inhabit it? We find similar statements in the Life Plan of the Misak people. In it, they speak of *"recovering the land in order to recover everything."* Their Life Plan entails a proposal for "constructing and reconstructing a vital space for being born, growing up, remaining, and *flowing.* The Plan is a narrative of life and survival, it is constructing a road to facilitate the passage through life, and not merely constructing a methodological planning scheme" (Cabildo, Taitas y Comisión de Trabajo del Pueblo Guambiano 1994; quoted in Quijano 2012, 263). What does "recovering everything" mean? What else if not recovering their capacity for worlding life, for making it into a world in accordance with their cosmovision, in complete autonomy? What do they refer to by "flowing" if not to a conception, both grounded and sophisticated, of the pluriverse, of life as an incessant and ever-changing flow, quite different from the modern conception that imprisons life in plantations, grids, and sterile GMOs? We should perhaps dare to assert that territory, so conceived, is the pluriverse given form.

Let us go back to the Nasa statements and look at some of the points in their "cosmoaction":

1. Recovering the earth. This means: land for the people! If we don't get land back, we can't even survive.

2. Liberating Mother Earth. It means more than recovering her: it's making different use of the earth than the death project [of capital] does. Developing economic models and Life Plans that have as their ultimate objective the defense and promotion of life. We must learn to live with the earth, not merely from her, using her up. We free ourselves with the earth, to live together in harmony. This is our plea and our commitment. This means not only freeing the earth and empow-

ering ourselves from the struggle, but also freeing our thoughts, our hearts, our wills, our identity, our joy, our awareness, and our hope.

3. Constructing territories for peace, dignity, and life on the Liberated Earth. . . .

4. Weaving the territories for life, peace, and dignity based on the capacities and realities of each people and process until we attain the necessary and possible nation for replacing and overcoming this regime of oppression and sorrow.[4]

Let us continue exploring this rich archive. The Nasa activist and intellectual Vilma Almendra observes:

So when we talk of peace, what are we referring to? To living in balance and harmony with Mother Earth; to all of us going back to freely walking the word of the peoples; to peacefully walking through the community without fearing death; to studying at school without it turning into a stronghold of bullies; to sowing and harvesting our crops on our piece of land without fear of being fumigated; to drinking water once more from the rivers and brooks; to seeing our mountains turn green again instead of seeing piles of chemicals and dirt dumped by mines; to sitting down once more at our assemblies with plenty of time and ample participation and to making decisions without time pressure; to joining together more fully among ourselves, not for burying our dead but for celebrating the miracle of life; to weaving ties of unity with other peoples and processes; to living, re-creating, and nurturing our dreams and life plans.[5]

We could offer other clear examples of statements in which territory, community, autonomy, and life are interwoven in what would seem to be a different discursive formation. Such is the case of the actions and statements by Francia Márquez, the resistance leader of the Afro-descendant community of La Toma, municipio de Suárez, against the illegal mining operations in that community's territory; I examine these statements in greater detail in the next chapter. She speaks, for example, of caring for territories and guaranteeing the territory "for our reborn" (*nuestros renacientes*), an Afro-Pacific concept (one might say an unmodern concept) reminiscent of the Kogui notion of "the circulation of life" as the foundation of the universe (Ulloa 2011, 2012). These statements point us to a discursive formation in which life remains in continual rebirth. What would it be like to think and live from that vantage point, beyond the separation between humans and nonhumans that is so alien to the ontology of the reborn? And what could we say in ontological terms about the concept of caring for territories, beyond reflecting that it presupposes an ethic of the conservation of life? What does "caring for" mean in a nondualist, relational cosmovision?

These are not easy questions to settle. Doing so would mean delving into the description of another discursive formation. These questions raise the issue of the possible paths and strategies for transitioning from the Man-form to the Earth~form of life. As the word of the liberation of Mother Earth moves forward, the territorial-ethnic movements do not merely add one more statement to a still-dominant but already-outdated discursive formation. From their territory and from the liberated lands, they release a statement to the winds, confident that it will sail above the roaring, anonymous muttering of the territory~peoples and land cautiously but firmly in other territories of existence, where it might contribute to other articulations of the visible and the enunciable, of the feel-thinkable.

B. Autonomy, Communality, and Buen Vivir

Speaking about transition points us to the political project of the collectives. We should conceive of this project in ontological terms, for two reasons: because neoliberal globalization entails the ontological occupation both of peoples' territories and of their lives. What are palm oil plantations, extensive cattle farming, or sugarcane production but strategies for occupying these territories? The indigenous and Afro-descendant communities of Northern Cauca and the Pacific coast know this full well. Then again, what resists this occupation are genuine worlds, relational worlds, like the worlds of these communities. Many territorial struggles can be seen as ontological struggles, in defense of other models of life. They resist the globalizing project of creating a One-World World (capitalist, secular, liberal), one that seeks to reduce all the worlds to a single world.

The form that these resistance strategies take on goes through three great concepts: autonomy, communality, and Buen Vivir ("Good Living"; see chapter 2). Let us get help from another statement in the Nasa archive: "Words without actions are empty. Actions without words are blind. Actions and words without the spirit of the community are death itself." This is why they speak of "cosmoaction," acting from their own discourse and cosmovision. But what I want to underline in this statement is the central place of "the community." We can have no doubt that the community—or, as the pro-autonomy movements in Oaxaca and Chiapas like to say, "the communality," which is to say, the fundamental fact of being communal—is returning both to the social and political field and to the realm of theory, after several decades in exile as the seat of tradition, various atavistic institutions, many forms of oppression, and everything that was supposed to disappear sooner or later under the domineering march of modernization. We have already suggested the reason behind this new round of interest in the communal: precisely because modernization, development, and globalization have also brought the destruction of everything collective in their eagerness to replace the communal-being (the habitual form of being for all social life, from time immemorial to recent eras) with the individual-being of modernity. Faced with the social devastation caused by the progressive and implacable establishment of the dominion of the individual and the market, communality seeks to assert itself as a strategy for reconstituting forces in defense of the Earth~form of life. We might say that the Earth~form has, as a necessary but not a sufficient element, the communal form of the human.

Implementing the communal means creating the conditions for the continual self-creation of communities. We are talking about autonomy. No one has theorized autonomy better than the Zapatistas. Autonomous Zapatista communities are grounded in the principle of "governing by obeying," the basic principles of which are as follows:

1. To obey, not command

2. To represent, not supplant

3. To propose, not impose

4. To serve others, not serve oneself

5. To work from below, not seek to rise

6. To unite, not divide

7. To construct, not destroy

8. To reveal, not conceal

9. To defend, not sell out

10. To offer your life, not take life away

The practices of Zapatista good government are founded on these principles, thus returning ethics to the heart of politics. In short, "The earth is in charge, the people give the orders, and the government obeys. Building autonomy" (and we might almost add that official governments work on the opposite principles!).[6] These are also the principles for building the pluriverse.

Communality is established through nonliberal, nonstate organizational forms. More than anything, they constitute relational worlds. Ecological anthropology abounds in examples of communities where no strict boundary line separates what to us are the biophysical, the human, and the supernatural domains. The Gaia theory, which sees the Earth as a single whole, a meshwork of organic and inorganic, also tells us that it is alive. These are also significant elements in the rise of the Earth~form. This is why we say that in the mobilizations of the territory~peoples we are witnessing not merely social movements but true worlds in movement.

Of course, all of this is taking place in the context of "actually existing communities." Communities are also spaces of intense capitalist exploitation, patriarchal domination, and consumerist modernity: profoundly affected by globalization, yet not completely determined by it. We might say, with Silvia Rivera Cusicanqui, that these are "motley societies," capable of re/defining a modernity of their own, a more convivial one than the dominant modernities precisely because they supply their own sense of things, intermingling sophisticated forms of the indigenous with things that are anything but, in such a way as to create worlds where strong cultural differences exist without melting together (Gago 2015; Rivera Cusicanqui 2014).

C. Toward an Ecological Episteme?

The political activation of relationality that I have schematically described is a process that goes beyond the indigenous, Afro-descendant, and peasant peoples. It is related to two great processes: on the political-theoretical level, to the constitution of what the Mexican ecologist Enrique Leff (2015) has called an ecological episteme; and on the social level, to the emergence of a multiplicity of discourses on the transition to different models of life from the globalized civilization model of contemporary capitalism. As Leff explains, the environmental episteme arises at the margins of the dominant economic and scientific rationality, as its exteriority, and as a source of alternative sustainable worlds. It is an aspect of the repositioning of being in the territories of life. It reunifies nature and culture, and with the movements to defend territories, it repoliticizes ontology; that is, it resumes the search for other forms of being-in-the-world. It helps activate the politics of cultural and ontological difference, fostering new territories of life. Beyond this, the ecological episteme and the political ontology resituate politics at the crossroads of civilizational transitions to worlds based on the preservation of life. This is a broad movement that involves emerging narratives and movements in both the Global South and the Global North, some of which could also be considered centered on the Earth~form of life. We find a statement about these global transitions in the Nasa archive:

> But there is an offensive from below. Many peoples, communities, groups have taken the initiative, are organizing, recovering factories, taking farms and roads, liberating territories, overthrowing laws on their own, founding *caracoles* [autonomous Zapatista communities], . . . sowing thousands of fields with healthy food crops, protecting the seeds, opening alternative schools, safeguarding forests, defending the water, liberating the airwaves and the internet. . . . The offensive from below confounds the offensive from above.[7]

IV. By Way of Conclusion: Weaving Life in Freedom

Let us go back to the questions we raised at the beginning of this talk. Are we witnessing the birth of a new discursive formation, the basic elements of which include territory as a living being, life as flow (the pluriverse), the harmonious coexistence of the human and the nonhuman in profound interrelation, sentipensar in autonomy, and communality as a model for existence? Among these elements, has Nasa discursive practice established a system of relationships determining the formation of concepts, objects, themes, and strategies that are significantly different—at the level of discursive regularities—from those of the episteme of modernity? It would take more time and much more collective research to justify this hypothesis. My intuition is that it is the case. We can get an indication of this by asking ourselves whether the currently popular concepts relating to the Earth and the environmental crisis—sustainable development, the green economy, carbon markets—would find any place in a Mother Earth liberation discursive formation: clearly that would not be the case. By the same token, the very statement of the liberation of Mother Earth could not be accommodated within modern discursive formations, even if the basic terms that it comprises might belong to them.

We are still left with a number of questions:

How can we best construct the archive of this new formation? What is the role of the nonhuman (the organic nonhuman, the inorganic, the affective, and the spiritual, in terms of the categories we still use)? What would it signify to do the archaeology of these discourses and the genealogy of their practices? What is the relationship between these discourses and the nondiscursive formations—if we still find the distinction useful—particularly capital's death project, on the one hand, and the struggles to foster the Earth~form of life, on the other?

What political role would we be taking on with this exercise? Wouldn't we simply be following the academic habit of interpreting a subaltern way of thinking in terms of an elegant theory out of the metropolis? Wouldn't we be engaging in "the prose of counterinsurgency," that is, reducing the thinking and experiences of insurgents and subalterns to manifestations of something else—the logic of modernity, of capital, of the dominant episteme, or resistance to all those forces associated with heteropatriarchal capitalist colonial modernity—instead of recovering them on their own terms? Or might we perhaps think instead that this is a matter of "provincializing" Foucault, of resituating him within the episteme that he so eloquently diagrammed and outside of which he never claimed to speak? In the end, isn't Nasa thinking, like the thinking of other subaltern groups, a powerful way to "provincialize" the episteme of modernity? The project of researching history from decolonizing perspectives has some undeniably important precursors, the most illustrious of which include the Andean Oral History Workshop (Taller de Historia Oral Andina), fostered by Silvia Rivera Cusicanqui and a committed group of Aymara intellectuals since the early 1980s with the aim of researching the oral histories of communities from a decolonizing perspective, and the Subaltern Studies Group from India.

This is what I feel: As this chapter draws to a close, I hope we will be left not so much with Foucault's famous laughter (upon discovering, with Borges, what is unthinkable for Western perspectives and adumbrating the death of Man), but rather with sadness, certainly, but also with the great joy that the Nasa people cultivate in their brave and illuminating struggles, or with the determination of the Afro-Colombian activists from the Pacific region who, in the face of the ecocide and ethnocide they have witnessed in their territories, insist on declaring the Pacific region to be a Territory of Life, Joy, Peace, Hope, and Freedom.

We should be clear about one thing: this is not about placing Nasa thought within a genealogy of epistemes in relation to modernity; Nasa thought hails from long before modernity began, and it aims far past it. Perhaps we should not even say that it constitutes another episteme, unless we unfold the episteme concept itself topologically and open it up to configurations that welcome sentipensar forms of knowing. The critical theory of modernity will have to continue to be provincialized until we can acknowledge that the state-

ments of indigenous and other territory~peoples today are often at the forefront of thought.

Toward the end of his book on Foucault, Deleuze asks whether the
Man-form that Foucault mapped out in such detail "has been a good one" for
life. He muses, for example: "Has it saved living men from a violent death? . . .
If the forces within man compose a form only by entering into a relation with
forces from the outside, with what new forms do they now risk entering into a
relation, and what new form will emerge that is neither God nor Man?" (1988,
130). To the first part of his question, our answer is no. Whether we think
about it from Colombia, or from the black and Latino neighborhoods of the
United States, or from the Mediterranean waters where forcefully displaced
Africans risk their lives to reach Europe, or whether we look at the apparent
calm of our hospitals, death continues to be a violent experience. Paradoxically it is sometimes the groups that have been hardest hit by violence who
maintain another form of death, more in community and in closer contact
with living spirits. Such, for example, is the case of death among the *renacientes*, the "reborn," of Colombia's Pacific region, with their *alabaos* (praise songs
on the passing of adults) and *chigualos* (funeral rituals for young children). To
the second question, about what new form "Man" will now enter into contact
with: we have suggested that this new form is the force of the Earth, and the
territory~peoples are more in tune with it; it is not "man" who will liberate
life but these peoples who will do so by liberating the Earth, as one of the first
quotations we read from the Nasa archive put it so well.

"Weave life in liberty": another Nasa statement. Let us conclude, then, by
listening once more to their thought:

> Then they will see clearly that this struggle comes out of Northern Cauca,
> but it is not Northern Cauca's struggle. It comes from the Nasa people, but
> it is not the Nasa people's. Because life itself is at risk when the earth is
> exploited in the capitalist way, which throws the climate, the ecosystems,
> everything out of balance. From Northern Cauca we say: enough, it's time
> to liberate her. Every liberated farm, here or in any corner of the world, is
> a territory that adds to reestablishing the balance of Uma Kiwe [Mother
> Earth]. This is our common house, our only one. Yes, indeed: come on in,
> the door is open.

So let's come on in!

My hope is that now we might understand a bit more clearly what it means
to accept this complex invitation. It means, in the powerful words of the Ma-

puche poet and *machi* (healer) Adriana Paredes Pinda (2014), nothing more and nothing less than "learning to walk anew on Earth as living beings." Because we've forgotten how.

Let us give the last word to the Nasa people, and walk it:

> The Liberation of Mother Earth is not a nesting place within the state or within capitalism. In liberating Mother Earth from capitalism, we liberate ourselves, to return to the time when we simply enjoyed life, eating, drinking, dancing, weaving, making offerings to the rhythms of Uma Kiwe. We are a nesting place on the road to Mother Earth. . . . So that all beings can be, we risk our own being.[8]

4

Sentipensar with the Earth

Territorial Struggles and the
Ontological Dimension of the
Epistemologies of the South

Other Knowledges, Other Worlds

Epistemologies of the South is one of the most compelling frameworks for social transformation to emerge at the intersection of the Global North and the
Global South, theory and practice, and the academy and social life in many
decades. The proposal does not claim to have arrived at a new land of general
theories and Big Ideas—in fact, this is explicitly not one of its goals—yet at the
same time it outlines trajectories for thinking otherwise, precisely because it
carves a space for itself that enables thought to reengage with life and attentively walk along the amazing diversity of forms of knowledge held by those
whose experiences can no longer be rendered legible by Eurocentric knowledge in the academic mode, if they ever were. The Epistemologies of the South
framework provides workable tools for all those of us who no longer want to be
complicit with the silencing of popular knowledges and experiences by Eurocentric knowledge, sometimes performed even in the name of allegedly critical and progressive theory. The Epistemologies of the South might also be useful to those who have been at the receiving end of those colonialist categories
that have transmogrified their experiences, translated them into lacks, or simply rendered them utterly illegible and invisible.

The Epistemologies of the South (ES) framework has been developed by
Boaventura de Sousa Santos over the span of three decades through a series
of books and political engagements with intellectuals and social movements
in various parts of the world.[1] These engagements include the author's central
role in the World Social Forum since its inception in 2001. Its main pillars are

what the author terms "the sociology of absences," effected by five "mono-cultures" (derived from the dominance of capitalist modernity, concerning knowledge, the classification of differences, scale, temporality, productiv-ity, and efficiency); the "sociology of emergences," which seek to redress such monocultures to bring to light the multiplicity of social experience (based on plural forms and ecologies of knowledge, temporalities, recognition of differ-ences, trans-scales, and productivities); intercultural translation across diverse knowledges and struggles; and the notion of cognitive justice as a necessary correlate of social justice. The framework explicitly attempts to build a non-Eurocentric approach to social transformation. More recently, the author has outlined a genealogy of a "non-Occidentalist West," that is, an account of au-thors within the West who transcended Eurocentric visions of the world, such as Blaise Pascal and Nicolas of Cusa. While the ES framework is solidly struc-tured in terms of these notions, it continues to evolve in the encounter with new actors and situations.

In identifying the infinite diversity of the world as one of its basic prem-ises, the ES framework clearly takes on an ontological dimension. By this I mean that in speaking about knowledges, the ES framework is also speaking about worlds. Simply said, multiple knowledges, or epistemes, refer to multiple worlds, or ontologies. The aim of this chapter is to draw out further the on-tological dimension of ES by setting it in dialogue with certain trends in con-temporary critical theory that share with ES its fundamental ethical-political orientation of learning at least as much from the experience, knowledge, and struggles of subaltern social groups as from the academy. These trends— broadly encompassed within a field that I call political ontology— stem from the proposition that many contemporary struggles for the defense of territo-ries and difference are best understood as ontological struggles and as strug-gles over a world where many words fit; they aim to foster the pluriverse. What this ontological angle adds to our understanding of contemporary struggles will become clear as the argument develops.

The chapter's first section offers some general remarks on the ontological character of ES, building on some of its key premises. The second section pro-vides an intuitive introduction to the concept of relationality and relational ontologies by engaging readers in an imagination exercise that asks them to situate themselves within a complex river landscape in a Colombian rain for-est. The third section outlines the framework for the political ontology of ter-ritorial struggles in Latin America, based on the defense of their territories by indigenous, Afro-descendant, and peasant groups, particularly against large-scale mining and agrofuels projects. It argues that these extractivist projects can be seen as strategies for the ontological occupation of the territories, and hence struggles against them constitute veritable ontological struggles. The fourth section engages in a reversal that is well known to the ES framework: it suggests that the knowledges connected with these struggles are actually more sophisticated and appropriate for thinking about social transformation than many forms of knowledge produced within the academy at present. This is so for two main reasons: first, because the knowledges produced from territorial struggles provide us with essential elements for thinking about the profound cultural and ecological transitions needed to face the interrelated crises of climate, food, energy, poverty, and meaning; and second, because these knowledges are uniquely attuned to the needs of the Earth. As the chapter title suggests, those who produce them *sentipiensan con la Tierra* (they feel-think with the Earth); they orient themselves toward the moment when humans and the planet can finally come to coexist in mutually enhancing manners.

I. The Ontological Dimension
of the Epistemologies of the South

The ES framework is based on a series of premises and strategies, often effectively summarized by its author in compact formulations and telling reversals that nevertheless point to crucial problems within contemporary theory (Santos 2002, 2007, 2014).[2] Perhaps the best starting point for our purposes here is the saying that the contemporary conjuncture is best characterized by the fact that *we are facing modern problems for which there are no longer modern solutions*. Ontologically speaking, one may say that the crisis is the crisis of a particular world or set of world-making practices, the world that we usually refer to as the dominant form of Euro-modernity (capitalist, rationalist, liberal, secular, heteropatriarchal, white, or what have you). If the crisis is then caused by this heteropatriarchal capitalist modern world, it follows that facing the crisis implies transitions toward its opposite, that is, toward a multiplicity of worlds we will call the pluriverse. This is precisely what one of the major premises of ES underscores, in stating that *the diversity of the world is infinite*; succinctly, the world is made up of multiple worlds, multiple ontologies or reals that are far from being exhausted by the Eurocentric experience or reducible to its terms.

The invisibility of the pluriverse points to the sociology of absences. Here again we find an insightful formulation of the ES framework: *what does not exist is actively produced as nonexistent or as a noncredible alternative to what exists*. The social production of nonexistence points to the effacement of entire worlds through a set of epistemological operations already mentioned. As we shall see in the next section, the worlds so effaced are characterized by relational ways of being that challenge the epistemological operations that effect absences. Conversely, the proliferation of struggles in defense of territory and cultural difference suggests that what emerges from such struggles are entire relational worlds. There are clear ontological dimensions to the two main strategies introduced by ES, namely, the sociology of absences (the production of nonexistence points to the nonexistence of worlds and often implies their ontological occupation), and the sociology of emergences (the enlargement of those experiences considered valid or credible alternatives to what exists entails the forceful emergence of relational worlds through struggles).

Finally, some principles of ES suggest the connection between the production of theory and ontology. The first is that *the understanding of the world is much broader than the Western understanding of the world*. This means that the transformation of the world, and the transitions to the pluriverse or the civilizations transitions adumbrated by some indigenous, peasant, and Afro-descendant activists, might happen (indeed, are happening) along pathways that might be unthinkable from the perspective of Eurocentric theories. Said differently, a glaring gap exists between what most Western theories today can glean from the field of social struggles, on the one hand, and the transformative practices actually going on in the world, on the other. This gap is increasingly clear; it is a limit faced by mainstream and Left theories alike, stemming from the mono-ontological or intra-European origin of such theories. Thinking new thoughts, by implication, requires moving out of the epistemic space of Western social theory and into the epistemic configurations associated with the relational ontologies of worlds in struggle.[3]

II. Yurumanguí: Introducing the Relational Worlds

Picture a seemingly simple scene from one of the many rivers that flow from the western Andean mountain range toward the Pacific Ocean in Colombia's southern Pacific rain forest region, inhabited largely by Afro-descendant communities, such as the Yurumanguí River:[4] a father and his six-year-old daughter, paddling upstream with their *canaletes* (oars) in their *potrillos* (local dugout canoes) at the end of the afternoon, taking advantage of the rising tide; perhaps they are returning home after having taken their harvested plantains and their catch of the day to the town downstream and are bringing back some items they bought at the town store—unrefined cane sugar, cooking fuel, salt, notebooks for the children, or what have you. On first inspection, we may say that the father is "socializing" his daughter into the correct way to navigate the potrillo, an important skill, as life in the region greatly depends on the cease-less going back and forth in the potrillos through rivers, mangroves, and estu-aries. This is correct in some ways, but something else is also going on; as locals are wont to say, speaking of the river territory, "Acá nacimos, acá crecimos, acá hemos conocido qué es el mundo" (here we were born, here we grew up, here we have known what the world is). Through their *nacer~crecer~conocer* (being born~growing up~learning), they enact the manifold practices by which their territories/worlds have been made since they became *libres* (free, not enslaved peoples) and became intermeshed with living beings of all kinds in these for-est and mangrove worlds.

Let us travel to this river and immerse ourselves deeply within it and expe-rience it with the eyes of relationality; an entire way of worlding emerges for us. Looking attentively from the perspective of the manifold relations that make this world what it is, we see that the potrillo was made out of a mangrove tree with the knowledge the father received from his predecessors; the mangrove forest is intimately known by the inhabitants who traverse with great ease the fractal estuaries it creates with the rivers and the always moving sea; we begin to see the endless connections keeping this intertidal "aquatic space" together and always in motion (Oslender 2008), including connections with the moon and the tides that enact a nonlinear temporality. The mangrove forest involves many relational entities involving what we might call minerals, mollusks, nu-trients, algae, microorganisms, birds, plant, and insects—a whole meshwork of underwater, surface, and above-ground life. Ethnographers of these worlds describe it in terms of three contiguous worlds (*el mundo de abajo*, or infra-world; *este mundo*, or the human world; and *el mundo de arriba*, or spiritual/supraworld). There are comings and goings between these worlds, and par-ticular places and beings connecting them, including "visions" and spiritual beings (e.g., Restrepo 1996). This entire world is narrated in oral forms that include storytelling, chants, and poetry.

This dense network of interrelations may be called a "relational ontology." The mangrove-world, to give it a short name, is enacted minute by minute, day by day, through an infinite set of practices carried out by all kinds of beings and life-forms, involving a complex organic and inorganic materiality of wa-ter, minerals, degrees of salinity, forms of energy (sun, tides, moon, relations of force), and so forth. There is a rhizome logic to these entanglements, a "logic" that is impossible to follow in any simple way, and very difficult to map and measure, if at all; it reveals an altogether different way of being and becoming in territory and place. These experiences constitute relational worlds. To put it abstractly, a relational ontology of this sort can be defined as one in which *nothing preexists the relations that constitute it*. Said otherwise, things and beings are their relations; they do not exist prior to them.

As the anthropologist Tim Ingold says (2011, 131), these "worlds without objects" are always in movement, made up of materials in motion, flux, and becoming; in these worlds, living beings of all kinds constitute each other's conditions for existence; they "interweave to form an immense and continually evolving tapestry" (10). Going back to the river scene, one may say that "father" and "daughter" get to know their local world not through distancing reflection but by going about it, that is, by being alive to their world. These worlds do not require the divide between nature and culture to exist—in fact, they exist as such only because they are enacted by practices that do not rely on such a divide. In a relational ontology, "beings do not simply occupy the world, they *inhabit* it, and in so doing—in threading their own paths through the meshwork—they contribute to its ever-evolving weave" (71). Commons exist in these relational worlds, not in worlds that are imagined as inert and waiting to be occupied.

Even if the relations that keep the mangrove-world always in a state of becoming are constantly changing, messing them up significantly often results in their degradation. Such is the case with industrial shrimp farming schemes and oil palm plantations for agrofuels, which have proliferated in tropical regions in many parts of the world, often built at the expense of mangrove and humid forest lands, with the aim to transform them from "worthless swamp" to agro-industrial complexes (Ogden 2011). Here, of course, we find many of the monocultural operations at stake: the conversion of everything that exists in the mangrove-world into "nature" and of "nature" into "resources"; the effacing of the life-enabling materiality of the entire domains of the inorganic and the nonhuman, and its treatment as "objects" to be had, destroyed, or extracted; and linking the forest worlds so transformed to "world markets" for profit. In these cases, the insatiable appetite of the One-World World spells out the progressive destruction of the mangrove-world, its ontological capture and reconversion by capital and the state (Deleuze and Guattari 1987; Escobar 2008). The dominant world, in short, denies the mangrove-world its possibility of existing as such. Local struggles constitute attempts to re/establish some degree of symmetry to the partial connections that the mangrove-worlds maintain with the dominant worlds.

III. Territoriality, Ancestrality, Worlds: Outline of Political Ontology

Elders and young activists in many territorial communities worldwide (including increasingly in urban areas) eloquently express why they defend their worlds even at the price of their lives. In the words of an activist from the Afro-descendant community of La Toma, also in Colombia's Southwest, which has been engaged in a struggle against gold mining since 2008, "It is patently clear to us that we are confronting monsters such as transnational corporations and the state. Yet nobody is willing to leave her/his territory; I might get killed here but I am not leaving."[5] Such resistance takes place within a long history of domination and resistance, and this is essential for understanding territorial and commons defense as an ontological political practice. La Toma communities, for instance, have knowledge of their continued presence in the territory since the first half of the seventeenth century. This knowledge is an eloquent example of what activists call "ancestrality," referring to the ancestral mandate that inspires today's struggles and that persists in the memory of the elders, amply documented by oral history and scholars (Lisifrey et al. 2013). This mandate is joyfully celebrated in oral poetry and song: "Del Africa llegamos con un legado ancestral; la memoria del mundo debemos recuperar" (We came here from Africa with an ancestral legacy; we have to recover the memory of the world).[6] Far from an intransigent attachment to the past, ancestrality stems from a living memory that orients itself to the ability to envision a different future—a sort of "futurality" that imagines, and struggles for, the conditions that will allow people to persevere as a distinct world.[7] As activists often put it, the essence of ancestrality is to make other futures possible.

Within relational worlds, the defense of territory, life, and the commons is one and the same. To this extent, this chapter's argument can be stated as follows: The perseverance of communities, commons, and the struggles for their defense and reconstruction—particularly, but not only, those that incorporate explicitly ethno-territorial dimensions—involves resistance and the defense and affirmation of territories that, at their best and most radical, can be described as ontological. Conversely, whereas the occupation of territories by capital and the state implies economic, technological, cultural, ecological, and often armed aspects, its most fundamental dimension is ontological. From this perspective, what occupies territories is a particular ontology, that of the universal world of individuals and markets that attempts to transform all other worlds into one single world. By interrupting the neoliberal globalizing project of constructing a single globalized world, many indigenous, Afro-descendant, peasant, and poor urban communities are advancing *ontological struggles*. They struggle to maintain multiple worlds; this struggle is best embodied in the Zapatista dictum "a world where many worlds fit."

Another clear case of ontological occupation of territories comes from the southernmost area in the Colombian Pacific, around the port city of Tumaco. Here, since the early 1980s, the forest has been destroyed and communities displaced to give way to oil palm plantations. Nonexistent in the 1970s, by the mid-1990s they had expanded to over thirty thousand hectares. The monotony of the plantation—row after row of palm as far as the eye can see, a green desert of sorts—replaced the diverse, heterogeneous, and entangled world of forest and communities. We should note two important aspects of this dramatic change: first, the "plantation form" effaces the relations maintained by the forest-world; emerging from a dualist ontology of human dominance over so-called nature understood as "inert space" or "resources" to be had, the plantation can thus be said to be the most effective means for the ontological occupation and ultimate erasure of local relational worlds. In fact, plantations are unthinkable from the relational perspective of forest-worlds; within this world, forest use and cultivation practices take on an entirely different form that ecologists describe in terms of agroecology and agroforestry; even the landscape, of course, is entirely different. Not far from the oil palm plantations, the previously mentioned industrial shrimp companies were also busy in the 1980s and 1990s, transforming the mangrove-world into a disciplined succession of rectangular, "scientifically" controlled pools. A highly polluting and destructive industry, especially when constructed in mangrove swamps, this type of shrimp farming constitutes another clear example of ontological occupation and politics at stake (Escobar 2008).

One of the main frameworks proposed for understanding the occupation of territories and resistance to such occupation is that of political ontology (Blaser 2010, 2013). On the one hand, political ontology refers to the power-laden practices involved in bringing into being a particular world or ontology; on the other hand, it refers to a field of study that focuses on the interrelations among worlds, including the conflicts that ensue as different ontologies strive to sustain their own existence in their interaction with other worlds. The framework's goal is to contribute to visualizing paths toward the planet's ontological reconstitution (de la Cadena 2010, 2015). It should be stressed, however, that this framework is not limited to ethnic minority territories. In different ways, it applies to all social groups worldwide, including to the ontological occupation of popular neighborhoods in many of the world's urban areas.[8]

It should also be made clear that the framework builds on, and does not seek to replace, the frameworks of political economy (which influence many liberation struggles of the twentieth century) and political ecology. We believe, however, that the onto-epistemic emphasis reformulates some of the questions and insights of previous perspectives.

Political ontology also helps us to understand the persistence of the occupying ontologies. A crucial moment in this regard was the conquest of America, which some consider the point of origin of our current modern/colonial world-system (e.g., Mignolo 2000). The most central feature of the single-world doctrine has been a twofold ontological divide: a particular way of separating humans from nature (the nature-culture divide); and the distinction and boundary policing between "us" (civilized, modern, developed) and "them" (uncivilized, underdeveloped), those who practice other ways of worlding (the colonial divide). These (and many other derivative) dualisms underlie an entire structure of institutions and practices through which the single world is enacted. Many signs, however, suggest that the globalized world so constructed is unraveling. The growing visibility of struggles to defend mountains, landscapes, forests, territories, and so forth, by appealing to a relational (nondualist) and pluri-ontological understanding of life is a manifestation of this crisis. The crisis thus stems from the models through which we imagine the world to be a certain way and construct it accordingly. This conjuncture and the questions it raises define a rich context for political ontology and pluriversal studies: on the one hand, the need to understand the conditions under which the idea of a single globalized world continues to maintain its dominance; on the other, the emergence of projects based on different ontological commitments and ways of worlding, including commoning (e.g., Bollier 2014; Bollier and Helfrich 2012; Nonini 2007), and how they struggle to weaken the dominant world project while widening their spaces of re/existence.

The pluriverse is a tool, first, for making alternatives to the one world plausible to one-worlders; and second, for providing resonance to those other worlds that interrupt the one-world story (Blaser, de la Cadena, and Escobar 2014). Displacing the centrality of this dualist ontology while broadening the space for nondualist ontologies is a sine qua non for breaking away from the one-world story. This implies a transition from one-world concepts such as "globalization" and "global studies" to concepts centered on the pluriverse as made up of a multiplicity of mutually entangled and coconstituting but distinct worlds. The notion of the pluriverse, it should be made clear, has two main sources: theoretical critiques of dualism and so-called postdualist trends stemming from what is called "the ontological turn" in social theory; and the perseverance of nondualist philosophies (more often known as cosmovisions or cosmologies) that reflect a deeply relational understanding of life, such as Muntu and Ubuntu in parts of Africa; the Pachamama or Uma Kiwe among South American indigenous peoples; US and Canadian American Indian cosmologies;[9] or even in the entire Buddhist philosophy of mind (see chapter 1). They also exist within the West, as alternative Wests or nondominant forms of modernity (Santos 2014). Some of the current struggles going on in Europe over the commons, energy transitions, and the relocalization of food, for instance, could be seen as struggles to reconnect with the stream of life; they also constitute forms of resistance against the dominant ontology of capitalist modernity. Worldwide, the multiple initiatives for the reconstruction of communal spaces and for reconnecting with nature constitute a perceptible political activation of relationality. Urban and rural territorial struggles and struggles over the commons are often examples of such activation. All of the foregoing are important elements of the ES, particularly of the sociology of emergences.

IV. Transitions to the Pluriverse, Buen Vivir, and the Politics of Theory

We are now in a position to return to our argument about why knowledges produced in the struggles for the defense of relational worlds are often more farsighted and appropriate to the conjuncture of modern problems without modern solutions than their academic counterparts. To substantiate this claim fully requires that we locate these knowledges within a twofold context: that of the need for civilizational transitions, on the one hand, and the planetary dynamics brought to the fore by global climate change, the destruction of biodiversity, and the Anthropocene, on the other. The first context involves a consideration of how discourses of transition have multiplied over the past decade; the second, the pressing historical need to become attuned again to what the ecologist and theologian Thomas Berry has poetically called "the dream of the Earth" (Berry 1988, 1998). Territorial struggles, as I will argue in this last section, are producing among the most insightful knowledges for the cultural and ecological transitions seen as necessary to face the crisis; these knowledges are also profoundly attuned to the self-organizing dynamics of the Earth.

Let us begin with the discourses of transition. The emergence, over the past decade, of an array of discourses on the cultural and ecological transitions necessary to deal with the planetary crisis is another powerful sign of the unraveling of single-world doctrine and the emergence of the pluriverse (see Escobar 2018 for an extensive discussion of transition initiatives). In other words, what globalizers call the Anthropocene points to the need for significant, if not dramatic, transformations and transitions. Transition discourses (TDs) are emerging today with particular richness, diversity, and intensity to the point that a veritable field of "transition studies" can be posited as an emergent scholarly political domain. Notably, writers on the subject are not limited to the academy; in fact, the most visionary TD thinkers are located outside it, even if most engage with critical currents in the academy. Transition discourses are emerging from a multiplicity of sites, principally social movements worldwide and some civil society NGOs, from some alternative scientific paradigms, and from intellectuals with significant connections to environmental and cultural struggles. Transition discourses are prominent in several fields, including culture, ecology, religion and spirituality, alternative science (e.g., complexity), futures studies, feminist studies, political economy, and digital technologies.

I can only hint at the range of TDs here, and we need a concerted effort at bringing together TDs in the North and the South. In the North, the most prominent include degrowth; a variety of transition initiatives (TIs); the Anthropocene; forecasting trends (e.g., Club of Rome, Randers 2012); the defense and economics of the commons (e.g., Bollier 2014; Bollier and Helfrich 2012); the economics of happiness (Helena Norberg-Hodge);[10] and some approaches involving interreligious dialogues and UN-related processes, particularly within the Stakeholder Forum for a Sustainable Future. Among the explicit TIs are the Transition Town Initiative (TTI, Rob Hopkins, United Kingdom), the Great Transition Initiative (GTI, Tellus Institute, United States), the Great Turning (Joanna Macy), the Great Work or transition to an Ecozoic era (Thomas Berry), the transition from the Enlightenment to an age of sustainment (Tony Fry), and transition design frameworks (e.g., Terry Irwin and Gideon Kossoff). In the Global South, TDs include the crisis of the civilizational model, postdevelopment and alternatives to development, Buen Vivir, communal logics and autonomía, food sovereignty, transitions to postextractivism, and autonomous design. While discussions of the new era in the North include postgrowth, postmaterialist, posteconomic, postcapitalist, and post-dualist features, those for the South are expressed in terms of postdevelopment, post/nonliberal, post/noncapitalist, and postextractivist (for a complete list of references, see Escobar 2011, 2014b, 2018).

I should point out that the ontological occupation of territories and worlds just described often takes place in the name of development; hence a renewed questioning of the civilizational imperatives of growth and development should be an important element of any transition. Like markets, development and growth continue to be among the most naturalized concepts in the social and policy domains. The very idea of development, however, has been questioned by cultural critics since the mid-1980s, who began to question the core assumptions of development, including growth, progress, and instrumental rationality (e.g., Escobar 2011; Latouche 2009; Rist 1997; Sachs 1992). These critics have argued that it is possible to imagine the end of development, emphasizing the notion of alternatives *to* development, rather than development alternatives, as goals for transition activists and policy makers.

The idea of alternatives to development has become more concrete in South America in recent years with the notions of Buen Vivir ("Good Living," or collective well-being according to culturally appropriate ways) and the rights of nature. Defined as a holistic view of social life that no longer gives overriding centrality to the economy, Buen Vivir "constitutes an alternative *to* development, and as such it represents a potential response to the substantial critiques of postdevelopment" (Acosta and Martínez 2009; Gudynas and Acosta 2011, 78). Succinctly, Buen Vivir grew out of indigenous struggles as they articulated with social change agendas by peasants, Afro-descendants, environmentalists, students, women, and youth. Echoing indigenous ontologies, Buen Vivir implies a different philosophy of life that enables the subordination of economic objectives to the criteria of ecology, human dignity, and social justice. The debates about the form Buen Vivir might take in modern urban contexts and other parts of the world, such as Europe, are beginning to take place. Degrowth, commons, and Buen Vivir are "fellow travelers" in this endeavor. They constitute important areas of research, theorization, and activism for both Epistemologies of the South and political ontology. Another vital area of discussion, debate, and activism in South America, linked to Buen Vivir, is that of the rights of nature. Together, Buen Vivir and the rights of nature have reopened the crucial debate on how Latin Americans want to go on living. The rights of nature movement is thus at the same time a movement for the right to exist differently, to construct worlds and knowledges otherwise (e.g., Gudynas 2014).

Buen Vivir and the rights of nature resonate with broader challenges to the "civilizational model" of globalized development. The crisis of the Western *modelo civilizatorio* is invoked by many movements as the underlying cause of the multifaceted planetary crisis. This emphasis is strongest among ethnic movements, yet it is also found, for instance, in peasant networks for which only a shift toward agroecological food production systems can lead us out of the climate and food crises (e.g., Vía Campesina). Closely related is the "transitions to postextractivism" framework. Originally proposed by the Centro Latinoamericano de Ecología Social (CLAES) in Montevideo, it has become an important intellectual-activist debate in many South American countries (Alayza and Gudynas 2011; Coraggio and Laville 2014; Gudynas 2011; Massuh 2012). The point of departure is a critique of the intensification of extractivist models based on large-scale mining, hydrocarbon exploitation, or extensive agricultural operations, particularly for agrofuels, such as soy, sugarcane, or oil palm; whether in the form of conventional—often brutal—neoliberal extractivist policies in countries like Colombia, Peru, or Mexico, or following the neoextractivism of the center-Left regimes, these are legitimized as efficient growth strategies.

Let us now move to the second context that makes the knowledges produced by those engaged in struggles for the defense of territories and relational worlds perhaps even more appropriate and meaningful than those produced from the detached perspectives of science and the academy. This context is none other than the fate of the Earth itself. One of the most compelling visions in this regard has been proposed by Thomas Berry. For Berry, "The deepest cause of the present devastation is found in a mode of consciousness that has established a radical discontinuity between the human and other modes of being and the bestowal of all rights on the humans" (1999, 4). He identifies governments, corporations, universities, and religions as the fundamental establishments that keep this state of affairs in place. We moderns have lost our integral relation with the universe and must restore it by bringing about a new intimacy with the Earth. As the first "radically anthropocentric society" (1988, 202), we have become rational, dreamless people.

Given that we cannot be intimate with the Earth within a mechanistic paradigm, we are in dire need of a new story that might enable us to reunite the sacred and the universe, the human and the nonhuman. The wisdom traditions, including those of indigenous peoples, offer a partial guide toward this goal of reembedding ourselves within the Earth. Within these traditions, humans are embedded within the Earth, are part of its consciousness, not an individual consciousness existing in an inert world. Every living being exists because all others exist. As a Nasa indigenous leader from southwestern Colombia put it, "Somos la continuidad de la tierra, miremos desde el corazón de la tierra" (We are the extension of the Earth, let us think from the earth's heart). Most Western intellectual traditions have been inimical to this profound realization.[11]

Given that the human has become a cosmic force itself, we (moderns and all humans) need to formulate a more explicit project of transformation and transition. Berry calls for a transition from "the terminal Cenozoic to the emerging Ecozoic era," or "from the period when humans were a disruptive force on the planet Earth to the period when humans become present to the planet in a manner that is mutually enhancing" (1999, 7, 11). Above all, we need to recognize that modern culture provides insufficient guidance for the Ecozoic era, and thus we need to go back to the Earth as a source—which is precisely what many relational struggles in defense of the territories and the Earth are doing.[12]

Activists at the forefront of these struggles will easily recognize Berry's dictum that "Earth is a communion of subjects, not a collection of objects" (2013, 4). The many functional cosmologies maintained by many peoples throughout history, including in the alternative Wests themselves, uphold this principle. Within these stories, the universe is a vast manifestation of the sacred, and the sacred is saturated with being and spirituality. The new stories seek to reunite the sacred and the universe. While indigenous traditions have an important role to play in this endeavor, so does a transformed understanding of science, one that would help humans reinterpret their place at the species level within a new universe story. By placing it within a new cosmology, science would move beyond the dominant technical and instrumental comprehension of the world to be reintegrated with the phenomenal world, and so it would contribute to the reencounter with the numinous universe. That Berry calls for a necessary complete restructuring of our civilization is perfectly understood by many activists of territorial struggles, activists of transitions to the pluriverse, and those who emphasize the need for a rediscovery of spirituality and the sacred.

V. Conclusion

Epistemologies of the South and political ontology are political-theoretical projects that aim to reinterpret contemporary knowledges and struggles oriented toward the defense of life and the pluriverse. They highlight ecologies of knowledge and ontological struggles in defense of territories and for reconnecting with nature and life's self-organizing and always emergent force, arguing that they constitute a veritable political activation of relationality. Moving beyond "development" and the economy are primary aspects of such struggles. They also show that, in the last instance, our human ability for enacting other worlds and worlds otherwise will depend on humans' determination to rejoin the unending field of relations that make up the pluriverse.

This geopolitical, epistemological, and ontological reflection deconstructs and allows us to see anew the social and ecological devastation caused by dualistic conceptions, in particular those that divide nature and culture, humans and nonhumans, the individual and the communal, mind and body, and so forth. It reminds those of us existing in the densest urban and liberal worlds that we, too, dwell in a world that is alive. Reflecting on relationality resituates the human within the ceaseless flow of life in which everything is inevitably immersed; it enables us to see ourselves again as part of the stream of life.

Epistemologies of the South and political ontology are efforts at thinking beyond the academy, with the *pueblos~territorio* (territory~peoples) and the intellectual-activists linked to them. In this regard, they show the limits of Western social theory; these limits arise from social theory's continued reliance on its historical matrix, the modern dualist episteme and ontology. Modern social theory continues to operate largely on the basis of an objectifying distancing principle, which implies a belief in the "real" and "truth"—an epistemology of allegedly autonomous subjects willfully moving around in a universe of self-contained objects. This ontology of disconnection ends up disqualifying knowledges produced not *about* but *from* the relation. It is thus that social theory comes to silence much of what brings life into being. To reenliven critical thought thus requires bringing it again closer to life and the Earth, including to the thoughts and practices of people struggling in their defense.

Coda

I would like to end by asking readers to imagine as vividly as possible two situations to understand intuitively what I mean by the ontological occupation of territories and the concomitant destruction of worlds (and, conversely, the importance of their defense). The first comes from the pen of the most eloquent chronicler of social and ecological devastation in Colombia over the past five decades, Alfredo Molano. In what I am sure was one of his gloomiest and most disheartening dispatches, written after the government declaration in 2012 of 17 million hectares as "strategic mining reserve" in the departments of Vaupés, Vichada, Guainía, Amazonas, and Chocó, largely inhabited by indigenous and Afro-descendant populations, he concludes:

> Today, half of the departments of Guainía and Vaupés are solicited in concession by large multinationals. These corporations have discovered—with the complicity and information from the government, no doubt—that this huge region is a vast gold, copper, uranium, and coltan reserve. Greed has been unleashed and will know no limits. What's most troubling, really

troubling, is that this entire zone is made up almost exclusively of indigenous resguardos, where any type of mining is legally possible, with government approval. Indigenous communities may enter into agreement with the corporations (as it happened between Cortés and Moctezuma and ever since). The locomotive of development [one of the Santos administration's government banners] will exhaust any valuable mining resource; it will divide and make enemies of indigenous communities to the point of death; it will destroy rivers, wetlands, and the vast moriche palm groves; it will exterminate tigers, tapirs, and toucans, at the same time that it imposes its vigorous cultural and economic control. There will not be a single shaman left who knows about the past. Nothing of what until now happened in the distant corner of the country—rubber, coca, Bible, salt, firearms, mercury, royalties, concessions—will compare with the civilizing brutality deployed by this new infernal machinery of extermination. Whoever did not know the region before will never realize it ever existed.[13]

Whoever did not know the region before will never realize it ever existed. I doubt there is a more accurate description of the destruction of worlds by the world made up of one (globalized) world.

The second example takes us to the black community of La Toma, Cauca, which we encountered in the previous chapters, and its resistance against gold mining and other threats to its territory. In November 2014, a group of twenty-two women started a courageous march from their homes in La Toma to the capital city of Bogotá, hundreds of kilometers away. They were greeted and joined by people in solidarity all along the way. Their march was motivated by the continued illegal presence of large backhoe machines owned by outsiders engaged in gold mining. As is well known, backhoe mining in combination with the use of mercury and cyanide is highly destructive. The mining was destroying their river and polluting the water; people who opposed the miners received death threats. Despite repeated protests, demands, and international letters in support of the community's efforts to get the machines confiscated or at least taken out of their territories, the state had taken no effective action to do so, which motivated the march as an action of last resort. The communiqués that the women released to the public invariably included the refrain "Movement of Afro-descendant Women for the protection of life and in defense of the ancestral territories," together with exemplary statements on territorial and ontological politics. I cite a few here, in ending:

We are black women from Northern Cauca, descendants of African men and women who were enslaved, with knowledge about the ancestral value embedded in our territories. We know how many of our ancestors had to pay for our freedom with their lives; we know that our ancestors spilled their blood to obtain these lands; we know that they worked for years and years in slavery to leave these lands to us. They taught us that you don't sell land; they understood that we needed to ensure that our people could permanently remain in our territory. . . . Four centuries have passed, and their memory is our memory; their practices are our practices, transmitted through our grandparents; our daughters and sons continue today reaffirming our identity as free peoples. . . . Today our lives are in danger and the possibilities of existing as Afro-descendant peoples are minimal. Many men and women are threatened with death. We women have lived from ancestral mining, an activity that enabled our ancestors to buy their freedom, and ours. This activity is linked with agriculture, with fishing, with hunting, and to ancestral knowledges that our elders and our midwives have inculcated in us so that we can remain as peoples. Because our love for life itself is stronger than our fear of death, we convene all the solidarity of those opposed to illegal mining and opposed to the threats against the people that protect life and the ancestral territories.

5

Notes on Intellectual Colonialism and the Dilemmas of Latin American Social Theory

Some Background to Intellectual Colonialism

To talk about intellectual colonialism today—a topic that paradoxically remains relevant, despite the development of a wide range of critical theories in Latin America and other regions of the world, especially since the 1950s—we have to bring the debate on Latin American social theory up to date with the current world situation, including ecological and social planetary crises, and of course the resurgence of political right-wing regimes across the continent after 2015. I think we may be at a particularly important and auspicious moment for doing exactly this.

Updating this debate is too large a project, however, to cover in a short text; to do so, we would have to cover the full genealogy of the question back to the nineteenth century, when the intellectual debates of the continent addressed issues that are still relevant to some degree, from discussions of the contrast between civilization and barbarism in the first half of the century to early debates on Latin American modernity as the century drew to a close (Rodó, Martí, Bello, Lastarria, and so on). The decolonial current would push us to explore even further back in the history of knowledge, to analyze every corner of history in search of examples of epistemic decolonization, as some colleagues who work on this issue have been doing; there we would doubtless find many voices of indigenous and Afro-descendant people and of women to fill out the archive of decolonial thought. Moving on to the early twentieth century, we would also have to consider Marxism, anarchism, indigenism, and the first precursors of feminism (such as María Cano in Colombia in the 1920s, of anarchist leanings); and later in the century, the famous debate between Leopoldo Zea and Augusto Salazar Bondy over the question of whether "a philosophy of Our America exists" (Salazar Bondy 1968; Zea 1969). Finally, we would arrive at the recent past and the radical critique of Orlando Fals Borda in his book *Ciencia propia y colonialismo intelectual* (A science of our own and intellectual colonialism, 1970), and Paulo Freire's influential book *Pedagogy of the Oppressed* (1968, with English and Spanish translations published in 1970); both books rattled the epistemic edifice of the academies and began to lay the foundations for us to begin to take seriously what we would now call *los conocimientos otros* (other ways of knowing) of subaltern worlds. Along the way, we would also come across perspectives such as dependency theory and liberation theology (see chapter 2).

What Does Epistemic and Intellectual Dependency Mean?

After this very incomplete genealogical note, let me now turn to the first question: What does "intellectual or epistemic dependency with regard to theoretical concepts and frameworks created in the central countries" mean?[1] We have many ways to approach this question; here I will point to just two of them. The first comes from the analysis of the modern/colonial world-system begun by Aníbal Quijano in the 1980s, and in particular the notions of the coloniality of power and of knowledge. I will not pause here to discuss this position, which I largely share, and has been immensely enriched by the contributions of a broad array of academics, intellectuals, and activists from two generations and counting, and a rich variety of themes and concepts. I will only mention two early contributions to the decolonial project that are still foundational to any analysis of Latin American social theory: the reinterpretation of modernity as "modernity/coloniality" from the very beginning (resituating all earlier debates on Latin American modernity on a more complex political-theoretical spectrum); and the concept of Eurocentrism as a pillar of the entire modern/ colonial framework, and of knowledge in particular.

A second way to approach the epistemic dependency of Latin American social theory is the Foucauldian concept of episteme. I feel that this second approach complements the first, which is why I like to use it, especially because it allows us to understand both contemporary social theory and *its limitations* in a different way. As mentioned in chapter 3, Foucault defines episteme as an intermediate level of knowledge, situated between the underlying domain in which the phenomenon of life takes place, on the one hand, and the space of the sciences explicitly constituted as such, on the other. Thus, in *The Order of Things*, Foucault analyzes three epistemes (corresponding to the Renaissance, the Classical Age, and the Modern Age), the rules that regulated each of them, and the discontinuities between them. He traces the vicissitudes of knowledge within each era in relation to the forms of thinking about life, work, and language. He discovers that the episteme of modernity, which crystallized around the end of the eighteenth century, is determined by the figure of "Man," which has been set up ever since as the subject, basis, and object of all knowledge, which constitutes the foundational anthropocentrism of modernity.

The Episteme of Modernity as the Background to All Academic Work

Contemporary social theory is necessarily situated within this episteme. Throughout my own academic practice, I have been discovering that the "modern academic space" runs on certain key epistemic practices, among which the following three stand out: (A) Three central paradigms (liberal theory, Marxist theory, poststructuralist theory) with their corresponding epistemologies, and their admixtures with other key factors such as gender, race, ethnicity, and sexuality; thus, for example, we can speak of a "Marxist feminist" approach, "poststructuralist critical race theory," "queer theory" in the poststructuralist vein, post-Marxist theories of social movements, and so forth. (B) The delineation, within the uninterrupted and complex flow of the real, of separate and supposedly autonomous spheres (for example, "economics," "society," "culture," "politics," "religion," "the individual," and so on), each of which has its own discipline devoted to uncovering its secrets (economics, sociology, political science, anthropology, psychology, and so on). (C) A series of constitutive dualisms that constrain knowledge (subject-object, mind-body, reason-emotion, nature-culture, human-nonhuman, secular-sacred, and many more). I would like to emphasize two points from this short explanation: First, all academic work must follow these rules if it is to be considered properly academic; for example, every master's thesis or doctoral dissertation must accept this epistemic structure to be approved (few escape this never quite explicit requirement). Second, the limits of knowledge production within this episteme are becoming clearer all the time, as I will explain shortly.

Let us turn back to the diagram of the modern episteme that I presented in chapter 3. If we place a particular discipline in it—anthropology, for example (but it could be any of the social or human sciences, making the appropriate adjustments)—we would situate in the center of the diagram the project of

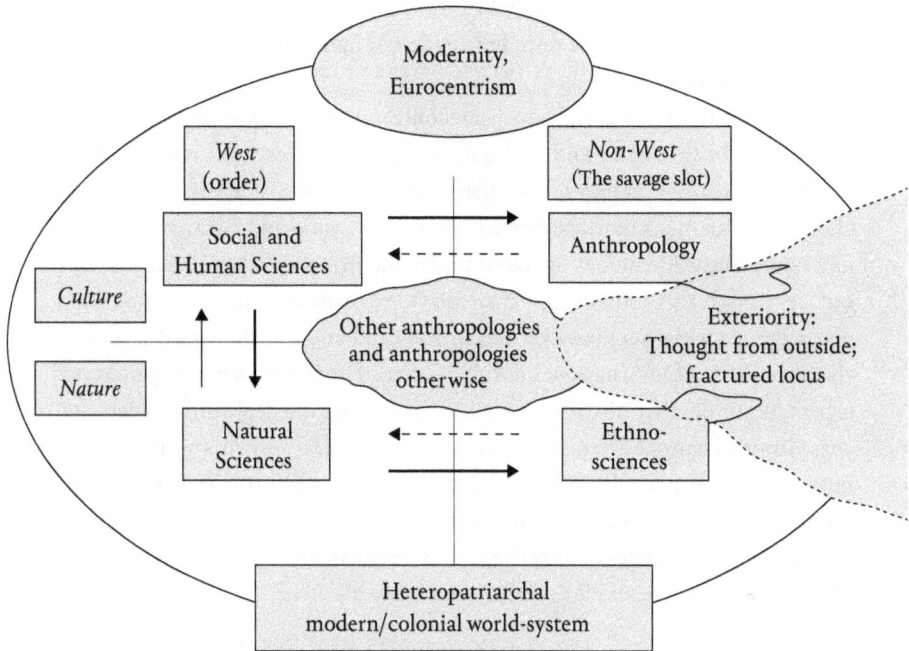

Figure 5.1. Anthropology and the episteme of modernity

constructing "other anthropologies and anthropologies otherwise," or what
we have called "world anthropologies" (Restrepo and Escobar 2005; Ribeiro
and Escobar 2006), as a potentially destabilizing force for the metropolitan
canons of anthropology, which can only think the field from their foundational matrices in the anthropologies of France, the United Kingdom, and
the United States (figure 5.1). However, it is a matter not just of making the
histories and contributions of other anthropologies from the rest of the world
(including Latin America) visible to what is called "anthropology," but also of
opening up the diagram to imagine "other anthropologies" (or other sociolo-
gies, or histories, or geographies, and perhaps even other philosophies, and so
on) about and from other worlds. This is a more radical project, one that will
find perhaps its greatest source of inspiration, as the diagram suggests, in the
space of "exteriority" and thought from outside, and within that space, in the
fractured locus created by the coloniality that we have learned about from
María Lugones (2010a, 2010b). That is where we find a whole series of trends in
contemporary thought that would have to be mapped out from that perspective; that is, trends (in both the Global North and the Global South, in diverse

ways) that can no longer be easily fit into the intellectual division of labor so zealously carved out by the onto-epistemic configuration of patriarchal capitalist modernity.

To be clear, there have always been contestatory efforts aimed at this episteme, from both within and without, which have sometimes caused significant ruptures (for example, the surrealism of the 1920s or the anticolonial thought of the 1940s to 1960s by authors such as Fanon and Césaire), but *taken as a whole*, the academy has operated under the iron rules that I have just laid out. Although this remains the case today (perhaps even more so than ever, given the growing neoliberalization of the academies at the world level and the imposition of international norms of alleged excellence), one encouraging aspect of our current historical condition is that we are beginning to perceive these limits. I cannot attempt to explain here how and why this awareness has been growing (especially since the 1950s), but I will point to a few of the main trends—interrelated with one another—that are causing fissures, if not actually moving at the edges of or perhaps outside the modern episteme. In the rest of the chapter, I give an idea of what these may be.

On the Edges of the Modern/Colonial Episteme

The constitutive dualisms of modernity, such as the split between nature and culture (humans-nonhumans) and between us and them (West–non-West; modern-nonmodern; in other words, the colonial divide), are increasingly coming into question. The questioning of the dichotomy between human and nonhuman in particular derives from two major sources: first, the Earth itself, Pachamama, which is giving clearer and clearer signs of how much it is suffering in the face of anthropogenic activity; second, the outbreak of a great movement to defend the Earth, especially the demonstrations initiated by a wide range of subaltern groups and territory~peoples whose very survival as worlds depends on the continuity and healing of Mother Earth.

Then again, the questioning of the colonial divide derives from all those who seek to situate their production of knowledge in the space opened up by colonial difference; that is, from the fractured locus of enunciation. Here we once more find two major strands. First, the ever more compelling emergence of the *knowledge* (perhaps we should call them "knowledges-emotions," or senti-pensamientos) of communities, activists, collectives, and movements—all those that never found a place within the academies, since they were not produced under the rules of the episteme, and some of which are now even beginning to insinuate themselves into those spaces, though not without difficulty and contradictions, as we well know. And second, a new series of critical lines of thought, often enough with ties to the academy, though in many cases produced by intellectuals who move among the social movements, communities, the academy, and sometimes the state itself; I will refer to these later.

I will make a couple of final observations on this whole emerging array of knowledges and theoretico-political preoccupations, from the perspective of the question: What does it mean to think about the social sciences from the vantage point of Latin America in the twenty-first century? Is there a Latin American perspective on thinking about current crises from the framework of social theory?[2] The first observation is that social theory and the social sciences (and this statement also applies to the human and natural sciences) already clearly show that they are at best *insufficient* for supplying the questions—much less the answers—that we need to face our multiple interrelated crises: of food, of climate and energy, of poverty, and of meaning. In other words, it seems to me that we can already assert more boldly and with a greater sense of reality that many of the key questions and ideas about the crises are coming not from the social sciences or the academy (without suggesting that they are no longer important, whether in a positive or a negative way) but rather from the epistemic space that is being created by the proliferation of *other* subaltern consciousnesses and knowledges, together with related critical trends (again, often in some sort of relationship to the academy, but independently developed). Second, with regard to all these other forms of knowledge, we must nevertheless ask the following questions: Do they constitute postpatriarchal/modern/colonial episteme forms of knowledge production? (That is, have they successfully left the Enlightenment episteme of modernity behind?) Or do they continue to function, entirely or partially and despite their radical nature and novelty, within the episteme of "Man"? This last question is key, in my opinion. I return to it at the end of this short chapter. For now, I would like to give an idea, however schematic, of the range of research projects that, I feel, form part of this emerging epistemic process.

Before concluding this section, I would like to mention a related theme that I have not touched on much in this book, which is the place of rational thought and design intentionality in working with communalitarian collectives. None of the sharpest critics of modern rationality (Illich, Varela, Plumwood, Leff) dismiss the practices of being, doing, and knowing that come with ontologies of dualism and separation, such as abstract knowledge, objectivizing representations, and cause-effect relationships, nor do they reject technology in itself; instead they object to their hegemony and the marginalization of other forms of being/knowing/doing that they carry out, while making visible their limitations for understanding experience and, in the final analysis, life. Their aim, then, is to resituate these practices as particular onto-epistemic and social practices. When they are resituated, their possible uses are resized, provided that they are subordinated to the principles of sentipensar and acting relationally. There is undoubtedly an inherent tension in this positioning, which Varela (1999; Varela, Thompson, and Rosch 1991), for example, seeks to address through his notion of "embodied reflexivity."

The Nasa activist and intellectual Vilma Almendra has recently put forward a notion that I find extremely thought provoking. Asking herself what the role of critical thought among indigenous communities is, she asserts: "Critical thought, as we see it and as it is expressed in our community, is one of the flows of life from Mother Earth; that is, communitarian critical thought is what has allowed us to keep moving" (2017, 61). Critical thought, in other words, arises from the dynamics of life itself, and at some point it becomes an essential tool for continuing to be a people in movement, for "thinking critically, not simply seeing and acting against the external enemy but also identifying the internal enemy and recognizing ourselves in the hydra that resides in us" (62). This is the source of the Nasa mandates of "being, thinking, and acting," "word and action in the spirit of the community," and "walking the word." Manuel Rozental (2017b, 65) continues this idea in his discussion of defiance in the face of the worsening capitalist hydra: "The defiance that challenges us to join words to actions is the recognition and addressing of critical topics or matters, threats and alternatives on which our survival depends, as does the survival of life itself in every territory and all throughout Mother Earth."

It seems to me that three forms of thought are at stake here: the thought that distances itself from the world it seeks to know (Cartesian thought, including in relation to the "enemy"); embodied reflection; and the sentipensar with the community-Earth that arises from grief and nourishes hope, perhaps the most important anchor for the desire to survive as a communalitarian people. This onto-epistemic transgressing would seem to characterize many struggles of territory~peoples today. We can conclude that the critical thought of communities arises from the depths of the situations in which they live. It arises as a necessity of communalitarian dynamics, of communal existence, of the historicity of relational worlds, perhaps as a leap in consciousness-complexity,[3] situating territory~peoples in a special place within critical thought.

The Three Realms of Critical Thought

In chapter 2, I argued that any genealogy or compendium of Latin American critical thought (LACT) today must include the knowledges and understandings of the communities and their organizations themselves, as these are among the most powerful expressions of LACT. This suggestion is the greatest challenge facing social theory, because the epistemic structure of modernity (whether in the liberal, Marxist, or poststructuralist register, whether on the right or the left) has been erected atop the effective erasure of this crucial level of thought, which is precisely the level that is now emerging most clearly and forcefully. In the same chapter, I identified three currents within LACT: Left thought, pro-autonomy thought, and Earth thought. I use the second current to refer to the ever more eloquent understandings that are emerging from the autonomic processes that have crystallized in Zapatismo but also include a wide variety of experiences and ideas from all over the continent, from southern Mexico to southwestern Colombia and to the Mapuche territory or Wallmapu. All these movements emphasize the reconstitution of communal ways—within noncapitalist, nonliberal, and nonstate conceptions of social organization—as the cornerstone of autonomy. Autonomy, communality, and territoriality are the three key concepts of this current.[4]

By "Earth thought," I am referring not so much to the environmental movement and ecology (though it is related to these) as to the dimension that every community inhabiting a territory knows is vital to its continued existence: its indissoluble connection to the Earth and to all living beings, and in at least some cases even to so-called inorganic and seemingly inert matter. This dimension is not confined to theoretical understandings, for it is eloquently expressed in art (weavings), in myths, in the economic and cultural practices of a given place, and in struggles for land and for defending Pachamama.

Latin American critical thought can be defined as the intermeshing of these three major currents: Left thought, pro-autonomy thought, and Earth thought. These are not separate, preconstituted spheres; rather, they overlap, sometimes feeding off one another, sometimes in open conflict. My argument is that social theory today must cultivate all three strands, keeping them in continual tension and dialogue, and must abandon any pretense of universalizing or of presenting a single truth. Put differently, we have to add a third fundamental building block to the Zapatista formula of fighting "from below and on the Left": "and with the Earth."

Emerging Research Areas for Another Social Theory
of Abya Yala/Afro/Latino América

We can also begin to visualize the contours of the post-modern/colonial episteme—that is, the configuration or configurations of knowledge that take place partially outside the structuring practices of the episteme of modernity—in terms of certain emerging areas of research. I tried to map out these trends a few years ago and was able to identify five major emerging areas, which overlap with the pro-autonomy and Earth currents (Escobar 2014b). Though I cannot elaborate on them in this text, I will mention them briefly: decolonial theory (including the new fields within this area, such as the coloniality of nature, decolonial feminisms, and decolonial aesthetics); studies of alternatives to development (including Buen Vivir, rights of nature, postdevelopment, alternative economies, and transitions to postextractivism); civilizational transitions; new approaches to heteropatriarchy; and communality, relationality, and the pluriverse (communal systems, communitarian meshworks, communitarian feminisms, and relational spirituality and ontologies). Many of these areas, which frequently overlap and intersect one another in mutually enriching ways, relate to the critique of dualisms in modernity and, beyond that critique, to the development of a political-theoretical framework that can generate a substantial space for research on the principle of relationality, which in my view has grown in importance since the renewed concern with ontology in social theory began.

Relationality signals that life is interrelationship and interdependence, always and at every level. Everything exists because everything else exists, as the Southern African principle of Ubuntu tells us. There are no intrinsically existing objects, subjects, or actions, as modernity has taught us to presume since at least the time of Descartes. In other words, the real is not made of isolated objects that interact with one another; the observer does not preexist what she observes (Maturana and Varela 1987); there is no external world for us to cling to; everything living is always an integral part of the ever-changing pluriverse. What we call "experience" is always coemerging with the experiences of many other beings. Scientific understanding, finally, is merely an intricate process of validating how the experts construct what is called "the real."[5]

At the intersection of the decolonial and relational currents, we find a fruitful output of political-theoretical works on gender and patriarchy, which take diverse yet converging forms in the works of different thinkers, up to a point. This is a basic trend for reorienting Latin American social theory as a

whole in a pro-autonomy direction. A basic premise of this current is a reread-
ing of patriarchy as the fundamental onto-epistemic matrix for all forms of oppression, even if entangled with multiple other forms—not simply because patriarchy historically got its start several thousand years before capitalism and
modernity (to which it loaned its foundations), but because that was where the
systematic erosion of the relational basis of life began, as can be seen in matriarchal or matriztic cultures, which value cooperation, respect for all other beings, the continual regeneration of life, cocreation, and the sacred. Patriarchy,
by contrast, displays values such as domination, appropriation, competition,
aggression, hierarchy, and creation through destruction (Escobar 2018).[6]

Another important development in this area is the reconceptualizing, or
even the abandonment by some writers, of the notion of gender as a principle
for classifying differences, for which relational, communal, and dual notions
of gender are essential.[7] The analysis of intersectionality has undergone an
important revival from the perspectives of race, sexuality, communality, spirituality, and nature on the part of indigenous, Afro-descendant, lesbian, and
environmental feminists, among others. This rich variety of work has given
rise to an emphasis on tackling depatriarchalization and decolonization simultaneously. An entire antiessentalist, relational (nondualist and thus nonliberal), and posthuman political-theoretical edifice is being built from these
converging but distinct currents. From that vantage point, it is possible to see
with greater clarity that a renewed understanding of communality and relationality constitutes a much-needed antidote to the hyperexploitation and extreme violence of capitalism against women, against society, and against life
as a whole.

Some Examples of Constructing
an Autonomous Social Theory

It will be useful to illustrate the arguments presented in the previous section
with works (actually, political-epistemic projects) that exemplify the elements
of a knowledge production that questions, and moves beyond, the modern
episteme, though I have space here only to present them in summary. These
include the many volumes recently edited by Xochitl Leyva in San Cristóbal de
las Casas; the collaborative work with communities in resistance coordinated
by Patricia Botero in Manizales; the feminist anthropology group at CIESAS in
Mexico City; the many works created in the space for decolonial thought at
the doctoral program in Latin American cultural studies at the Universidad
Andina Simón Bolívar (UASB), edited by Catherine Walsh in Quito; and the

events and texts produced over the past decade by academics and activists at the Universidad del Cauca, mentioned in chapter 2.

Some of the characteristics of these works include the following:

A. They are conceived and constructed from the epistemic space of communities in resistance, collectives, and movements. They therefore do not depend on mediations, nor do they incorporate major translations into the logocentric categories of social theory, though they might be in conversation with it; in fact, they dislodge those categories from their central place in interpreting the real.

B. They are the products of profoundly collective forms of working, which come under many names (collective action research; "hearting" (*corazonar*); colaboring; decolonial pedagogies; sentipensar; networks and mingas for Buen Vivir). From this perspective, they are related to the militant research epistemologies and methodologies proposed by groups such as the Colectivo Situaciones in Buenos Aires since the early 2000s.

C. They explicitly circulate among the subaltern political spaces in which colonial difference is inhabited and reconstructed—that is, where other worlds and forms of knowing are constructed. They are not produced solely or mainly for circulation within the academy, though that could also happen.

D. Their relationship with the academy is based on their maintaining autonomy in their categories of thought and subaltern experiences.

E. Their basic aim is to contribute to the struggles for (re)constituting worlds based on the categories and experiences of actors in the struggle and the resistance.[8]

Of course, these are not the only works that deserve to be singled out, just the ones that I am most directly familiar with. I am not saying that all social theory must follow the trail these works have blazed, but rather suggesting that they illustrate what we might characterize as "a Latin American perspective on thinking through current problems from the framework of social theory."[9] Nor are they free from contradictions, and with regard to all these trends, it is worth maintaining a kind of epistemic vigilance in relation to how far they stray from the established episteme. But it is from experiences such as these that what I have called a post-Enlightenment episteme is emerging.

Some Characteristics of More Autonomous Social Theories

It occurs to me, by way of conclusion, that the political-theoretical perspectives and proposals that display greater autonomy with regard to the dominant episteme share the following characteristics, among others:

They go beyond the modern epistemology and ontology of subjects, objects, and actions understood as intrinsically existing.

They underscore the coloniality of power, of knowledge, and of being, and they situate themselves firmly in the onto-epistemic space of the fractured locus of enunciation of discourse and of knowledge.

They problematize the disciplines and interdisciplines as currently constituted.

They question the anthropocentrism, androcentrism, and logocentrism that are constitutive of academic ways of knowing, taken as a whole.

They are oriented toward a nondualist or postdualist episteme, and they are open to a perspective of understanding reality through its profound constitutive relationality.

They therefore embrace the repressed poles of the binaries of modernity, such as the body, the emotions, the spiritual, the senses, intuition, and artistic inspiration.

From this new onto-epistemic space, they propose innovative rereadings of heteropatriarchy, capitalism, racism, and modernity, as well as the many resistances to them; and they promote dialogues and practices for reconstituting worlds in decolonial, postdevelopmentalist, and pluriversal ways.

It is from this post-Enlightenment space that people are once again tackling, with renewed energy, the core questions that contemporary social theory has worked on so assiduously, but the understanding of which was reaching an impasse: domination, capitalism, heteropatriarchy, racism and white dominance, and inequality. Indeed, it would be from this new episteme (or these new epistemes) that we might finally glimpse an end to the figure of "Man," which might perhaps now disappear at last, "like a face drawn in sand at the edge of the sea" (Foucault 1970, 387). This would be a postcapitalist, postpatriarchal, nonracist, and nonliberal pluriverse made up of posthuman worlds in which knowledge and sentipensamiento would once more serve life and the complex human and nonhuman meshworks that incessantly, despite the hierarchy-loving and homogenizing strategies that seek to dominate it, have always constituted life.

6

Postdevelopment @ 25

On "Being Stuck" and Moving Forward, Sideways, Backward, and Otherwise

Soy el desarrollo en carne viva
I am development in the flesh

—CALLE 13, "LATINOAMÉRICA"

(*Ritmo de bambuco, acompañamiento de guitarra*)
Una historia que me ata
Un pueblo que no se olvida
Un sendero en la montaña
El calor de la mañana
La manera en que se habla
La simpleza que se extraña
Las riquezas de sus aguas
El olor de la manigua. . . .
No, que el discurso del progreso
Es riqueza petrolera
Es pobreza en la vereda . . .
No, que el discurso del progreso
No se mezcle por las aguas
De mi tierra y de mis venas
No, que el discurso del progreso
No me arranque de este suelo
La riqueza de mi tierra.
No, que estas Aguas no se tocan
Esta tierra no está en venta
Y éste pueblo no se entrega.

(Bambuco rhythm, guitar accompaniment)
A history that binds me
A village I can't forget
A trail in the mountains
The heat of the morning
The way the people talk
The simplicity that I miss
The riches of its waters
The smell of its wild lands. . . .
No, for the discourse of progress
Is wealth for the oil companies
Is poverty in the village . . .
No, for the discourse of progress
Must not mix in along the rivers
Of my homeland and of my veins
No, for the discourse of progress
Must not rip from my soil
The richness of my land.
No, 'cause these rivers aren't to be touched
This land is not for sale
And this pueblo won't give up.

—JUAN VÁSQUEZ, "EL DISCURSO DEL PROGRESO" (2017)

This chapter involves a conversation between Gustavo Esteva and myself, on the occasion of the twenty-fifth anniversary of the publication of *The Development Dictionary* (Sachs 1992). Our aim was to assess what has happened since in development debates, and to rearticulate some of the postdevelopment insights and proposals.[1]

Arturo: It's been almost thirty years since that memorable week of September 1988, when we sat around the convivial table at Ivan Illich's house on Foster Avenue in University Park (where Penn State University is located), summoned by Wolfgang Sachs and Ivan. Out of the intense and enjoyable discussions of those days there emerged the task of writing our respective chapters for what a few years later would emerge as *The Devel-*

opment Dictionary. The book made a "splash" of sorts when it made its debut in print. For some, the splash has been enduring and one of the most essential elements behind what came to be known as the postdevelopment school. Other, less generous, retrospective analyses of the *Dictionary* (and postdevelopment) argue that it was interesting but ineffective and that, in any way, it is superseded by now, since development has certainly not died, as the *Dictionary* appeared to prognosticate. Many mainstream scholars and development practitioners, harsher in their appraisal, consider it to have been a terribly misguided endeavor and a disservice to the poor.

Aram Ziai's invitation comes at an auspicious time to take stock of what has gone "under the bridge" of the *Dictionary* and postdevelopment waters in the intervening years, and to renew our understanding and critique. You were not only one of the pioneers of the critique, but your position regarding development has, if anything, become even more radical than in 1992—at least that's how I read your most recent texts on the subject (Esteva, Babones, and Babcicky 2013). To remain for now on a historical register, I would like to ask you, to start this conversation: How do you see now the intellectual-political ferment of those early days, when the radical problematization of development was first launched, as compared with the conditions that exist today for radical critiques? Is there something you think that our group could have done differently? Where do you hear echoes from those conversations in current debates?

Gustavo: "Development" is no longer an unquestioned category. At the grassroots, I have seen in recent years open resistance and opposition to development itself, not only to certain forms of development—and some have a long history. Such opposition is now fully incorporated in people's discourses, something they did not dare to do before. In my contribution to the *Dictionary*, I celebrated the emergence of new commons, which I saw as an alternative to development. The *Ecologist* described such emergence that very year. And the commons movement is today in full swing, everywhere, in what we can legitimately call a posteconomic society, not only beyond development.

Salvatore Babones's classification of the current development panorama is very illuminating. He associates it with three Sachses (Esteva, Babones, and Babcicky 2013, 22–23):

The "Goldman Sachs" approach expresses a pretty general consensus that dominates in governments and international institutions. Goldman Sachs defines development through their commodities trading desks, their infrastructure projects and their exploration units. Their approach could be symbolized by an oil platform located ten kilometers offshore, safe from harassment by local indigenous militants.

The "Jeffrey Sachs" approach blindly believes in development and capitalism but is concerned with massive hunger and misery, which Jeffrey and his colleagues see not as the consequences but as the shortcomings of development. Well-meaning people like Sachs, Gates, and major NGOs in the United States and Europe focus on alleviating obvious suffering. They stand for a chicken in every pot, a mosquito net over every bed, and a condom on every penis.

The "Wolfgang Sachs" approach circulates in university critical development studies departments (which paradoxically focus on postdevelopment) and among indigenous leaders, independent intellectuals, and a motley group of people basically ignored by academia and the 1 percent. In my view, this approach corresponds today to the awareness and experience, not necessarily the discourse, of millions, perhaps billions, of ordinary men and women around the world who are increasingly "beyond" development.

The adventure of the *Dictionary* started for me a few months before that meeting on Foster Avenue. Ivan invited us to his house in Ocotepec, Cuernavaca, Mexico, to talk about "After Development, What?" Majid Rahnema, Jean Robert, and Wolfgang [Sachs] were there. One of the things that I remember very well from that meeting was that we abandoned the expression "after development" for the implicit periodization that Wolfgang retained. We knew that the developmentalists were still around and would continue their devastating enterprise. We wanted to explore how *to be* beyond development.

As you know, I am not a scholar. I read a lot, but my ideas, my words, my vocabulary, my inspiration, come from my experience at the grassroots, in my world of *campesinos*, *indios*, and urban marginals. Ivan knew that. At one point in the conversation, he asked me, "Gustavo, if you could only use one word to express what is to be beyond development, what word would it be?" My immediate answer was "hospitality." Development is radically inhospitable: it imposes a universal definition of the good life and excludes all others. We need to hospitably embrace the thousand different ways of thinking, being, living, and experiencing the world that characterize reality.

This was not just a witty remark; it drew from my experience. In the early 1980s, we who had been classified as "underdeveloped" were frustrated and enraged with always finding ourselves at the end of the line. We knew by then that "development," as the universalization of the American way of life, was impossible; that we would never catch up with the developed, as Truman promised; that we would be permanently left behind. For many of us, this new awareness was a revelation: we still had our own notions of what it means to live well, and they were feasible. Instead of continuing the foolish race to nowhere, we should reorient our efforts. In my experience, it was not dissident vanguards trying for alternative development strategies or alternatives to development, but many grassroots groups reaffirming themselves in their own path, in many cases simply to survive in the dramatic 1980s, what was later called "the lost decade" in Latin America. For me, they were already beyond development.

I bought into underdevelopment when I was thirteen years old. I mean that I fully assumed my "lacks": I wanted development for me, for my family, and for my country, to satisfy all the "needs" that had suddenly been created for me. Let me clarify. When I was a child, the word "necessity" had only one practical application: taking a shit. It was used when my mother told us: "When you get to your uncle's house, ask him where you can do your necessities." We *did* our "necessities"; we didn't *have* them. This way of talking applied to everything: our "needs" were defined by our own capacity, our tools, the way we used them, and they were strictly personal, imponderable, and incommensurable. It was in the course of my lifetime that all current "needs" were created and we were transmogrified into needy, measured, and controlled people. Professionals defined our needs, and we were classified according to them.

When I was a child, people would talk to me. Words were symbols, not representations or categories, and only one of every ten of them addressed me as an undifferentiated member of a crowd. As I grew, words became categories, and I was addressed as a member of a class of people: children, skinny, underdeveloped—according to our "needs": education, nutrition, development.

As you know very well, in the early 1970s, the recognition that the development enterprise was causing hunger and misery everywhere produced the Basic Needs Approach. The goal became to satisfy a package of "basic needs." There was no consensus about the definition of those needs, but that orientation still characterizes most development efforts—and it has shaped the UN Millennium Development Goals and the Sustainable Development Goals (SDGs) today.

In 1976 I was in immediate danger of becoming a minister in the new administration of the Mexican government, after my success as a senior official for more than a decade, coming up with and implementing great development programs. I quit. I started to work autonomously with people at the grassroots. By then I knew that instead of "development," people sought autonomy, as we expressed in the name of an independent organization that some friends and I created (Autonomía, Descentralismo y Gestión). I also knew that the "state" was a mechanism for control and domination, useless for emancipation. Similarly, after observing how much damage the professionals did as transmission belts for creating "needs" and dependence, I began the complex process of deprofessionalizing myself.

In the early 1980s, there was increasing awareness of the failures of the development enterprise and the folly of adopting a universal definition of the good life. The idea of postdevelopment began to get around: people were reclaiming

their own feasible ways of living well. In the 1985 conference
of the Society for International Development in Rome, invited
by Wolfgang to discuss the future of development studies, I
suggested it lay in archaeology: only an archaeological eye
could explore the ruins left by development. I saw development as a thing of my past, not my present, and even less my
future. I was exploring those ruins in my own world and already looking for hospitality for our ways of being—the ways
captured in the expression "Buen Vivir" now coming from
your part of the world.

   A few years ago, when Salvatore Babones approached me
with a proposal to write a book about development, he observed that "we" in the postdevelopment school don't use statistics. He was right; we hate them. Salvatore is a quantitative
sociologist, well acquainted with development statistics. He
wanted to incorporate them into our analysis. He also observed that people studying development are often concerned
with the real problems of the world, interested in making a
difference. But we closed the door on them by proclaiming a
firm "No" to development. Couldn't we open a decent door
for them? He was right. And he appeared at a time when I
was adopting, with many others, the position of "One No and
Many Yeses," following the Zapatista suggestion to create a
world in which many worlds can be embraced. Yes, I agreed,
we can share a common "No" to development but be open
to thousands of "Yeses": the many paths people are following around the world beyond development; people studying
development can accompany and support them. That is why
we wrote and published *The Future of Development: A Radical
Manifesto*.

Arturo: There are so many interesting dimensions to your answer,
          Gustavo. I would like to explore a few and perhaps provide a
          counterpoint to some of them (as in musical counterpoint,
          where a theme is developed in various directions). But first
          there is something I remembered as I read your comment on
          "needs," something I heard Ivan saying once; I am not sure
          if it was at Penn State or perhaps Berkeley, in the early 1980s
          when he came to do his then-controversial lectures about

his book *Gender.* He said that *Homo faber* had given way to *Homo miserabilis* (needy man), who eventually gave rise to *Homo oeconomicus.* The history of needs was one of Ivan's long-term interests, and it still has to be worked on, for instance, in today's digital age and given the expansion of consumerist middle classes in many world regions, for whom "needs" have seemingly skyrocketed. How do we treat needs "postdevelopmentally"?

Here I arrive at my first substantive question. It is a question often asked of me, so I thought we ought to give it our best answer. I think it is a significant obstacle to getting people to embrace the thinking of postdevelopment. And it is: You speak about the grassroots as the space par excellence to explore how *to be* beyond development. In doing so, are we not romanticizing the grassroots (in your case) or ethnic communities and social movements (in mine)? Are they not also, now and increasingly, subject to needs and desires, including those that development and capitalist modernity promise and eventually deliver (though in limited ways; cheap cell phones, more consumer goods, second-rate overcrowded schools and health services)? Let me give you my answer to this issue, and then I would like to hear yours. The first part of my answer is a simple reversal: faced with the social and ecological devastation brought about by patriarchal capitalist modernity, coupled with the fact that things are not getting better (skyrocketing inequality, climate change), isn't it more romantic to think that "more of the same," in whatever guise (new World Bank prescriptions, green economy, SDGs, or the new "Green Revolution for Africa" advocated by J. Sachs), is going to lead to lasting improvement? In this context, the alternatives emerging at the grassroots and with social movements are genuinely more realistic and less romantic. I would rather bet on them than on the world bankers and mainstream NGOs.

This links up with the historical dimension of my reply to the "romanticism" charge. I was remembering Walter Benjamin's injunction: "To articulate the past historically . . . means to seize it as it flashes up at a moment of danger." He associates this moment with "the politicians' stubborn faith in progress" (Benjamin 1968, 258). Are we not going through one of these moments again, with technology promising humans anything they wish, from unlimited information and immediate communication to eternal life, a "life beyond biology"? At the same time, we are, as Boaventura de Sousa Santos puts it, at a conjuncture where we are facing modern problems for which there are no longer modern solutions. And yet the slogan of the moment seems to be "Everything for the corporations! Everything for the super-rich!" What is the danger, then? That of an even more profound ontological occupation of people's territories and lives. Land grabbing and extractivism are the ugliest heads of it, but they also include growing consumerism and individualism. It is not romantic, in my mind, to be on the side of those who oppose these tendencies, especially when Earth itself is "on our side," considering the warnings she is giving as we wound her ever more deeply and extensively.

Finally, on the theoretical side, I am pondering the question of how to understand "actually existing communities" without falling into the trap of endorsing or reenacting modernist traps. Here I find the recent debates on autonomy and the communal (or the communalitarian, as you call it in Mexico) that have emerged in Chiapas, Oaxaca, and Northern Cauca in Colombia's Southwest new and hopeful. Both of us have written about this recently, though largely in Spanish (Escobar 2014b; Esteva 2015). Here we might also locate the intense South American debates on Buen Vivir over the past decade. This is not the place to even try to summarize these currents of thought and action. But I would like to speak briefly about two recent works that conceptualize communities in all of their entanglement with global forms of capital and modern technology without reducing them to the terms of capitalism or modernity. I am referring to the recent books by Silvia Rivera Cusicanqui (2014) and Verónica Gago (2015). As they show, the communities are also the sites of intense forms of capitalist exploitation, patriarchal domination, and consumerism. They are significantly affected by globalization, and yet they are not completely determined by it. Rivera Cusicanqui emphasizes this feature of many of today's indigenous and popular communities, referring to their capacity to define their own forms of modernity, more convivial than the dominant ones precisely because they also find nourishment in their own histories, intricately weaving indigenous and local practices with those that are not; the result is worlds composed of different cultural strands that nevertheless do not fuse into one single world. These groups find sustenance in the complementarities among diverse worlds without overlooking the antagonisms, articulating with market economies while remaining anchored in indigenous knowledge and technologies. "There is no 'post-' or 'pre-' in a view of history that is not linear or teleological but rather moves in spirals and cycles, that always traces a path but never fails to return to the same point. *The indigenous world does not conceive of history as linear; the past-future are contained in the present*," she says (Rivera Cusicanqui 2014, 57, emphasis added).

I would say that social groups in struggle, at their best, move in several directions at once: adding to and strengthening their long-standing practices while engaging selectively and effectively with the "modern world," its practices, and its technologies. This ability is crucial for deepening the autonomous and communalitarian foundations of social life. I suspect you'll have much to add in this regard.

The second aspect of your reply that caught my attention was the idea of "opening a door" to those genuinely concerned with the world's problems. You add that you are talking about saying one no to development and many yeses to "the many paths people are following around the world beyond development; people studying development can accompany and support them." Are you here suggesting opening a door to those working with progressive development organizations? Could you please clarify? Whatever your answer, I'd like to share a reflection that came to mind recently as I was responding to an interview on "development cooperation" in Barcelona. I came up with three paths for thinking about cooperation, as follows:

(1) *Cooperation as development aid.* This is the standard form of cooperation, practiced by institutions such as USAID, the World Bank, and mainstream NGOs. It takes for granted the dominant world (in terms of markets, individual actions, pro-

ductivity, etc.). Cooperation under this rubric might lead to some improvements for some people, but viewed more broadly, it can only reinforce colonialist understandings of development, and it thus opens the door to dispossession. To this I say: Let's keep the doors tightly closed on them.

(2) *Cooperation as, or for, social justice.* This is the kind of cooperation practiced with the intention of fostering greater social justice and environmental sustainability; it embraces human rights (including gender and ethnic diversity), environmental justice, the reduction of inequality, direct support for grassroots groups, and so forth. Oxfam might serve as paradigm for this second trajectory. In this case I would say: Let's keep the door open while applying pressure on them to move toward the third trajectory.

(3) This third option could go under several names, such as *Cooperation for civilizational transitions* or *Cooperation for autonomy*. Those practicing this option would be, in my view, the natural allies of radical postdevelopment. What is interesting is that this form would go beyond the binary of "us" (who have) and "them" (who need) and embrace all sides in the same, though diverse, movement for civilizational transitions and interautonomy; that is, coalitions and meshworks of autonomous collectives and communities from both the Global North and the Global South. There are no ready-made models for this third kind of solidarity cooperation, but there are groups here and there that approach it (like a few I know in Catalunya).

Do you see any value in this distinction? Is it helpful to raise the question of "allies" for the project of moving beyond development?

Gustavo: My hope, Arturo, is that some readers may enjoy our conversation as much as I am enjoying it!

You are right, of course: we still have a lot of work to do about what are called "needs." A good starting point is the chapter on this concept by Ivan Illich for the *Dictionary*. He clarifies how, for thousands of years, being human meant submitting to the communal norm for needs in a particular place and time. He explains the transition to the dictatorship of universal needs, the subject hooked on alleged needs, as part of the story of *Homo miserabilis*.

We should remember that in classical political economy, for Malthus, Ricardo, or Marx, the vague idea of a "standard of living" alluded to an acceptable subsistence income, the reproduction cost of the labor force. That notion, however, was transmogrified into a *desired* form of living, presented as a condition to aspire toward, and finally a normalized definition of a *necessary* standard defined by basic needs. In that process, the idea of the good is turned into a quantity. The diverse forms of the art of living vanish in the academy, the state, and the powers that be, to be replaced by standards that homogenize individual pursuits. Serge Latouche, also in the *Dictionary*, urges us to view this fetishistic object "standard of living" skeptically and to rediscover the multidimensionality of life.

To discuss "needs" today, we have to acknowledge that more than ever they are created through dispossession, in the classical tradition of the enclosure of the commons that marked the beginning of capitalism. The commoners, dispossessed of their means of subsistence, became people in need of jobs, shelter, food, everything. As Illich explained in the *Dictionary*, development changed the human condition through a grotesque transformation of necessities and desires into prescribed needs. For the dominant mind, it is difficult to recognize the historicity of needs and to understand that before the enclosures, the commoners were eating, learning, healing, living under their own roofs—within the limits imposed by nature and their culture; they had no "needs" for food, education, health care, housing.

We should also explore questions like those examined by Agnes Heller in her critical analysis of the notion of needs in Marx, especially alienated needs and the distinction between desire and need. What she and others observed in the Soviet Union as "the dictatorship of needs" (Fehér, Heller, and Markus 1986) can be applied today to all contemporary societies, through means such as compulsory schooling, marginalizing or outlawing alternative ways of healing, repressing the art of house building, eliminating self-mobility in a world organized to create dependency of the automobile and other vehicles, and so forth.

In exploring what grassroots people are doing, we must carefully draw a line between market- and state-imposed needs and people's own uses of technology. Around the year 2000, more than half of people on Earth had never made a phone call. Even when phone booths came to their villages, many people never used them because they did not have anybody to call: their family and friends had no phones. Today the situation is entirely different. Even the poorest people have access to cellular phones and use them intensely. Yes, as we all know, many young people are now pathologically plugged into this technology and alienated from their communities. But there are people of all ages who are effectively using phones for their own purposes in their own way. In a conversation with David Cayley, Ivan Illich observed that the change he had anticipated when the industrial form of production took off ultimately went in a different direction: that of millions of people "misusing" or tweaking for their own purposes the failing, counterproductive institutions as well as the market (Cayley 2005).

Of course, we must resist any romanticization of rural communities and people at the grassroots. "Don't idealize us," the Zapatista Subcomandante Moisés insists all the time. All kinds of horrors happen at the grassroots. If women are taking the lead in many communities, in a very radical post-patriarchal attitude, it is because for them the combination of traditional patriarchy and modern sexism has become a kind of hell.

At the same time, we must acknowledge that these communities, particularly the indigenous communities, are today a source of inspiration for many of us. They have been struggling for centuries with the predicaments we are facing today; they have the experience. They know well how to deal with modernity. Many of them successfully resisted modernization and were able to protect their own traditional ways. We need to seriously explore the notion that we will not find modern solutions to modern problems—because modernity itself has already collapsed. We are transitioning to another era (which is not postmodernism!) in the uncertainty created by the fact that our old rationalities and sensibilities are obsolete while new ones have not yet been clearly identified. Based on the experience of similar periods in the past, we should turn to the artists, who can often sniff out the coming of a new era; they produce their creations not by using the old logic but with new insights.

The communities were never isolated; this was an invention of British anthropology. All the global forces affect and infect every community and barrio everywhere. Nobody is beyond the reach of globalization. But in the communities we also observe the creative construction of a contemporary art of living. The Zapatistas are amazingly autonomous and self-sufficient. They don't get any funds from the government. They don't need the market or the state to live their lives. If they were suddenly besieged and blockaded, their way of life would basically remain the same. But they have x-rays and ultrasound machines in their health clinics, and they buy in the market equipment for their community radios, mobile phones, computers, bikes, vehicles, and so on. The difference is, they know how to use those technologies instead of being used by them.

An increasing number of people are resisting old and new enclosures, thus preventing the creation of new needs. Yes, they are exposed to all kind of pressures, and they often surrender to old or new dependencies. But what I am increasingly observing at the grassroots is how people dismantle the need for state apparatuses or the goods and services offered by the market. Many people are producing their own food (small farmers, mainly women, feed 70 percent of the people on Earth); learning in freedom (beyond the school system, escaping from education); "healing from health care" (trusting again their own healers and their own notions and traditions of how to be sane or heal—with a little assist from modern technologies); recovering the art of house building (constructing their own homes and buildings), and so forth. This is, in my view, living beyond development. It does not mean going back to the Stone Age; it means saying no, for sheer survival or in the name of old ideals, to a tragic path destroying Mother Earth, dissolving the social fabric and dooming millions to hunger, misery, and homelessness . . . even in prosperous societies like the United States.

Silvia is right, of course. If you live among indigenous people, sometimes you don't know if what they are talking about is happening now, happened yesterday or a thousand years ago, or will happen tomorrow. Time is not real for them. They pack into the present as much past and future as they can. They live in cycles, natural and social cycles, and the image of the spiral or of the Zapatista caracoles may represent changes in which they come back to the same place, but at a different level.

I agree with all your reflections on aid and cooperation. In 1994 and 1995 there was a flow of people and goods coming to help the Zapatistas. At one point, the famous Subcomandante Marcos produced a communiqué in which he stated that he was now forced to carry a broken red high-heeled shoe in his backpack, just to remember what was happening. In one of the many boxes of charity that had been sent to the communities, that red pump arrived—just one shoe, not the pair, for walking through the jungle. For him it was a symbol of what was happening. "If you want to offer aid to these poor Indians struggling against a bad government: thanks, but no thanks. We don't want or need your aid. However, if you think that our struggle is also your struggle, please come. There are plenty of things we need to talk about—and do together." Yes, we need alliances and coalitions now more than ever. There are many things that we can do together with people who want to make a difference in this tragic world in which we all live today, people who also want to resist the horror, the destruction of Mother Earth and culture and the social fabric, and hunger and poverty. We can join forces with them.

After the US election on November 8, 2016, it seems evident that very diverse groups in the United States should join forces and find new forms of articulation. Instead of issue struggles—for the environment in the face of climate change, against racism or racist police violence, against all forms of machismo and sexual discrimination, against chronic debt,

unemployment, or homelessness—what is needed is to struggle together: first, to resist the horror, to resist specific measures, policies, decisions, behavior, offensive language; and
second, to construct a better society, more humane and sen-
sible. This is the time to come together, to hold each other
tight, both inside every country and between people of different countries.

I don't see a lot of conventional developmentalists around
me these days. Public developmentalists no longer have large-
enough budgets. Private developmentalists are increasingly
focused on grabbing and dispossessing, not really on developing. The rich are accumulating more money than ever, but that
money is not transformed into capitalist social relations, into
hiring workers. Many of us are increasingly becoming, as the
Zapatistas warned, disposable human beings. What we are calling *extractivismo* in Latin America (mining, urban, and financial
extractionism, but also labor and services extractionism) cannot be described as development—not using any notion of that
monumentally empty concept, as Wolfgang used to say.

The long agony of development as a myth and as an enterprise is coming to a close. Do we really think that the American dream is still intact? That the American way of life is still
the universal definition of the good life?

From my point of view, development is no longer a myth,
a taboo, a promise or a threat. It is an obsession, an addiction,
a pathological mania that some people suffer, in their minds,
their emotions, or their behavior—and it is also a tool of domination and control. I don't see people mobilizing to achieve
development in all its masks and shapes, the way they used to.
Of course, we still have capitalism. But it's hard to keep calling this capitalism—this society filling up with zombies, the
"living dead," capitalist enterprises that blame their falling
profits on the banks, the state, immigrants, whomever; enterprises controlled and bled dry by a group, a very small group,
of vampires who suck from them and from all of us the blood
of profit, income, goods, everything. As we all know, these
vampires are not only devastating the planet to the point of
endangering the survival of the human species; they are also
killing the goose that laid the golden egg, by accumulating

through extraction and speculation instead of production; by reducing both salaries and employment and exhausting resources, thus preventing or limiting the reproduction of the very system in which they thrive.

We are no longer in the age of TINA (there is no alternative). There are now thousands of alternatives, and a new one emerges every day; many of them, perhaps most of them, offer alternatives to development or express conditions beyond development, in spite of the ominous march of vampires and do-gooders in governments, international institutions, NGOs, and academia still threatening or harassing the social majorities and the planet itself.

Arturo: Your answers pose many challenges, Gustavo. I am only going to take on two of them, for the sake of space: the idea that modernity has already collapsed, and what you so insightfully refer to as "the creative construction of a contemporary art of living" by many communities resisting capitalism and development. They are interrelated, and there is a reason why I want to take on the question of modernity here, which is the angst that the "death of modernity" causes among so many friends and potential allies, particularly otherwise critical academics in both the North and the South.

I have found the following paraphrase to be true: it is easier to imagine the end of the world than the end of modernity. I would like to attempt two displacements of modernity's centrism, starting with Ashis Nandy's telling reversal that the pathologies of science-driven modernity have already proved to be more lethal than the pathologies of tradition.[2] And yet we seem utterly unwilling to consider a creative retrieval of the history-making potential of traditions, a task that Nandy's "critical traditionalism" embraces. Beyond a handful of philosophical treatises, critical academics rarely entertain seriously the end of modernity; most scholars react disdainfully against such a proposition, disqualifying it as utopian or even reactionary. Nevertheless, it is implicit (though rarely stated out loud) in most discourses that speak of the need for civilizational transitions. The revered Buddhist teacher Thich Nhat Hanh has spoken openly about it in his critique of consumerism (he could well be referring to development as addiction): "This civilization of ours will have to end one day. But we have a huge role to play in determining when it ends and how quickly. . . . Global warming may be an early symptom of that death" (Nhat Hanh 2008, 43, 44). He goes further, inviting us to actively accept the end of our civilization by meditating on this thought: "Breathing in, I know that this civilization is going to die. Breathing out, this civilization cannot escape dying" (55). He is calling us to move beyond a civilization that has become antithetical to the ontology and ethics of interexistence.[3]

For us moderns (I include myself here), actively facing the ontological challenges posed by the idea of the end of modernity—of a world significantly different from the current one—is not easy; it fills us with a sort of fright that is deeply unsettling. How can we articulate this civilizational anxiety effectively? After all, most other worlds have had to exist (still do) with a similar fright and, not infrequently, with the reality of their vanishing.

I have found several responses among European and Latin American academic friends. Perhaps the most common is that what they perceive as a condemnation of modernity is not fair because the West itself is plural, inhabited by dissenting voices and plural modernities. This is an important corrective to the tendency, in our critiques, to homogenize the West/the modern. We need to acknowledge the many nondominant, peripheral, and alternative forms of modernity, the nondominant Wests that exist within the West. At the same time—I say to these colleagues—we need to do it decolonially and post-developmentally, in other words, without denying the privileges accorded to all things European (especially white European people and things), and without reinforcing Western modernity as the de facto (naturalized) site of reason, progress, civility, and so forth, as opposed to the alleged barbarism or unviability of other worlds. And, in my view, the best way to do so is to see clearly how we are all in this together, that is, that the liberation of Mother Earth (as the indigenous Nasa people of Colombia call it) and the defense of the pluriverse are a project we should all embrace, from wherever we are, be it in the Lacandon forest or in Europe or Cali or Mexico City.

So our critique is not really anti-European or anti-West, but in favor of Mother Earth liberation and the pluriverse; and *the Earth and the pluriverse are all of us*, not just indigenous peoples. These concepts have been created by indigenous and ethnic movements not just for them but for all. They apply to all. It is incumbent on those of us "in the belly of the beast" who would like to defend those other nondominant modernities to set their differences with the dominant West *effectively* in motion, thus joining forces with those opposing the assemblages of heteropatriarchal, Eurocentric, and racist capitalist modernity from the peripheries of the Global South, those struggling daily to construct territories for reexistence in mutually enriching ways with the planet. This is the meaning, for me, of inhabiting ethically and politically the civilizational crossroads in which we are enmeshed at present. And this means that we all need to make serious efforts to *vivir entre mundos*, to live in between, with, and from multiple worlds, as we attempt to recommunalize our daily existence.

Said differently, we need to resist endowing modernity with the ability to fully and naturally occupy the entire field of the social, making invisible or secondary other ways of instituting it, including what have been called "traditions." This brings me to the second aspect of your answer I want to comment on, that of constructing other forms of reexistence. This would include the question of how we might cultivate ourselves as subjects who desire noncapitalist, nonliberal, and nonmodern forms of life—more autonomous, convivial, and communal. In the field of transition visions and narratives, the relocalization of food, energy, transportation, health, and so on, and the recommunalization of social life (reconnecting with other humans and nonhumans, including the spiritual worlds) are emerging as two principal criteria for moving in this direction; these are the sine qua non conditions for living beyond development. Autonomía—autonomy—is the name given by Latin American grassroots struggles to this attempt at creating conditions for reexistence and a thoroughly contemporary art of living. Again, this concept is not just for those in the peripheries, but for all. How do we think about autonomous living and communities everywhere, and perhaps particularly in the densest and most consumption-oriented liberal worlds, namely, those of today's urban middle classes worldwide? This is one of today's greatest challenges, and debates on degrowth and postdevelopment have lots to contribute to making it tangible and realizable.

Gustavo: The end of modernity, in my view, comes first in the form of disillusionment, as Wolfgang Dietrich brilliantly describes in his "Call for Many Peaces."[4] Modern people increasingly doubt the universal truth of the modern paradigm—a social project characterized by Newtonian physics, Cartesian reductionism, the nation-state of Thomas Hobbes, and the capitalist world-system. This doubting derives from everyday experience. The subsequent scholarly reflection has not been very productive. As a consequence, we have confusion, a loss of values and orientation, or the insight of a pluriverse: instead of dissolving plurality, the idea is to celebrate it, to demand respect for and coexistence with difference, as expressed in the Zapatista dictum you mentioned before: a world in which many worlds fit.

Many academics and universities are already engaged in the search for a new unitary system of reference to replace the exhausted modern paradigm. But their search is becoming something like the old definition of metaphysics: looking in a dark room for a black cat that doesn't exist. As Einstein observed, we cannot find a solution for a problem within the frame that created it. Some of us are beginning to believe that the new paradigm already exists, not in academic rooms but in reality—in the form of an alternative practice that is in itself a theory. The Zapatistas are the best example, but many groups are engaged in the same path. It is not the impossible effort to turn back history or to toss out the fresh fruits of scientific or cultural achievements along with the rotten fruits of the modern mentality and paradigm. It is the autonomous construction of a contemporary art of living. Instead of cutting a head off the capitalist hydra only to see how it regenerates other heads, people are drying up the soil on which the hydra can grow; that is, they are escaping from the habit of "needs" and thus dissolving their dependence on the market, on the state, and on capitalism. That is precisely the nature of autonomy for many in Latin America. And this is the attitude, by the way, that the so-called progressive governments of Latin America refuse to understand.

Indigenous peoples have a long experience in dealing with modernity and are a real source of inspiration for those imagining its end. I see again a very creative alliance with those inside modern thinking who are seeking alternatives. Foucault, for example, spoke repeatedly about the insurrection of the great diversity of subjugated knowledges, when erudite knowledge is juxtaposed with empirical knowledge to generate historical knowledges of struggle. Similarly, the commons movement is today everywhere, not only in the so-called Global South. Everywhere, people exposed to hyperindividualism, consumerism, exploitation, and climate change seem to have had enough. They are rescuing old terms to give new meanings to their contemporary social constructions—sometimes in contradictory ways—which in my view are clearly beyond development, and beyond the conventional, modern, capitalist paradigms.

A recent UN report, prepared for the Quito conference Habitat III in October 2016, titled *Urbanization and Development: Emerging Futures*, has some pertinent gems buried in its mass of bureaucratic jargon. It mentions the failure of urban policies, which can be translated as the failure of development policies—entirely visible and of devastating consequences. According to the report, prosperity used to be described as a tide that raises all boats, but it has become clear that it raises only the luxury yachts.[5] I can adopt that kind of obituary for development without any reservations. I don't think we said in the *Dictionary* (or today) that the developmentalists are dead; they continue their destructive enterprise. What is dead is their promise. We can no longer argue seriously that development can bring justice, sustainability, dignity, or a good life, or that it eliminates hunger and poverty, or that it is a tide raising all vessels.

Of course, we should continue exploring the conditions that shape the desire to be led and to have others regulate our lives, which generates a herd instinct, massively displayed in the 1930s and still at work today. We must once more, and seriously, ask ourselves Wilhelm Reich's question: "How could the masses be made to desire their own repression?" Foucault (1983) made his observations on Reich's question fifty years ago, in his preface to the English edition of *Anti-Oedipus*, by Deleuze and Guattari. Today they are more pertinent and urgent than ever, given the increasingly destructive ethos of the dominant economic and political system we now suffer. We need to resist the current horror, and the best way to resist is to construct a new society, in the many shapes it will take in our pluralist world.

Arturo: Unfortunately, Gustavo, we must bring this conversation to an end—for now. To conclude, could you summarize succinctly how your views on development have changed over the past twenty-five years?

Gustavo: Have I changed my views about development in the last twenty-five years? Yes and no.

I still look at development with an archaeological eye: I explore the ruins that the enterprise of development has left behind, and I can't see it in my present, much less in my future, as I argued back in 1985.

Today I insist on my call to public debate and political action to stop the current madness that is still being packaged as development or "progress." Today, like twenty-five years ago, I denounce the cynicism of those still promoting development, even when they pose as do-gooders and pretend to help the poor.

But there is a change. Twenty-five years ago we were not explicit enough in showing how development was just the slogan used by capital to facilitate the implementation of its neocolonial enterprise. We all know well that capitalism has permeated the whole society through every pore.

I am fully aware that today there are still many millions whose desires are shaped by the belief that development defines a universal norm of the good life. Many people still believe in the Western or American way of life, no matter how far they experience its negative consequences: the immense price to be paid by adopting it in terms of decency, joy, freedom, and humanity; the radical impossibility of extending it to all people on Earth, or even of restricting it to those who are already "developed"; the degree to which it endangers the survival of life on the planet.

I am also aware that the current ecological, economic, social, and political limits to that irresponsible race are stimulating violent and blind reactions, of a fundamentalist character. We are living in a moment of extreme danger that was not so clear twenty-five years ago.

Yet today, most of all, I am enjoying the surge of a new hope. I wrote, twenty-five years ago, that it was "time to recover a sense of reality, time to walk with one's own feet, on one's own path, to dream one's own dreams, not the borrowed ones of development." Millions, perhaps billions, are following that path and experiencing what is to be beyond development. Capitalism is not an almighty and omnipresent monolith. The current wave of violence and destruction is fostering struggles against capital, which involve the heart, the head, and the hands of people increasingly discontent with the situation. A new social force, transforming rebellion and indignation into a political revolution, is thus beginning to take shape.

There is no place for optimism in this tragic circumstance of the world, in this transition to a new era. Many of those millions are struggling under extreme conditions, and everywhere the struggle requires lots of courage and lucidity. But there is room for hope, the opposite of the expectations defining the economic society, development, and capitalism; hope is not the conviction that something will happen in a certain way, but the conviction that something makes sense, whatever happens. What makes sense today, as always, is to reclaim our human condition and decency.

7

Cosmo/Visions of the Colombian Pacific Coast Region and Their Socioenvironmental Implications

Elements for a Dialogue of Cosmo/Visions

We have the dream of leaving to our renacientes ["reborn," i.e., descendants] what we have learned and are learning from our elders: resistance, reexistence, which are only possible *in community, in collective, by being a people!* Resistance and reexistence are integral parts of our being black women, of our being black men, they are in our cultural-historical-territorial DNA. We will therefore continue resisting the onslaught of this Western rationality, which does not want to let us be, which wants us to be like "the developed ones," for us to see life with its eyes, to think with its thoughts, from its senses. So just as more than four hundred years ago we knew that they do not respect the other ways of living, that they do not keep their word, now we know that they will continue disrespecting, destroying life, trying to impose their ways and their decisions. The spaces for dialogue and consultation will be used to make them understand that we are here and that here (in our territories) we will stay. The ancestral territories that we have defended and will continue to defend will go on being spaces for life in all its expressions, they will be defended by us all, remaining the legacy of Maroon women and men.

—MARILYN MACHADO, PROCESO DE COMUNIDADES NEGRAS DE COLOMBIA
(PROCESS OF BLACK COMMUNITIES OF COLOMBIA, PCN), 2017, 253

Preamble: The Civilizational Crisis as Macrocontext

This chapter explores the idea that humanity is facing an unprecedented crisis and that climate change, the mass destruction of species, and the rapid acceleration of inequality are merely its most acute manifestations.[1] For many observers in Latin America and other parts of the world (indigenous, Afro-descendant, and peasant collectives; some scientists, intellectuals, and spiritual teachers; and theorists and activists of the transitions), the current moment is proof of a civilizational crisis. What is in crisis is the modern liberal (capitalist, racist, and heteropatriarchal) model that has spread over the past several centuries all across the world in its zeal to create a single, globalized model. From within this conjuncture, the question of the possible futures of the Pacific rainforest region of Colombia shows some very special features. The Pacific *potentially emerges as a cutting-edge territory for transitioning to models of life in which humans and the Earth can at last coexist in mutually enriching ways.* For this notion to be taken seriously, however, the leaders of the region and state and academic experts will first have to be open to the possibility of a genuine and profound *dialogue of world visions,* as some activists, communities, and intellectuals from the region have been suggesting for more than two decades. What this exercise could lead to is a vision of the Pacific as a *special territory of life,* able to imagine new ways of existing for the region, for the country, and for humanity in general.

What Is a "Cosmo/Vision"?

To discuss "Pacific Vision: Sustainable Territory" in the context of a civilizational crisis, we must analyze in depth the categories contained in the topic.[2] What is a "vision" or better, to problematize the term, a cosmo/vision (from here on just cosmovision), since I am referring to contrasting perspectives on life and the world? What is "the Pacific"? What is a "territory"? Finally, what is "sustainability"? Without this preliminary discussion, we will automatically be endorsing the dominant vision of the region—what we will call the "developmentalist liberal" view. We cannot take the meanings of these terms for granted if we want to open ourselves up to the possibility of imagining a design for the Pacific that differs significantly from what we have now.

Let us start by observing that *every vision of what life is constructs a world.* In fact, that is what the cosmovision concept means. This applies as much to the cosmovisions of ethnic groups as it does to the dominant cosmovision of modernity, European in origin, even if modernity is considered the true or most accurate way to think and thus to exist. Every vision of the world is based on a series of implicit premises, arises from particular histories, and has implications for the sort of world it constructs. We must therefore make these premises explicit, render the histories visible, and examine the implications of each vision as a precondition for having an effective dialogue between different conceptions.

Thinking about the Pacific (a sizable humid forest region extending between Panama and northern Ecuador, and between the westernmost Andean mountain range and the Pacific Ocean, also known as the Pacific littoral or the Pacific bioregion), we can identify four cosmovisions: (1) The developmentalist-liberal cosmovision, which is the dominant vision, held by a good part of the state, the academy, and the elites of the region. (2) The neoliberal cosmovision, which is an extreme variety of the first. (3) Modernizing and developmentalist but noncapitalist visions of the Left, such as those that have predominated in Ecuador and Bolivia in recent years. (It remains to be seen whether in the post-conflict period a nonextractivist Left vision will arise in Colombia, closer to the communities and to the Earth.) And (4) the pro-autonomy and communal vision articulated by a number of territorial-ethnic communities in the region. In this discussion, I set aside the neoliberal and Left cosmovisions to concentrate on the dominant vision and the emergent alternative vision proposed by many of the communities and their organizations.

The Developmentalist Liberal Cosmovision

The developmentalist vision of the past six decades grew out of a vast civilizational complex, which emerged in Europe and has taken centuries to consolidate, with the major milestones of the scientific revolution in the seventeenth century, the industrial revolution in the eighteenth, the cultural orientation known as modernity, and the economic structure of capitalism. Its fundamental principles, drawn from liberal philosophy, are private property, the self-regulating market, and the individual as pillars of society, supplemented by the "rights of man" (the French Revolution) as a means for defending society from the excesses of capitalism, the market, and the state. The liberal vision is based on economic growth and "progress" as the goals of social action. Its consolidation, especially beginning in the late eighteenth century, shored up by colonialism, made Europe the model of society for the rest of the world—that is, the social ideal of so-called modernity. Today this local European history has produced a global design, which we call "globalization."

The modern cosmovision is based on an ontology (a way of seeing and constructing the world) of separation. On the one hand, it divides the human from the nonhuman (culture from nature); on the other, it divides the "civilized"

(Europeans, moderns, rational people) from the "noncivilized" (primitives, barbarians, underdeveloped people, nonmoderns, terrorists). These binaries give rise to many other divisions (mind-body, reason-emotion, secular-sacred, individual-community, material-spiritual, masculine-feminine, white-black, Indian, or "people of color," and so on) in which the second pole of the binary is subordinated to the first (thus, for example, the emotions and the feminine are subordinated to the rational and the masculine). This is why modernity constructs a world that privileges the individual (versus the communal), the material (versus the spiritual), and the modern (versus the traditional).

The modern world is a profoundly anthropocentric (man-centered) world, not a biocentric (Earth-centered) one, as the worlds of many territory-peoples are. Finally, another distinguishing feature of modernity is the division of the uninterrupted flow of all that exists into supposedly self-contained spheres such as "the economy," "society," "politics," "culture," and "the individual," each with a science devoted to extracting its secrets (economics, sociology, political science, anthropology, psychology; see chapter 5). All these features are specific to the modern cosmovision. Despite the enormous productivity of this ontology or way of constructing worlds (made possible by science, technology, capitalism), we are becoming more and more aware that these same features *are the root of the environmental, cultural, and social crisis we are going through in the world today.* Put another way, the world that the moderns created is killing us, and thus we can assert, anthropologically, that "the modern tribe" is destined to disappear, for it has been unable to invent ways of life for coexisting with the Earth. Let us look at why not.

Among the consequences of the modern way of constructing the world (clearly visible in regions such as the Pacific coast of Colombia and Ecuador and Northern Cauca), we find the following:

The compulsion for "development": after more than seven decades of the development era, society is more unsustainable than ever, and social problems are perhaps worse than ever.

The systematic destruction of nature (erosion of biodiversity, climate change, environmental devastation wherever we look).

Persistent and growing social inequality.

The systematic occupation of ethnic and peasant territories (oil palm and sugarcane plantations, cattle ranching, and various megadevelopment projects are truly strategies for occupying these territories, if not for emptying them of people).

Massive displacement, poverty, violence, and femicides.

European and white supremacy (persistent racism) and male supremacy (patriarchy).

The idea of expert knowledge as the only truth.

The marginalization and destruction of worlds with different visions and knowledges.

The creation of a world where only one world fits: the so-called globalized world, based on the ontological premises of the liberal cosmovision.

In short, we can state without exaggeration that the modern cosmovision has allowed for the establishment at an ever more global level of an ethic of economic growth, appropriation, hierarchy, control, the negation and subordination of the other, and war. (Or is this somehow not what is going on in Colombia, despite how many people are bravely struggling to create the conditions for a different way of life?)[3] Furthermore, we can conclude that in Colombia and throughout Latin America, *we are still living out the European design of the world from the late eighteenth century*: so-called modern society, which is at one and the same time capitalist, racist, and patriarchal, or the "modern/colonial world-system," as theorists of decolonial thought call it. That is where the liberal cosmovision has gotten us; it is about time now for us to re/learn how to live and construct worlds in a different way.

It Is Possible and Essential to Go beyond the Dominant Cosmovisions!

Thinking the unthinkable, making the unthinkable believable, and making the believable achievable are part of what is at stake in the creation of a different imaginary for another possible Pacific. Let us listen to a few ideas that urge us to undertake such an exercise; we should think of them as provocations for opening ourselves up to a different way of thinking:

> *We cannot resolve the problems of one era using the same mental frame that created it* (attributed to Albert Einstein). The central problems of any era demand a paradigm shift.

> *We have modern problems for which there are no modern solutions* (the Portuguese sociologist Boaventura de Sousa Santos 2012, 46). Modernity has, despite its achievements, produced poverty, inequality, and climate change, problems for which it can offer no effective solutions. The

"green economy" and carbon markets could perhaps mitigate planetary unsustainability to some extent, but not enough to prevent the coming catastrophes.

The pathologies of modernity have already proved to be more lethal than the pathologies of traditions (paraphrasing the Indian political psychologist Ashis Nandy 1987, 51). Doesn't it make more sense now to revitalize and re/create traditions critically, beyond idealization, than to insist on implementing modernity in every corner of the world, by force if need be, as not only the United States but practically all the governments of Latin America continue to do?

These three provocations lead to an inescapable corollary: *We cannot construct the postconflict (and postcarbon) world using the categories that created the conflict*, such as "progress," "development," "competition," "efficiency," "growth," unlimited energy and material consumption, megaprojects, market globalization, and so forth. Opening up a space for the collective and the communal, for example, is a good start for creating a lexicon for a postaccord period that will not depend on the categories of the past, or at least not only.[4] Perhaps what we most need, in this sense, is a profound discussion of the development model, starting from the hypothesis that "development," at least as we know it, will never bring peace but will only perpetuate the social, economic, and cultural conditions responsible for the conflict.

What Is a "Territory"? The Pro-Autonomy, Territorial, and Communal Cosmovision

Throughout their long history, the black and indigenous communities of the Pacific have maintained and reelaborated cosmovisions of their own, rooted in their own territories. For these communities, territory is the collective space for existence, a vital space that ensures their survival as a people in profound interdependence with nature, the human, and the spiritual. This is why the defense of life and of territory has arisen in recent decades as the fundamental action principle for many of these communities and their organizations. The notion of the Pacific as a *region-territory of diverse ethnic groups* arose in the mid-1990s in light of the struggles for territory, conservation, and the affirmation of cultural identity. We find lucid expression of the defense of territory among people young and old in these ethnic groups. As one young leader from Río Yurumanguí put it so well, "The economy is causing a mental deterritorialization among our young people. The young person is there, in the river, but his mind is somewhere else. Remaining in our ancestral territories protects life."[5] And the Nasa leader Mauricio Dorado expresses the relationship between physical expulsion and the destruction of the communal world with powerful frankness when he says, "They don't just take people out of the territory, they take the territory out of the people"—that is, they make people live according to individualized and commodified dynamics. This is how the communalized worlds of ethnic collectives are dying out.

The struggle against physical and mental deterritorialization and displacement has led to a broad defense of the communal and territorial, giving rise to pro-autonomy visions, often articulated by territorial-ethnic organizations, as in some of the examples mentioned in earlier chapters.

In these struggles, ancestrality, territory as life and as place for existence, autonomy, dignity, and the ethic of care are categories underlying a very different cosmovision from that of the modern liberal capitalist and developmentalist world. Territory is the vital space that ensures survival as a people, as a culture in coexistence with nature and the spirits. Based on what activists call *ancestralidad* (ancestrality), territory keeps the traditions of communities alive, while looking forward; it is the collective space of existence that makes peaceful coexistence among peoples possible. But we must be clear that none of these notions implies a static conception of territory or community. Quite the contrary: this is a dynamic vision in which the communal is ever changing in its encounters with other peoples and worlds, including the so-called modern world. This is why activists speak of the relationship between resistance and *reexistence*; these groups persist by reinventing their cultural existence and their modes of subsistence. The Afro-Pacific concept of renacientes, "the reborn," referring to the continual renewal of life (see chapters 3 and 4), embodies a local way of thinking about the sustainability of the lifeworlds of the region's black communities. It is important to point out that appealing to ancestrality as a principle has nothing to do with a desire to "remain mired in the past," as critics often adduce. On the contrary, although defending territory for the sake of the renacientes is conceived in terms of an ancestral mandate, it is oriented toward the future—a future, however, in which the communities will be able to decide on their ways of life autonomously. As a woman from a mining family in La Toma put it so well, "The essence of ancestrality is looking to the future. All this has to serve not only me, but it has to serve all the generations that come after me," which is to say, future generations (quoted in Weitzner 2017).

Territory is the subject of *care*, not the object of development. *What is cared for is a whole world, that is, a way of creating and living life*: a way of "worlding" life,

CHAPTER SEVEN

of making it a communal world. This is the main lesson of the examples of relational ways of worlding discussed in previous chapters, whether La Toma or the Yurumanguí River, or the Nasa or Arhuaco peoples. If one takes interexistence as the point of departure, the only possible ethic is an ethic of care: rather than "development," what we need are *strategies of care* for the meshworks of humans and nonhumans that make up local worlds. Some groups call these strategies "good living," or Buen Vivir.[6]

How different this vision of territory as an uninterrupted intermeshing of interexistence is from what the modern cosmovision offers us, a vision of a universe populated by subjects and objects each independent of all the others, which we can manipulate at will! The expansion of palm oil and sugarcane plantations, industrial shrimp farming, megaprojects, large-scale mining, and coca production in regions such as the Pacific and other Afrodescendant, indigenous, and peasant territories: all these are strategies that deny the cosmovision of interexistence and so are fatal to local worlds (see chapter 4; Escobar 2008). The classic case in the southern Pacific region has been oil palm, and to a lesser extent shrimp cultivation on the mangrove forest, which in the 1980s and 1990s began to occupy territories and displace local populations, sometimes assisted by paramilitary violence (coca cultivation spread along many of the region's rivers after the early 2000s, pushed by paramilitaries and guerrillas alike, and more recently even by Mexican drug cartels). These *strategies of occupying territories and local lifeworlds* have often been justified in terms of progress and development, but in reality they have caused displacement, death, violence, and especially the destruction of worlds. Defending territories is therefore the same as defending the communal and relational way of living; it develops from partly communitarian and noncapitalist roots, though it implies a whole history of relationships with capitalist modernity. We can say without exaggeration that neoliberal globalization is a *war on relational worlds, on everything that is collective*. In the Pacific, the escalation of extractivism implies racialized practices of plunder; the worlds being destroyed are nonwhite (black and indigenous).[7]

I must call attention in particular to the role played by violence against women in the strategies for capital accumulation, development, and ontological occupation of territories in the region. This problem is not only endemic but getting worse. Commenting on several cases of femicide in the Pacific in 2017, the Cali-based Afro-Colombian feminist sociologist Betty Ruth Lozano, one of the organizers of the International Forum on Feminicides and Global Accumulation held in Buenaventura, in the heart of the Pacific region in April 2016 (mentioned in the preface), asserted:

Our insistence on making these violent attacks visible and reporting them is because we consider that they are directly related to the processes of deterritorialization and individuation in the communities. Violence against women, I insist, is a strategy for deterritorialization and decommunalization, of fragmentation, rupture, the dismantling of everything communitarian, which is an obstacle to the advance of capitalism. The killing [of women] has broken, or has reinforced the rupture of, the community; it has created feelings of hatred and vengeance among people from a single pueblo, who will never again be able to look at each other as brothers.[8]

She likewise remarked that, in an environment of violence and impunity, every murder committed against a woman reinforces hegemonic masculinities. Impunity only reinforces violence against women. In the face of generalized decommunalization, especially as effected through violence against women, all alternative strategies for the region must consider recommunalization and depatriarchalization as interrelated and crucial goals. They must take into account the black feminisms that are appearing in the region with strength and lucidity.

The notions briefly presented here are all keys to a dialogue of visions for the Pacific: an ethic of care, relationality, interexistence, autonomy, the communal, depatriarchalization, black feminisms. In conclusion, let us analyze some elements of this dialogue.

Transition to a Sustainable Pacific?

It is important to clarify the reasons why the modernizing liberal cosmovision will never create the conditions for a genuinely sustainable Pacific, if by sustainability we mean the long-term survival not of the conventional economic model or the modern liberal society but rather of the plurality of worlds that inhabit it. The developmentalist cosmovision will only bring about, at best, a reduction of unsustainability, but it cannot halt the devastation already underway. This is the lesson we learn from all the plans that have been introduced, one after the other, in the Pacific, from PLADEICOP in the 1980s and Plan Pacífico in the 1990s to the "Buenaventura Master Plan 2050" and the "We Are All PAZcífico" Plan from the second Santos administration (2014–18). Each of these plans, announced with great fanfare in its time, called on the same actors (Inter-American Development Bank, World Bank, USAID, experts from the Department of National Planning, and so on); each was derived from the same vision that continues to mold perceptions of the region today; and we can assert that, despite some accomplishments (such as certain infrastructure projects), they each had the same results, which were at best questionable in terms of the welfare of the communities and the environment. We cannot overlook the fact that massive displacement, femicides, casas de pique,[9] and sheer poverty have descended on the region in the wake of these development strategies. This is not a mere coincidence. Today, neither the "green economy" nor carbon markets nor megaprojects will achieve different results. They will only perpetuate the structural unsustainability (see Escobar 2008 for a thorough analysis of the development strategies for the Pacific since the early 1980s).

Based on this brief analysis, we can propose two provocative "antiformulas." First: *It is not a "lack of development" that is doing in the Pacific, as is generally taken for granted, but rather too much of it*—at least, too much of a certain sort of development. Second: *Therefore, it is actually the developmentalist vision that is anachronistic and romantic, not the communal vision held by ethnic-territorial organizations, as is widely thought.* What could be more romantic than an insistence that "more of the same" (more capitalist development) will bring about a sustainable territory? We insist: conventional strategies can only reproduce the sustainability of the capitalist model of world construction, which cannot halt the ongoing devastation.[10]

Let us look at how the territorial-autonomic cosmovision offers possibilities for the transition to another possible Pacific. From the perspective of this vision, there is a great principle for sustainability: *restoring the conditions for the continuous self-creation of life*, which in return requires restoring, re/constructing, and revitalizing territory for the re/production of life in the face of the avalanche of violence and destruction caused by conflict, modernization, and development. This principle, in turn, is based on two types of interrelated strategies: first, genuinely intercultural strategies, which is to say, strategies that enable a world in which many worlds fit (the opposite of imposing a unitary world of capitalist globalization as the natural result of the liberal-modern cosmovision); and second, strategies that *realize the communal mode of life*, based on ancestrality but oriented toward a future of autonomous and free communities.

The latter strategies could be based on the Life Plans or Buen Vivir plans (as opposed to development plans) of the communities, or on what many Afrodescendant and indigenous communities call development in accordance with their cosmovision or their own vision of the future. It should also be said that these concepts of territorial-ethnic organizations are supported by numerous national and international legal tools that defend the right of a people to develop in accord with their own cosmovisions and aspirations, beginning with the International Labor Organization (ILO) Convention 169.[11]

Creating the conditions for the continual self-creation of life in biodiverse regions such as the Pacific requires a new "dialogue of visions," as I have suggested. Recent trends in the field of design provide useful tools in this regard (beyond expert-led, vertically imposed planning). These trends emphasize codesign based on the principle that every community practices its own designing. Design is no longer for experts alone; we all design our own existence, and this applies with even more relevance to communities that are defending their own ways of life. It would be impossible to specify all the major components of a codesign strategy for the Pacific in this short text, but we can mention that the first step would be to create a team and a space for collaborative design with multiple actors, including at least the following: territorial-ethnic organizations, traditional authorities, and communitarian councils; groups of women and young people along the rivers and in the cities; academics, intellectuals, and artists; NGOs; the media; and the state (see chapter 8 for an elaboration and application of this idea to the Cauca Valley region).

The first job for this group would entail creating a different imaginary of the region than that of the prevalent narrative based on megaprojects, growth, consumerism, trade, "productivity," development, and so on. Put succinctly, this other imaginary would aim for a vision of *the Pacific as a pluriversal bioregion, which is to say, one inhabited by many diverse worlds.* These worlds would consist of relational meshworks of humans and nonhumans, and they should be thought out based on the principle of *an alternative productivity: a productivity for life.* At minimum, this new vision would generate a robust interethnic and intercultural perspective founded on a respect for the integrity of collective territories and biodiversity. The strategies arising from this exercise in codesign would be oriented toward the self-sustained reproduction and transformation of the web of life. As for economics and investment plans (including those in the private sector), they should be subordinated to these principles. Economic and infrastructure strategies should thus serve the communities and their Buen Vivir, not the other way around, as is generally the case today. It will also be important for the rights of nature to be recognized, as they already are in other countries (the so-called biocentric turn, transcending the anthropocentrism that constitutes the modern cosmovision). This would form the basis for environmental agreements.

Within this codesign strategy for the needed transitions, the essential ingredients for deliberating and designing concrete policies turn out to be the knowledges of communities and territorial-ethnic organizations. These knowledges exhibit a number of important characteristics: a profound understanding of the continual self-creation of life that implies being in tune with the Earth; a relational vision of the fabric of life; a cutting-edge political strategy centered on the relationship between territory, autonomy, dignity, and the defense of life; a keen awareness of the global situation and of the option for civilizational transitions; and a realistic utopia for re/constructing the meshworks of worlds, aiming at a Pacific as a pluriversal Region-Territory of diverse ethnic groups.[12]

Adopting a communal perspective of codesign or of autonomous design thus suggests a major turning point in the thinking and politics of development for the Pacific. From the perspective of this book, however, we clearly see that this is a new vision of the real and of the possible. Let me repeat the idea that I stated at the beginning of this chapter: we are facing a global crisis within which the Pacific has special potential for a cutting-edge design for the transition to a new model of life different from that of "development." Some organizations are giving shape to this historical possibility with the imaginary of "Another Possible Peacific."[13] This slogan is another way to describe the concept that emerged from some territorial-ethnic organizations in the region during the 1990s: The Pacific as Territory of Life, Joy, Hope, and Freedom. As Carlos Rosero, an intellectual and activist from Buenaventura, puts it, this is a Pacific "where all of us, those from here and those from the outside alike, shall have the right to eat *bocachico* fish and to swim in the rivers that are now polluted with mercury, and where all of our children, everyone's children, can enjoy and delight in the landscape and not merely see it nostalgically in the photographs, videos, and the few memories we manage to convey to them."[14]

Making the Unthinkable Thinkable, Believable, and Achievable

Many will argue that the communitarian-autonomic codesign proposal presented here is utopian and impractical. As I have already stated, however, the most romantic and ultimately self-destructive strategies are those that do not pay serious attention to the cosmovisions of the communities and are not profoundly in tune with the Earth, as expressed in a deep concern for the well-being and Buen Vivir of communities, the integrity of territories, and the preservation of biological diversity. Given the severe crisis that the region, the country, and the very planet are going through, only a prospect of transitioning to a nondevelopmentalist model can help us think that the unthinkable may transform into the thinkable, the thinkable into a *credible alternative to what exists,* and the credible into the achievable.

Even amid the debacle caused by the model of regional growth and development, a codesign for the transition of this beautiful, special region is not unthinkable. For designers of the transition, it is relatively easy to put forward a new imaginary for the region. We can reimagine it, for example, as a genuinely intercultural and pluriversal region of small and midsize farmers, forest producers, and fishers; of autonomous communities creatively transforming the worlds of the rivers, without losing the deep relationality, in their encounter with digital technologies and media, global youth cultures, music, and arts, and echoing the resistances and ideas of other pueblos in the process of reinventing themselves with a basis in their traditions; a decentralized and functional network of small villages along the rivers and small and midsize cities along the coast, of mixed economies oriented toward Buen Vivir and equipped with renewable energy and modes of transportation adapted to the environment; the gradual restoration of landscapes, of ecosystems, of the mangrove~world, the river~world, and the tropical forest~world (and thereby of biodiversity); the effective appropriation of the territories by the communities with the guarantee that they will always be there for their renacientes, in all their fullness, beauty, and vitality. To get to this point, however, the current macrostrategies of development, cooked up in elite universities and led by the region's major capital investors, or the de facto capitalist strategies of armed actors and narcotraffic, are of little use. Little or none.

Easy to imagine, perhaps, but still unthinkable to the experts and elites, and even perhaps to the majority of the population. Do we still have time to carry out this sort of exercise for the Pacific, so that the ravaged and decommunalized present that we see today in the Cauca River valley (see chapter 8) does not become its future, and so that the diversity of actors who inhabit it can generate their own Pacific visions and—why not?—their own utopias. The state and the media could play a defining role in this regard if they open themselves up to a true dialogue between visions, especially with organizations that genuinely represent the interests of the communities because their struggle to defend biodiversity, territory, and culture has demonstrated it.

Finally, a brief clarification of an undoubtedly important topic. This text could be challenged for focusing solely on two major visions and neglecting other conceptions of the Pacific and many other expressions and voices of the ever-widening and more vocal Afro-Colombian intellectual sector. It is a just critique. However, my own challenge to these other conceptions—at least those that truly aim to differentiate themselves from the neoliberal and developmentalist-liberal Afro-Colombian frameworks—is to show us how they go beyond the latter. I fear that in most cases, the answer is that they still work within the basic premises of the capitalist economy and the liberal-modern cosmovision. In this respect, I think it will help to bring in an important work on the African cosmovision and philosophy of the Muntu by the Cameroonian philosopher Fabien Eboussi Boulaga. In his opinion (Eboussi Boulaga 2014, 167):

> The liquidation of the colonial heritage will not take place as long as knowledge continues to play the same roles as in the past. . . . The ways our society relates to knowledge have not altered. . . . And to be "educated" meant to climb up the ladder of Being to get nearer to the white master. . . . [The] instrumentality [of knowledge] was eaten up by its symbolic function of social integration. Its acquisition became a preliminary rite before the enjoyment of a good life. It is from such knowledge that the present elite draws their legitimacy and privileges, without any practical test or services rendered, due to proximity to the master, the consecration needed to replace the master, to speak and act in lieu and instead of one.[15]

For Eboussi Boulaga, the only antidote to this (liberal) politics of knowledge is a new order of knowledge that will build on those long-standing practices that draw people closer to the community and to the Earth (indeed, where the communal takes precedence over the modern/individual), practices that entail an ethical relationship with ancestrality and, precisely because they recognize their limits, are oriented toward a future of hope. Regarding any current Afro-Colombian proposal about the Pacific region, we could ask, in the spirit of Eboussi Boulaga: To what degree does it depart from the capitalist cosmovision of life? Does it actually go beyond liberal politics, defined in terms of "progress," "individual opportunities," and the criterion of "success" in terms of the market and economic advancement? Isn't the idea of "moving ahead" trapped in the liberal language of self-improvement, of concepts of empowerment, innovation, and entrepreneurship that are adapted to a decommunalized vision of life? What sort of "leadership development" are we talking about? Leaders for what? By fostering the development of an educated elite that can guide the affairs of the region in a better direction, haven't they already accepted the distancing of that elite from the community and the people?

Some of these developmentalist-liberal strategies could be useful to certain groups and individuals, helping them to improve their life circumstances and social positions; moreover, they could be important elements in a comprehensive strategy to fight discrimination and racism.[16] But can they go beyond being pragmatic individual solutions to the prevailing economic system? To what degree could they be said to be collective? From the territorial-ethnic perspective, one could raise serious doubts about their capacity for stopping the wave of devastation that continues its relentless march across the region, or for generating a vision of the Pacific that will resonate with the Region-Territory of Life, Hope, Peace, and Freedom imagined and desired by many organizations and communities in the region.

Appendix

The following "shopping list with the aim of contributing to the understanding of our reality, to the sustainability of the Pacific Region-Territory, as a patrimony for all men and women" was presented by Carlos Rosero of the Proceso de Comunidades Negras (PCN) at the Foro Semana. I reprint it here because, in addition to being incredibly clear and eloquent, it seems to me entirely consistent with what I have called a dialogue of visions.

1. We all need to take the same course in geography and history. I learned, in elementary and secondary school, that Santiago de Cali was the capital of the department of Valle del Cauca. It is not the capital of the Pacific.

2. We need to think together about how the equation T + C = BD (Territory plus Culture equals Biodiversity), coined by the indigenous and black movements in the 1990s, is like $E = mc^2$.

3. We need to think about how the inhabitants of the Pacific Region-Territory are not needy; they do not have needs. They have rights. And to think about our relationship with the state as a relationship between rights. The rights of the residents of the Pacific Region-Territory, in this case the blacks, are also recognized in Law 70, the National Constitution, and in the corpus of constitutional law.

4. We need to think about new principles for talking about the Pacific Region-Territory: authority, compensation, integrality, sustainability, self-determination. These principles were created by the movement in 1994; indicators for monitoring the situation of the region and its inhabitants can be created around them.

5. We need to think and plan about the Pacific Region-Territory, privileging what is collective, that is, the family, communal, social, and planetary over the individual.

6. We need to think and accept that time does matter, as the distinction between fast food and slow food matters. There are those of us who

prefer a *sancocho* (stew) cooked in the traditional way to one prepared in a pressure cooker. Every pueblo and at times every region has its own particular way of measuring time and of talking, from within, and in relation to time, about their own urgent issues.

7. The Pacific was defined from within as an ancestral Region-Territory of diverse ethnic groups. We need, based on the documented fact that it is a culturally and environmentally diverse territory, to think together and to accept that it requires: (a) a special statute of autonomy; (b) a special model for "development" that must differ from the modern notion of development.

8. The Pacific Region-Territory and its indigenous and black residents were and remain severely impacted by the internal armed conflict. We need to think of novel ways to restore the territory, the cultural identities, the appropriate logics for Buen Vivir, the appropriate forms of government. We need to accept that the conditions of not repeating [the conflict] will never come about if we do not undertake a discussion of historic reparations to the indigenous people and the descendants of the enslaved, we who are the majority living in this important and strategic region, for colonialism and the crimes against humanity of enslavement and trafficking in the enslaved.

9. We need to finish what has been started: rulemaking for Titles IV, V, VI, and VII of Law 70 of 1993. We need to move forward in the implementation of ILO Convention 169, referring only to Prior Consultation.

10. We need for the institutions and high officials of the state, private sector, the academy, NGOs, and all of us to accept that participation, prior consultation, and free, prior, and informed consent are not an inconvenience to be grudgingly fulfilled. They are rights intrinsically associated with the protection of the cultural identity of the pueblos who inhabit the Pacific Region-Territory and thus of the sustainability of the biodiversity that all of us speak of.

11. If we want there to be sustainable development in the Pacific Region-Territory, we need for there to be a new dialogue from the territory and its communities with the country and its institutions. A dialogue among equals.

8

Beyond "Regional Development"

A Design Model for Civilizational Transition in the Cauca River Valley, Colombia

When the image is new, the world is new.
—GASTON BACHELARD, *THE POETICS OF SPACE* (1969), 79

(Salsa rhythm)
They're burning the sugarcane, there in the Cauca Valley
They're burning the sugarcane, there in the Cauca Valley
Now the sun rises
And with it the farmers
If my work is so hard
I do it for my children
The sugarcane carts pass by
Carrying the wild cane
And the farmer on bicycle
Crying as he rides
And with the midday sun
Burning his back
The farmer laments
And sings to his family.
. . .
Campesino, you who sweeten
Our dinners and our tables
How bitter is your life
How bitter is your workday.
(Chorus) The land roars, the cane on fire.
The wind carries ashes
From the cane harvest burn
And the whole valley knows

That the cane is being burned.
Skin truly black
And you give me white sugar
Watch out, life is hard
For the humble cane cutter
(But keep on going)
With pride and dignity
Facing the harvest bravely.

—YURI BUENAVENTURA, "ESTÁN QUEMANDO LA CAÑA" (2000)

Preamble: Meditation Preliminary to Reading

In a tribute to Don Luis Enrique Dinas Zape, an Afro-Colombian elder from the city of Puerto Tejada, that took place in Cali on October 28, 2015, he referred to the sudden expansion of sugarcane production in his region as the era "when the bandits arrived" and did away with the productive cacao farms and other polycultures that black farmers had managed to maintain all across the Cauca River valley until the middle of the twentieth century.[1]

Although black resistance to sugarcane expansion has not ended, today that resistance is led by indigenous Nasa people from Northern Cauca, through their movement for the Liberation of Mother Earth (see chapters 2 and 3). For more than a decade, their movement has engaged in concrete land occupation actions; they begin by manually uprooting sugarcane from the fields that they reclaim, planting instead food crops using what could be called agroecological practices.

Let us think actively, perhaps alongside Don Luis Enrique and the Nasa commune members, about the long ecological history of the Cauca Valley before the arrival of sugarcane, and about the history of resistances to sugar plantations, and let us undertake the following meditation with our full attention: *Breathing in, I recognize that sugarcane is coming to an end; breathing out, I am convinced that it will come to an end. Breathing in, we uproot the cane; breathing out, sugarcane disappears entirely.* Let us imagine ourselves participating in a great collective minga with indigenous, black, peasant, small-town, and big-city people of every background, variety, and color, a great wave of people uprooting one by one every sugarcane plant, from north to south and from east to west, plantation by plantation, property by property. Then let us actively reseed this vast and bountiful territory of flatlands, foothills, mountains, and prolific flora and fauna with every kind of food crop and ornamental plant, and with freshwater springs, creeks, wetlands, wild bamboo stands, and forests of native plants and animals, a multitude of landscapes; and in the midst of this newly revitalized living landscape let us imagine friendly, beautiful, and healthy towns and cities with smiling people finally living with a certain modicum of peace, solidarity, and harmony. This meditation will help us enter into the following intellectual exercise, an exercise of the design imagination, with open minds and another sense of what is possible.

Another Cauca River Valley Is Possible: An Exercise in Imagining a Regional Transition

Many regions around the world are ripe for embarking on substantial cultural and ecological transitions, though few are prepared to do so. To a certain extent, as we briefly saw in the previous chapter, some of the Afro-descendant movements in Colombia's Pacific region have devoted themselves to this sort of project, though in a limited way owing to the onslaught of developmentalist and defuturing projects since the year 2000. In this region, the recalcitrant regional elites and the institutions of the state continue to impose economic strategies that only add to the ecosocial devastation, violence, and unrest—against all scientific evidence, and against ecological, social, and cultural common sense. Faced with the developmentalist liberal project, some social movement organizations are trying to produce a postcapitalist alternative, despite the opposition. The Pacific region of Colombia and Ecuador is, in fact, a favorite laboratory for local and regional transition projects and can provide rich lessons for alternative pluriversal imaginations.

Across the Western Cordillera of the Andes, traveling east from Buenaventura, the main Colombian port on the Pacific, lies the fertile Cauca River valley; this region could well serve as a symbol of the development debacle. Capitalist development, based on sugarcane plantations in the flatlands and cattle ranching in the foothills, began to gain momentum in the early decades of the twentieth century. It picked up speed in 1950 with the creation of the Corporación Autónoma Regional del Cauca (CVC), supported by the World Bank and modeled on the famous Tennessee Valley Authority. Today it is obvious that this development model, based on sugar and cattle, has not only reached a dead end but caused ecological devastation to hillsides, aquifers, rivers, wetlands, forests, biodiversity, and soils, in addition to massive, deeply painful, and unjust social and territorial dislocations of peasants and Afro-descendant communities in the region. The region could easily be reimagined as *a true bastion of agroecological production of organic fruits, vegetables, grains, and tropical plants, and as a multicultural region of small and midsize agricultural producers, and a working, decentralized network of towns and midsize cities.* Other attractive futures can doubtless be imagined for this region.

However, these futures are currently *unthinkable*; such is the grip that the developmentalist imaginary holds over most people in the region, as of course does the power of the elite. Though the region is ripe for a radical transition, this proposition is unthinkable to the elites and to most townspeople, and of course to the middle classes of the region, whose intensely consumerist lives are inextricably linked to the current model. Under these conditions, is an exercise in designing a transition even possible? Moreover, could it have any real influence on public policies, mentalities, actions, or practices? In this chapter, I try to show, albeit tentatively and as a hypothesis, that even under these contrary conditions, a transition design can be set in motion. I begin by presenting some critical elements of design theory. In the most substantial section, I present some major design elements for the transition in this region. Finally, in a short section, I discuss a few useful elements for thinking about design for transitions in urban areas, based on certain critical trends in architecture and urban planning.

Notes on Autonomous Design and Design for the Transitions

Critical theory has shown little interest in the nature and impacts of design on social practices, but design is emerging as an important realm of thought and action for reimagining the world as a pluriverse, perhaps because designers are rediscovering people's capacity for shaping their worlds through collaborative tools and solutions (Manzini 2015).

Design has unquestionably been a basic political technology of modernity, from objects to services, institutions, and cities. We can say that the current crisis is the result of deeply rooted ways of being, doing, and knowing, and these are closely tied to design. Reclaiming design for the construction of other worlds thus appears to have great relevance as an intellectual and political project. It demands a new and effective awareness of the historicity of design and its relationship to the patriarchal, capitalist, modern, and colonial onto-epistemic formation. I address this proposition in a recent book, whose argument I will briefly outline in this section as a prelude to tackling a design exercise for the transitions in a particular region (Escobar 2018).[2]

The most fitting way to enter into the issue of reorienting design toward the construction of other worlds is ontological. Why might design be considered ontological? The initial response to this question is easy: "We encounter the deep questions of design when we recognize that in designing tools [technologies, institutions, spaces, infrastructures, even discourses] we are designing ways of being" (Winograd and Flores 1986, xi). Design is a conversation about possibilities of being, doing, and knowing. Every society generates inventions whose existence alters the society itself. The new digital technologies, of course, represent dramatic examples of radical innovations (much as the printing press, the automobile, and the television were in the past) that have opened up unprecedented new possibilities and transformed a whole set of daily practices. Put differently, by designing tools, we humans design the conditions of our existence and at the same time the conditions of our design. We design tools, and those tools design us. "Design designs" is the apt and telling formula for this circularity, coined by the Australian theorist of design Anne-Marie Willis: "We design our world, while our world acts back on us and designs us" (2006, 80).

There is no such thing as a neutral design. But, we might ask, what could be more seemingly neutral than a living space, a container for the body? I often give the example of the *maloca*, the longhouse of indigenous people in the Colombian Amazon, versus the archetypal nuclear family home of the suburban United States. The maloca can house dozens of people under one roof, even if the way in which they reside in it obeys certain rules of distribution and use of space. As I joke, "Give me a maloca, and I'll give you a relational world," one based on deep interrelationships between humans and nonhumans. On the other hand, give me a house in the suburbs, and I'll create a world of decommunalized individuals alienated from the natural and often from the spiritual worlds. A sugar plantation, as we shall see, is a design and as such is very different from the multidiverse parcels of free black farmers that used to exist in the Cauca River valley before the sugarcane boom. Undoing the "sugarcane design" must form an integral part of a design for the transition of this region to a different model.

Understood ontologically, design develops through our existing ways of being in the world, and it deeply affects the kind of beings we are. For Winograd and Flores, pioneers in this field:

> Ontologically oriented design is therefore necessarily both reflective and political, looking backwards to the tradition that has formed us but also forwards to as-yet-uncreated transformations of our lives together. Through the emergence of new tools, we come to a changing awareness of human nature and human action, which in turn leads to new technologi-

cal development. The designing process is part of this "dance" in which our structure of possibilities is generated. (1986, 163)

In ontological designing, we are doing more than asking what can be built. *We are engaging in a philosophical discourse about the self—about what we can do and what we can be.* Tools are fundamental to action, and through our actions, we generate the world. The transformation we are concerned with is not a technical one but a continuing evolution of how we understand our surroundings and ourselves—of how we continue becoming the beings that we are. (1986, 179)

We shall see the importance of this abstract formulation when we apply it to the redesign of the Cauca River valley. The problem with modern design is that it has structured unsustainability as the dominant way of being. Designing another way of conceiving design means critically examining the dualist ontology of separation, control, and appropriation that has become dominant with Western capitalist patriarchal modernity, and examining the actual existence or potential creation of other rationalities and ways of being, especially those that emphasize the profound relationality and interconnectedness of all that exists. We might call this relational design.

Can design be reoriented, beyond the rationalist and functional tradition from which it emerged and within which it still operates, so that it can help create worlds based on the relational ontologies of many pueblos and collectives? If it can, these forms of design would entail reconnecting with nonhumans, with things in their "thingness," with the Earth, with the spirit, and, of course, with humans in their radical alterity (decolonially understood, bearing in mind the inclusion of many worlds, rather than their exclusion). They would help dismantle dualisms and would take nondualist ways of existing seriously. Moreover, might this new way of designing assist communities' struggles against extractivist models of development and foster their autonomy? (See Escobar 2018 for an extensive development of this argument.)

We should note (see chapter 4) that this type of design by communities will take place under conditions of ontological occupation of their territories and lifeworlds. Is it possible to think about design under such conditions of intense repression and violence? It is precisely in cases like these that ideas of autonomy and communality are flourishing (see chapter 1) and the premise of autonomous design acquires meaning. This does not mean that the proposition cannot and should not be questioned. Isn't autonomous design a contradiction in terms? To put it prospectively, the possibility I am suggesting is that design, conceived ontologically, can be design for, and based on, autonomy. For this possibility to make sense, we must think whether design can be decoupled from its unsustainable, defuturing modernist practices and reoriented toward other ontological commitments.

The starting point for this exercise is the realization that *every community practices the design of itself*: its organizations, its social relationships, its daily practices, its ways of knowing, its ways of living, its relationships with the environment, and so on. This was the case with most communities throughout history; they practiced a sort of "natural design" independent of expert knowledge (ontonomy, diffuse design). Today, however, things are more complicated and entail both embodied (place-specific) forms of reflection and abstract, objectifying forms; that is, ones based on so-called scientific rationality.

Based on this brief discussion, we propose the following elements for thinking about autonomous design (especially in certain Latin American contexts). Autonomously oriented design

has as its primary aim the realization of the communal, understood as creating the conditions for the continual self-creation of communities and their successful structural coupling with their seemingly ever-more-globalized surroundings;

embraces both ancestrality, because it arises from the history of the relational worlds at issue, and also futurality, understood as a declaration of futures for communal achievements;

privileges interventions and actions that foster nonpatriarchal, non-liberal, nonracist, non-state-centered, and noncapitalist forms of organizing;

creates spaces conducive to the life projects of communities and to the creation of convivial societies;

carefully considers how community articulates with technologies and with heteronomous social actors (including markets, digital technologies, extractive operations, and so on), from the perspective of preserving and strengthening the autopoiesis and autonomy of communities;

takes seriously the transition design imperatives of place building, relocalization, renewed attention to materiality and to nonhumans, and the creation of collaborative interepistemic organizations;

pays special attention to the role of the commons in realizing the communal and develops effective means of "marginalizing the economy" while bolstering diverse economies, social and solidarity economies, and noncapitalist economies;

is consistent with the Buen Vivir and nature rights trends, and with similar tendencies elsewhere (such as degrowth and the defense of commons);

fosters openings to the pluriverse and in this sense is a design for the pluriverse, for the flourishing of life on the planet;

thinks deeply about, and creates spaces for, strengthening the connection between the realization of the communal and the Earth (its relational fabric in every place and everywhere), in ways that allow humans to relearn how to live on the planet with nonhumans in mutually enriching ways;

brings hope to the ongoing rebellion of humans and nonhumans defending the principles of relational life.

Autonomous design, thus conceived, can be thought of as a response to the drive for innovation and for creating new ways of life, a drive that arises from the struggle, the forms of counterpower, and the life projects of politically motivated relational and communal ontologies, for example, in the movements against extractivism. This is undoubtedly too ambitious for any political-theoretical imaginary. But as Gustavo Esteva (2009, 22) notes, "Hope is not the conviction that something will happen but rather the conviction that something makes sense, whatever happens" (see chapter 6).

So now, with these ideas in mind, let us proceed with the exercise of imagining the design of another possible Cauca Valley.

The Cauca River Valley:
An Example of Failed Regional Development

The Cauca River, the second largest river in Colombia, with a total length of 1,360 kilometers, flows north from its headwaters in the Colombian Massif, a group of high Andean mountains in southwestern Colombia that is said to be the source of 70 percent of the fresh water in the country. In the massif, the Andean range splits into two branches, giving rise to inter-Andean valleys, including the Cauca River valley. The Cauca Valley gradually opens up between the Western and Central Cordilleras (the latter featuring several snow-covered peaks over five thousand meters high). The first stretch of the great Cauca River basin (the focus of this exercise) gradually widens, following the river for more than five hundred kilometers from the Salvajina Dam to the northern tip of the valley in the Risaralda department, with a width that varies between 15 and 32 kilometers and an area of about four hundred thousand hectares. It is an incredibly beautiful valley, flanked by two high mountain ranges and crisscrossed by numerous smaller rivers and creeks. The flat bottomlands lie at an altitude of one thousand meters above sea level; the average temperature is 25°C (77°F). A traveler admiring the valley in the 1940s with a relational mind-set would have concluded, undoubtedly, that it could easily support an extremely pleasant and culturally and ecologically rich life for a large population. The locals have named the valley after one of the most famous colonial-era haciendas still standing: El Paraíso. Paradise. This future, however, was already being frozen out by the 1950s as defuturing processes gained speed and strength.

In terms of jurisdictions, most of the valley belongs to the department of Valle del Cauca, but a significant part of it to the south lies within the department of Cauca, starting at the old colonial capital of Popayán. What is known as the Alto Cauca begins at the Salvajina Dam, constructed in the mid-1980s by the CVC to regulate the river's water volume and generate electricity for the growing agroindustrial complex centered in Cali and for the growing middle class of that city (with a current population of 2.5 million). Geographically, the Cauca Valley is a bioregion composed of some forty smaller basins, several lakes and ponds, and extensive wetlands (though many of the ponds and wetlands have been drained for sugar production). Its soils have historically been extremely fertile, well drained, and relatively low in salinity. Its surface and deep aquifers have served as a rich source of high-quality water for agricultural and human consumption. Historically, this ecological complex of mountains, forests, valleys, rivers, ponds, and wetlands has been home to hundreds of plant and animal species. All these features (which actually constitute a genuine meshwork of worlds, a pluriverse) have been systematically undermined by agroindustrial operations.

Though the valley population is majority mestizo, it has a major Afro-descendant presence. Several municipalities in Northern Cauca are predominantly black, such as the municipality of Buenos Aires, which includes the community of La Toma (mentioned in chapters 3 and 4), which also lies within the Salvajina Dam's sphere of influence. A bit more than 50 percent of the population of Cali is black, according to some estimates, largely as a result of migration and forced displacement from the Pacific coast over the past thirty years; Cali has the second largest black urban population in Latin America, after Bahia in Brazil. This is an incredibly important social fact for any design project, especially a project of autonomous design. The majority of the black population is poor. At the other end of the spectrum is a small and extremely rich group of elite whites who pride themselves on their European ancestry. These elites have traditionally controlled most of the land and owned the sugar plantations. In 2013, some 225,000 hectares were devoted to sugarcane and 53,000 to cattle pasture. Although only about sixty properties are larger than five hundred hectares, this figure is deceptive because the big landholders rent land or buy cane produced on a large number of small and midsize farms that are exclusively devoted to sugar. Sugarcane uses water intensively, some 10,300 cubic meters per hectare in this region. The sugar sector consumes 64 percent of all the surface water and 88 percent of the underground water here. Moreover, though I will not examine this aspect in depth, more than 670,000 hectares of foothills (more than half the total surface area) have been affected by extensive cattle ranching.[3]

Driving up and down the valley on the main highway, you can spend several hours viewing what most locals consider a "beautiful green landscape," hectare on hectare of sugarcane growing almost uninterrupted in the flatlands, and cattle peacefully pasturing in the foothills of the mountains. But this landscape is the result of more than a hundred years of ontological occupation of the valley by a heterogeneous assemblage of white elites, cattle, cane, water (the dam supposedly built to control flooding and regulate irrigation, plus the irrigation canals found everywhere in the cane fields), chemicals (the tons of pesticides and fertilizers used on crops), the state (the political elite, totally wedded to this model), the experts (particularly the CVC experts), global markets (the demand for refined sugar), and of course the black cane cutters, without whom the entire operation (despite growing mechanization) would have been and would still be impossible. The black cane cutters speak of sugarcane as the green monster and associate it with the devil; for them, this landscape is not beautiful (Taussig 1980). The whole ensemble is structured by an extensive network of highways, trucks (the "sugar trains," huge tractor trailers loaded with sugarcane, impossible to avoid if you go by car, since cane is grown year round in this fertile valley), and the entire industrial, financial, and service infrastructure of Cali and the surrounding towns.

After more than a century in which the well-oiled machinery of this heterogeneous assemblage has hummed along with seeming smoothness—a fact that the local elites proclaim as a development miracle and popular culture celebrates in numerous ways, from telenovelas to salsa music—its deeply defuturing effects are finally coming to light. They can be seen in the depletion, silting, and pollution of rivers and aquifers; the draining of wetlands; the erosion of biodiversity; the deforestation and severe erosion of hills and slopes;

the respiratory problems among black workers and nearby populations caused by the ash produced when the cane is periodically burned for harvesting; the repression of black workers' attempts to organize and win better living conditions; and the persistence of racism and profound inequality, all integral to the sugarcane model. Linked to inequality and the inevitably resulting poverty in which 60 percent of the people live, there is a high level of "insecurity," denounced by middle-class people, often in a racialized and class discourse, who try to avoid it by living in heavily monitored condominiums and apartment complexes and by restricting much of their social life to the growing number of well-guarded, globalized shopping malls.[4] One wonders how this model continues to function year after year, in spite of its flagrant shortcomings, which are obvious wherever one looks: problems that some activists and a handful of academics and intellectuals are now beginning to identify, despite the seeming lack of awareness among most people and the absence of critical voices in the mainstream media, which continue to celebrate the model in so many ways. This is the challenging background (not unusual in many regions of the Global South) within which any strategy for transition design will have to be devised. I will now discuss some of the main aspects of this project.

Generating a Transition Imaginary for the Cauca Valley

Even a purely theoretical exercise in transition design for a region such as this is a task of enormous proportions; more so if there is any hope that some aspects of it might be implemented in some way. However, bearing in mind the large number of "successful" and influential cases of regional capitalist re/development around the world (including the Cauca Valley after the construction of the Salvajina Dam), the question arises: why not give it a try? Conventional regional development, it goes without saying, has been built on a naturalized history of capitalist development, whereas the sort of regional transition envisaged here would be carried out against the grain of that history and of the current structuring conditions of unsustainability and defuturing.

I could cite many trends in the field of critical design and architectural studies (Escobar 2018) in support of this exercise. However, as the Colombian design theorist Andrea Botero of the Media Lab at Aalto University in Helsinki argues, "Despite these advancements, our understanding of how to go about setting up, carrying on, and more broadly, sustaining collaborative and open-ended design processes in explicit ways is still limited" (A. Botero 2013,

13). We have great need of methods that will allow for collaborative design to be sustained over longer periods of time than usual; for construction to be based on the designers' changing roles over the course of that extended time frame (beyond being, say, the initiators or facilitators); and for taking seriously the distributed nature of agency in design—including, we should add, the non-human actors. The articulation of design-in-use practices in the context of collective design activities over longer time frames is particularly important at this moment.

As ecologists, activists, and transition designers, it is relatively easy to propose scenarios to motivate a new imagining of regional design. Earlier I proposed just such a scenario. Let us recall, first, the staggering landscape of omnipresent sugarcane and cattle, and their in/visible effects. Next, let us re-imagine the region as *a true bastion of agroecological production of organic fruits, vegetables, grains, and tropical plants, and as a multicultural region of small and mid-size agricultural producers, and a working, decentralized network of towns and midsize cities.* Easy to imagine, perhaps, but locally unthinkable, so far. Next I present some factors that might enter into a transition design exercise for the Cauca Valley over a period of years (or rather decades). We'll call it Cauca River Valley in Transition, or CRVT.[5]

There are two crucial tasks to be carried out early in the project: forming a codesign team, and creating a design space together with which the collaborative design team will evolve.[6] It might be useful to create an attractive identity for the design space, but that is only the beginning. The design space involves tools for mapping out design activities with the aim of identifying the participants' possibilities along a continuum that goes from consumption to active creation. Design spaces are always coconstructed and explored by multiple actors through their social interactions, including technologies, tools, materials, and social processes. Through the activity of design in process, it becomes "the space of potentials that the available circumstances afford for the emergence of new designs" (A. Botero 2013, 188). The concept thus goes far beyond the focus on objects, workplaces, and design briefs; it embraces design-in-use and codesign in all their complexity, including the contributions and designs of multiple users. This expanded notion of design spaces could be particularly effective in what Botero (2013, 22) calls "communal endeavors," which "stand midway between being the project of a recognized community of practice . . . or teams [such as, say, La Toma or its territorial organization, or the indigenous communities of Northern Cauca], and being simply the coordinated actions of unidentifiable collectives or ad-hoc groups."

In this dialogic space, the design coalitions would create a new and radical vision for the geographical Cauca River valley and a vision for a sustained transformation that would go far beyond the usual adjustments. In years one and two of the project, the participating collaborative organizations and coalitions would have the job of constructing an initial framework for the transformation(s). You might think of the design space as a sort of laboratory or set of labs in which the jobs of constructing a vision and of codesign would meet, producing conversations intended for actions—for example, a "Valley Design Lab" or "Northern Cauca Lab," but also a "Cali Lab," given that city's imposing presence in the valley, and subregional laboratories; or labs organized in terms of spheres of social and ecological actions.[7]

In view of this general aim (and of the highly charged, political, and controversial nature that the process will no doubt take on as it evolves), at least in the early stages of the VCT process, only a limited number of actors will take part in the codesign team. It will be essential for the main actors to share the fundamental aims of the exercise in the widest sense. This said, the actors should include at least the following sectors: social movement organizations (urban and rural, Afro-descendant, indigenous, peasant, and various urban groups); women's and youth organizations, especially from marginalized rural and urban areas; the academy, NGOs, and intellectual sectors; and the arts, communications, and alternative media. It will also be essential for the team to be seeded with diversity—epistemic, social (in terms of race/ethnicity, gender, generation, class, and territorial base) and "cultural" (ontological) diversity—from the outset, since that will the only reasonable guarantee of a genuinely pluriversal design result. The activists, intellectuals, NGO members, and academics, including those in the natural and physical sciences, are in principle good candidates for the team—it is not uncommon in Latin America for people to perform more than one of these roles (or even all of them) simultaneously or sequentially; in fact, in Northern Cauca and in parts of Alto Cauca, there is a significant "natural reserve" of people who are already prepared to take part in interepistemic conversations. It will also be crucial for the team to develop the capacity to think "communitarianly" and relationally, in onto-epistemic terms (though, of course, not necessarily in these theoretical terms).

The real transition exercise would begin to evolve from this initial process. It will have to continually generate contexts that feed into the idea of a transition and also concrete projects aimed at developing specific design aspects of transitions in a collaborative and communalitarian way.[8] Some objectives and activities in this phase of the project might include the following:

- Making visible the "civilizational ruptures" and defuturing practices of the current model. What are the main ecological and social manifestations of unsustainability and defuturing? (These might include the systematic impoverishment of black workers and their families; the virulent racism and violence directed against black women; the depletion of the soil; the effects on water and on air quality; the unfettered consumerism; the destructive forms of extractivism, including gold extraction—to mention only a few.)

- Creating a sense of the region different from the prevailing "popular" regional narrative, especially in Cali, which is dominated by sugarcane, salsa music, sports, and commerce. This will mean articulating a *pluriversal bioregional notion* for the whole of Alto Cauca, beyond the merely geographic or popular notions.

- Becoming familiar with the various life projects of the communities and collectivities involved, including those in marginalized urban areas and even those that apparently no longer have any home or community.

- Encouraging a diversity of actions, such as digital platforms to allow for greater participation in the codesign process; thematic constellations and design labs; traveling interactive exhibits and labs for fostering and helping to generate new imaginaries about and for the region in small cities and rural areas; compilations of real-life cases (particularly useful for showing that "other economies are possible"[9]); diversity in metanarratives, even if in tension with one another; the collective creation of scenarios, whether rooted in existing cases that can be extrapolated to fulfill the vision of a community (indigenous, Afro-descendant, peasant, urban, and other communities) or speculatively imagined to elicit open thinking about design.

- Actions favoring design methodologies and tools that are bottom-up, horizontal, and peer-to-peer, while using top-down items when necessary, though they should always be subordinated to the aims that emerge from communal dialogues. There are bound to be many methodological obstacles to achieving this goal, for example, figuring out how to design spaces in which collaborative organizations can create conditions honoring the multiple memories of the past that exist, recognizing the existence of multiple overlapping worlds, and thereby amplifying the numerous futures that inevitably fill the discursive and emotional space of the wide range of inhabitants of the region.

- A "Cali Lab" series intended to determine the range of responses to the question "What do you want Cali to be?," followed by constructing scenarios in which the diverse visions can be presented, together with the possible transformation and the speculative design imaginaries developed by the codesign team—so that more and more people will begin to play with the idea of Cali as a truly welcoming space for living in and not as an unsustainability machine.

- Designing methods and tools to mobilize the multiple communal design histories, such as vernacular, diffuse, autonomous, and other sorts of design (Gutiérrez Borrero 2015a, 2015b), that are found in so many rural and urban groups and in so many places in the valley, and their intersections with professional design.

- The impact of climate change on the various local worlds (places, communities, and ecosystems) must be an important aspect in imagining the transitions, drawing on all the initiatives around the world already working on this issue (such as the Transition Town network) while strategically invoking broad transition imaginaries (such as Buen Vivir and degrowth). This aspect of design has the potential to affect everything: agriculture (as Vía Campesina [2009] puts it, "small peasant farmers cool the earth"); energy and transportation (slowing the exponential growth of private vehicle usage, supporting decentralized and light transportation systems); urban planning (such as parks and recreation areas); and so on. The concept of resilience, repositioned in the ontological context of autonomous worlds, could be important in this area.

- An integral part of the design task will be creating art and new communication media for the transitions, such as performance art (including performances that could be done about/with nonhumans—for example, on how to "liberate" soil ruined by cane and cattle and bring it back to life); music and dance for the transition (based on the strong musical traditions of the region, including salsa and the black musics of the Pacific and Northern Cauca); and social media and new content for conventional media to destabilize the "popular" discourse on the region and position the new discourse in the collective imaginary. This aspect will be based on the education and popular communication sectors that have been active in the region since the 1980s. Imagining the transition has great potential for generating an unprecedented wave of cultural activism.

Other questions could be addressed through the transition design framework, such as the relationship between diffuse or popular design and professional design; the creation of knowledges that can "migrate" from one situation to another; the learning process as the project moves forward; the role of research in design; the use of prototypes and maps, SLOC (small, local, open, and connected) scenarios (Manzini 2015), and digital and live storytelling; tool design by and for communal spaces; and issues of scale, among others.

Can Cities Be Rethought?

In the Cauca River valley today, we can see clearly both life's and matter's capacity to create complex meshworks of life, with intense forms of differentiation and cohesion—as crystallized in the region's beautiful landscapes, ecosystems, and some of its human accomplishments—and also the enormous human capacity for going against the grain of that natural capacity.[10] The landscape is the great witness of all these transformations, if we know how to read it. The modern human propensity for producing designs that go against nature is perhaps nowhere quite so visible as it is in Cali and the midsize cities of the region. Here, climate and territory intermingle on the one hand with social dynamics and human activity (including the mass displacement of entire populations, especially since the 1970s, and their convergence on Cali), and on the other hand with urban planning and architecture, producing urban sprawl whose serious problems—real estate bubbles, the marginalization of hundreds of thousands of people, particularly Afro-Colombians, the "mallification" of the middle class, the patent inadequacy of services, growing congestion, generalized "insecurity," and so on—seem to resist any attempt at a solution.

We find the same features in many cities around the world, of course, especially in the Global South. Many of these cities are proof of the failure of urban planning and its buckling to the pressures of the dominant economic interests and capital accumulation. Thus the urban systems of transport, norms, services, and infrastructure have systematically favored these interests at the expense of popular or working-class groups and places, which remain marginalized though they are precisely the ones that most need effective use of such services. In their retrospective look at Latin American urban planning, in preparation for the United Nations Conference on Housing and Sustainable Urban Development (the Habitat III conference, Quito, October 17–20, 2016), Jordi Borja and Fernando Carrión (2017) show the many ways in which urban planning has aligned itself with private interests. Given this situation, no national or international strategy—such as the so-called New Urban Agenda that emerged from Habitat III—can be anything more than a summation of pious and inadequate declarations, "catalogues of rights that sound like letters to Santa Claus" (50), to the degree that they do not at any moment question the real powers that define the transformations of cities (developers, builders, landowners, corporations, banks, and the financial system), all of this with the active complicity of the professionals.

Faced with the tremendous spatial injustice of cities, these critical urban planners echo the call for *the right to the city* on the part of many urban social movements and grassroots groups. This right becomes a platform for promoting

> a radical transformation of the city and of the organization of territory. It questions the right to own property, does not accept private management of common assets, and is opposed to growthism at the expense of the environment, basic resources, and the quality of life. It proposes a deliberative democracy with limits on institutions of representation in favor of civic forms of governance and management, prioritizes the objectives of equality and freedom, of recognizing all the inhabitants of a territory equally, and so on. . . . In sum, the right to the city constitutes a horizon that helps us keep walking (as Eduardo Galeano might have said); it expresses the aspiration for a more just, kinder, and happier society. (Borja and Carrión 2017, 52)

This is a premise for a whole program for redesigning urban planning itself and for starting to rethink specific cities such as Cali and the smaller cities around it.[11] What does the right to the city of Cali mean but the right for Afro-descendants, women, poor people of every stripe, and, we might add, pedestrians, to live, work, and walk through the streets in dignity and freedom? By confronting the conventional view of urbanism or urban planning with this apparently simple question, we can begin to read the city from the creativity of its (profoundly pathologized) peripheries, rather than from its already exhausted center, much less from what the Dutch architect Rem Koolhaas straightforwardly calls "Junkspaces," such as shopping malls, veritable temples to the entertainment and consumerism of the global middle classes (when they are not in cyberspace), even more desperately so in the Global South. Going beyond "the generic city" imagined de facto by the measures outlined in Habitat III (which are functional to the interests of giant investors and global capital), cities such as Cali would find their own identities if urban planners dared to look genuinely from the viewpoints of pedestrians, of people with other abilities ("the handicapped"), of women, of black people, of indigenous people, of the displaced, and thus forge new ways of creating neighborhoods and recommunalizing social life.[12]

Koolhaas himself reflects on this other kind of urbanism:

> If there is to be a "new urbanism" it will not be based on the twin fantasies of order and omnipotence; it will be the staging of uncertainty; it will no longer be concerned with the arrangement of more or less permanent objects *but with the irrigation of territories with potential*; it will no longer aim for a stable configuration but for the creation of enabling fields that accommodate processes that refuse to be crystallized into definitive form.... Since it [urbanism, or the growth of cities] is out of control, *the urban is about to become a major vector of the imagination.* (1995, 29)

A new imagining of the city would have to think of Cali as a metropolitan region that functions as such and not in name only; to cite Borja and Carrión again, "metropolitan or highly urbanized areas should be structured as polycentric networks of cities with a collective mobility system and nonurban interstices" (2017, 38). Instead of the ongoing neoliberal rollback of democracy, which only sees purely individual solutions for social problems, Cali as a metropolitan city would become a zone of democratic renewal. We will have to keep this principle in mind in any collective design for the city.

This is not the place to describe the current state of Cali or what Cali and its neighboring cities might become in the future, but I would like to conclude this section with a short reference to the substantial and visionary work of the Cali architect and urban planner Harold Martínez Espinal. His architectural perspective could be said to be founded on a deeply relational cosmovision and thus may be considered foundational for new urbanisms. It resonates with views of cultural and ecological transitions that are considered civilizational (Escobar 2019). He begins, in fact, by stating that "behind the ecstatic presumption surrounding the concepts of modernity, progress, and globalization, Western men and women are beginning to perceive, for the first time and in a fragmentary way, both the collapse of their civilizational paradigm and its resulting catastrophes—social, economic, and particularly ecological" (Martínez Espinal 2016, 13). It is a crisis for a way of being, doing, and living that can be traced back to classical Greece, when, given the particular anthropocentrism of that society, the basis of earlier lifeways based on "terrestrial habitability" in synchrony with the self-organization of matter began to erode. Therefore, he argues, we must return to a view of the increasing, systemic complexity of life, based in part on the "thermodicity" of matter (defined by the entropy of the universe) and in part on the "associative interaction" that is indispensable to creating successful living forms and processes (which in these essays I have called radical relationality). From this new perspective, we could address the task of rethinking "the existence of all beings [as] spatially systemic, as part of a global network of networks within networks. Network of networks, which we know by the name of habitat" (2016, 18).[13]

The associative interaction between organism and environment (which Martínez Espinal understands in terms of autopoiesis) has been constructing habitats since the dawn of the planet, constituting a genuine ethos that over time produced the conditions that made Earth inhabitable. From this perspective, inhabiting (*habitar*) can be defined as the recurrent associational interaction between living things and their environment, creating the conditions for well-being. For a good portion of their history, humans knew how to practice this form of inhabiting the habitats they found. This ethos began to crack with the Greek polis, with its geometrical forms and layouts, conceived by humans who had begun to think of themselves as superior to and apart from the natural world. Here began the long civilizational journey of the Western ontology of separation and dominion over the natural world; the habitat is transformed into "an out-of-focus, scarcely noticed background" to the polis and its function of inhabiting. The rest of the living world was thus exiled from this form of inhabiting. What we see in cities like Cali today has its genealogy in practices that can be traced back to that time, founded on the famous *logos* and *anthropos* of the Greece of the Acropolis and their many subsequent developments in patriarchal Western culture.

One can anticipate Martínez Espinal's project and conclusions based on these premises. How can humans reclaim terrestrial habitability? In philosophical terms, it will require creating a new way of being in the world (*ser-al-estar-en*, or "being-while-existing-in," an echo of Heidegger) and even a new human, unlike the disembodied and decontextualized human that Western civilization has imagined and molded through many spatial practices and other means. It will mean designs in which "it will only be possible to continue existing and being-there through collective *habitus* in cities where the urban merges as a collective entity with its natural *habitat*, which as we already know is by its essence a collective entity. Cities where humans could just exist, like other living beings, simply as occupants of a living soil to which they owe an ethos of reciprocity and complementarity, and more specifically, of *associational interaction*" (22).

Martínez Espinal finds hopeful signs in many social and environmentalist movements from the past few decades, and he senses particular potential in Latin America: "Bit by bit, in the pueblos of Latin America and the Caribbean, the profound significance of *being-while-existing-in* the natural world has begun to be valued and positioned as the structural pillar of the great battle of ideas that humanity is currently undergoing" (197). It opens up the possibility of a new bifurcation, the birth of "a new era in Latin American identity where we will begin to realize that the value of its history does not reside in the European invasion of the fifteenth century [nor in the route of modernization, development, and globalization]; instead, it actually begins some 12,000 years ago with the First Peoples, who have been able to resist the past 500 years of oppression and extermination by protecting, enjoying, and preserving the *habitus* of associational interaction" (196).

The Cali architect helps us visualize the possibility that a beautiful new display of the power of self-organization of matter might act as an agent of urban revitalization and creative innovation. As a design imagination, this perspective requires a new temporality that will allow us to think about effects and transformations on a larger scale, changes that will go far beyond the time-limited reformist proposals that have come out of Habitat III and the regional and urban planning offices of our cities. It will thus have to operate on a multitude of scales and temporalities, from geologic time scales to the microorganism level, from the genetics of life to the structure of matter, from the associational ethos of nonhumans to the new ways of being human. The challenge is to translate these philosophical and scientific principles into tools for people and for pueblos to use, rather than into political technologies for the state or corporate prescriptions that will necessarily vitiate them. It is a matter of conceptualizing "infrastructure as complex ecology" (Bélanger 2015, 12) so that it will really support the re/design of life, for thinking about new articulations of live systems and living infrastructures. What would it really be like to inhabit a living valley of the Cauca River, fertile and full of forests and living waterways, of hardworking folks who are able to interweave urban and nonurban spaces with their environments as they seek collective wellness, comfort, and playfulness?

Today, critical architecture is open to questions of this sort. It asks, for example: "Could space be liberated for alternative, slower yet more motile forms of life, where growth is defined metabolically?" (Bélanger 2015, 37). It questions the production of "outlaw territories," spaces proscribed by the neoliberalized administration of our cities, of the whole apparatus of biopolitics engineered by state experts and planners, with their devastating instrumentalization of displaced persons, refugees, the poor, racial minorities, and the marginalized, whose objective is nothing but "security" and "order" for the powerful and who make any sort of real cohabitation almost impossible (Scott 2016). It imagines, and practices, *forensic architectures*, using a number of techniques to make visible the lethal effects of the destructive technologies of modernity—wars, drones, displacements, great environmental conflicts—on infrastructures, inhabited spaces, and ecosystems (Weitzman 2017).

An exercise in forensic architecture for the Cauca River valley would reveal all the damage that more than a century of "development" has wreaked on its soils, its waterways, its habitats, and of course on its cities.[14] From the opposite direction, to conclude, let us practice for a moment what might be called an *architecture of interrelatedness* and reconnection, carrying out (perhaps collectively) a great exercise in reimagining the region, from meticulous new inventories of living forms—flora, fauna, minerals, landscapes—toward a new production of space. Let us situate ourselves in some high place somewhere in the valley (as the legendary Scottish urban planner Patrick Geddes used to do) and ask ourselves: What layouts of vegetation, territories, human groups, jobs, vocations, and professions would produce pleasant configurations of spaces and places, territories and cities? What healthy, comfortable, and playful meshworks of infrastructures, cities, humans, and nonhumans can we collectively construct? Finally, how can we get this minga (collective labor) going, on the ground?

A Final Note

This transition idea is, of course, tentative and general. I offer it more as an indication of what sort of questions might be at stake in the efforts for a transition, not as a road map to follow. I am perfectly aware of the exceedingly ambitious nature of what I have proposed. Let us say that it is meant, to a large extent, as an exercise in theory and a contribution to critical design studies. It also means to bolster the idea that "another way of designing is possible," a design for the pluriverse. It could be considered, too, as an example of the dissident imagination of design; or perhaps as my flawed attempt at doing an ontological-political analysis, taking advantage of those ultradesigned spaces that are the academy, the book, and the writing process.

Let us listen once more to the farsighted words of the Nasa people to learn what is at stake and what sort of alliances could be formed:

> We know that we know little, as an elder from distant lands and times put it; that we can do little and that we can only learn and succeed by banding together. Not only as a gang (*montonera*) of Indian women and men: a gang with peasants, a gang with Afrodescendants, a gang with people in the cities. It is true that doubt has been sown and that it is strong. We

invite you all to turn off the TV and look us in the eyes: our history, our struggle, our words, clumsy but sincere. Then you will see that we, Indian men and women, are not the ones stealing or grabbing your land or banks or oil or gold or banknotes. You will see that there are powerful enemies who are trying to leave us with nothing and to hide themselves they point at us. Ardila Lülle among them. Light the lantern and shine it on them. Then you will see clearly that this struggle comes out of Northern Cauca but it is not of Northern Cauca. From the Nasa people, but not of the Nasa people. . . . Every liberated farm, here or anywhere in the world, is a territory that is joining in to reestablish the balance of Uma Kiwe. It is our common home, our one and only. So: please come on in, the door is open.[15]

Preface to the English Edition

1 The practice of personal and group blogs in many languages, I believe, resembles the intellectual style I am describing here.

2 Charles Hale, personal correspondence, November 20, 2017.

3 These themes recur in the questions by audiences during oral presentations and in review processes connected with the material presented in this volume.

4 Modernist forms of politics have enshrined a naturalized political culture in which only certain practices and institutions, largely those associated with liberal representative democracy or with their socialist counterparts, count as political (Alvarez, Dagnino, and Escobar 1998). This "political" domain is taken for granted as real. Within this domain, objectivity and truth are possible. It is relational in that the political stands in some relation to other equally naturalized domains, particularly the economy. This relationality is limited when compared with the radical relationality of the emergent forms of ontological politics featured in this volume. In these latter forms, even the very existence of pregiven domains is questioned. This is why it is important to highlight equally the ontological dimension of the political and the political dimension of ontology.

5 The Global Tapestry of Alternatives (GTA), launched in May 2019, is devoted to catalyzing convergences of this sort among transformative initiatives worldwide. See Kothari et al. 2019, 341–42; and the GTA website, www.globaltapestryofalternatives.org. See also Vikalp Sangam, a confluence process spearheaded in India by Ashish Kothari, http://www.vikalpsangam.org. Some of these initiatives use the concept of weaving. In the art world, the project Antropoloops, by Rubén Alonso, an architect and ethnomusicologist from Seville, Spain, maps and weaves world musics in ways that could perhaps be applied to struggles. See https://www.youtube.com/watch?v=oatdM-jsVaI&feature=youtu.be. Thanks to Alberto Corsín for bringing this neat project to my attention.

6 A well-known collection of Zapatista texts includes Subcomandante Galeano's own rendition of the question of the master's house. As the group involved in the anecdote concludes, it would not make sense to fix a house "that does not serve to live," because it only maintains well those on top, while they trample on those below and destroy the house along the way. Better to build a new house/world, while preparing for the eventual collapse of the old one (Comisión Sexta del EZLN 2016, 8). I thank Anthony Dest for reminding me of this passage.

7 I will not deal here with anarchism as a theoretico-political perspective and practice, although its role in renovating political debates in Latin America, in-

cluding in homegrown approaches to *autonomía* and the communal, is clear and understudied.

8 The zones to defend, or ZADs, are sites or territories that have been occupied by activists resisting mega development projects. The term was first used by protesters blockading the construction of a large international airport at Notre-Dame-des-Landes, near the city of Nantes. The village that resulted from the occupation has lasted more than a decade, despite heavy police repression. This has been an inspiring struggle, replicated in other places in France and Europe. It may be seen as an instance of Klein's "Blockadia" (2014). See the movement's website, https:// zad.nadir.org/?lang=en (accessed July 31, 2018). I visited the ZAD at Notre-Dame -des-Landes on June 7, 2018. My thanks to Christophe Bonneuil for the invitation for this visit, and to the *zadistes* who welcomed us that day.

9 I dedicated *Designs for the Pluriverse* (2018) to exemplary figures of radical relational politics and the struggle for the pluriverse, including Bob Marley, the Zapatistas, and the Afro-Colombian and indigenous movements of Colombia's Southwest, some of whose thoughts and deeds are told about in this volume.

10 From the album *Survival* (Kingston: Island/Tuff Gong Records, 1979).

11 Bogues's work, I believe, as well as the work of Caribbean writers such as Sylvia Wynter, Paget Henry, Lewis Gordon, Édouard Glissant, and Nelson Maldonado-Torres, anticipated some of today's discussions on black radical thought from ontological perspectives.

12 "War," from the album *Rastaman Vibration* (Kingston: Island Records, 1976). The inextricable relation between racism and war has been carefully treated by the Puerto Rican philosopher Nelson Maldonado-Torres (2008).

13 Warren situates his work within the critique of metaphysics in Western philosophy (particularly Heidegger and Vattimo), on the one hand, and a series of historical archives concerning the invention of the Negro and the black person as nothing through scholarship, science, law, and pictorial representations, on the other. In commenting on his work, I do not claim to be an expert on Afro-pessimism, black radical thought, Black Optimism, and Afro-futurism, or even to have a complete picture of the map of these illustrious scholarly trends. It seems to me, however, that the questions raised by these trends about blackness and antiblackness (its ontology; the social life and social death of the black subject; the question of how to understand black existence in an antiblack world; the dismantling of white supremacy; the articulation of refusal and affirmation; the resilience and perseverance of black people in the face of the continued trauma of slavery and antiblackness; the ways in which antiblackness confers meaning on nonblacks as human; and the questions of agency and politics) are of utmost importance to all those wishing to comprehend these very issues in relation to other subaltern groups and those interested in different understandings of whiteness. These trends are often associated with Saidiya Hartman, Hortense Spillers, Frank Wilderson, Orlando Patterson, Jared Sexton, Christina Sharpe, and Fred Moten. (Moten is identified with Afro-mysticism by Warren; see Warren 2017.)

14 From the forum's declaration: https://movimientos.org/es/content/declaraci
%C3%B3n-del-foro-internacional-sobre-feminicidios-en-grupos-etnizados-y
-racializados, accessed October 30, 2019. See also the forum's blog, http://foro
feminicidios2016.blogspot.com.

Prologue

1 The terms *sentipensar* and *sentipensamiento* were first reported by the Colombian
sociologist Orlando Fals Borda (1984) as the living principle of the riverine and
swamp communities of Colombia's Caribbean coast. They imply an art of living
based on thinking with both heart and mind, reason and emotion. See http://
www.youtube.com/watch?v=LbJWqetRuMo. They were popularized by Eduardo
Galeano; see, for example, http://www.youtube.com/watch?v=wUGVz8wATls.
Approximate translations in English would be "feeling-thinking" or "think-
feeling."
2 The election of the right-wing politician Iván Duque as president of Colombia in
May 2018—and the increasing repression and assassinations of social activists that
have ensued since then—is having a strong impact on the conditions for popular
protest and mobilization; these, however, have not stopped altogether.

Introduction: Another Possible Is Possible

Epigraph: My thanks to Gabriela Merlinsky for this quote by the great Argentine
environmentalist Héctor Alimonda, who died a few weeks after sending Gabriela
a text containing this marvelous phrase.
Epigraph: From the version featuring the great black singers Susana Baca and
Totó la Momposina singing the refrain. https://www.youtube.com/watch?v
=DkFJE8ZdeG8.
1 This is why I sometimes use the notion of "the real/possible" in this book,
without meaning to imply that they are one and the same. I explain these terms
in chapter 1.
2 See the excellent analysis by the Colombian activist and doctor Manuel Rozental
(2017a, 2017b) of worldwide war (Syria, Libya, the Middle East, Venezuela) as the
essential mechanism for the accumulation of capital.
3 I explain these and other aphorisms in chapter 7, where the references will also be
found.
4 An effective way to counter the accusation is to turn it upside down by showing
that the accusers, not the accused, are the true romantics. I often try out ways of
turning conventional perceptions upside down with my students, coming up with
formulas such as the following: The problem with the world isn't extreme poverty but extreme wealth; Africa isn't being "killed" by too little development but
by too much; The greatest "failed state" is the United States, where elections are
for sale, wars are manufactured, everything gets handed over to the corporations,
and people don't bat an eye; The more elitist a university is, and the closer it is
to the circles of power, the more conventional its view of the world, and therefore

the more cut off from people's true experiences and needs (this, to denaturalize the glorification of universities such as Harvard). And to denaturalize the value assigned to choosing a profession in business, engineering, economics, and so on, because these are "productive" careers, and to overturn the subsequent devaluation of the arts and humanities, I might say: "It is the knowledge produced by these conventional careers that keeps helping to destroy the world; on the other hand, the knowledge produced by the humanities and social sciences is what has the potential to guide us in the process of reconstructing the worlds we are destroying." It's important to be mindful, however, that these strategic reversals imply a return to the idea of a real world with a single truth.

Chapter 1: Theory and the Un/Real

1 With the use of the tilde (~), I am suggesting that the terms are not completely separate, but are in continuity with each other.

2 Colombian and Latin American anthropologists and political ecologists also tell us that the Kogui and Arhuaco peoples of the Sierra Nevada consider themselves the "elder brothers" of humanity, in charge of maintaining world balance, beginning with their own territories.

3 This argument has been developed since the 1970s by the German feminists Claudia von Werlhof, Maria Mies, and Veronika Bennholdt-Thomsen. See von Werlhof 2015 for an introduction to this literature and von Werlhof 2019 for a discussion of the "new matriarchies." This research program (and the related work of Silvia Federici, Ariel Salleh, Wendy Harcourt, and Latin American feminists such as Rita Segato, María Lugones, Sylvia Marcos, and Silvia Rivera Cusicanqui, among others, as well as communitarian and decolonial feminists) is independent of the feminist theories that prevail in the Anglo-American academy, where they have often instead been criticized as essentialist. See Escobar 2018 for a discussion of these analyses.

4 Humberto Maturana and Ximena Dávila have been carrying out a research and action project on matriztic cultures and the biology of love with colleagues in Santiago de Chile for many decades. See the Matriztic School (Escuela Matríztica, a formulation that combines the words "matristic" and matriz or "matrix"), http://matriztica.cl/.

5 The Buddhist teacher Thich Nhat Hanh (2008) offers the well-known example of the "flower," which interexists with the planet, soil, water, pollinating insects, even the sun, all of which are essential to its existence. It should be added that in Buddhist meditation, interdependence goes hand in hand with equally important reflections on impermanence and compassion; only then can the vision of interbeing be realized. The ultimate objective is to be able to *practice interdependence and not remain trapped in philosophical or conceptual reflections about it.*

6 The Buddhist literature (and secondary literature) on the mind is so vast that it is almost ridiculous to mention any particular sources. However, for a useful introduction to the question of mind by an eminent Buddhist teacher, see Mingyur Rinpoche 2007. A key, basic Buddhist text from the twelfth century can be

found, with contemporary commentaries, in Thrangu Rinpoche (2003; see especially chapter 17 on the perfection of wisdom). A classic guide to Tibetan Buddhism for dealing with the nonexistence of the self and attachment to the ego (a guide to the practice of cultivating compassion, known as *lojong*) is found in Kongtrul 2005. For an introduction to Tibetan Buddhism, see Kyabgon 2001. Finally, from the Dalai Lama (1994), see his reflection on a life devoted to compassion, or the way of the Bodhisattva. Francisco Varela drew on the cognitive sciences as well as on Tibetan Buddhism for his theory of enaction, and he participated in fruitful dialogue with the Dalai Lama and other Buddhist scientists and teachers.

7   This is admittedly an extremely partial presentation of these currents; there are other alternative sources in the physical and natural sciences, and still more in the humanities and arts, that should rightfully be listed as well.

8   Of crucial importance in this "biology of love," as Maturana terms it, is the recognition that the act of emotioning is the basis of biological existence, and social coexistence is based on love rather than any sort of appropriation and conflict. See also Maturana and Verden-Zöller 1993, 2008.

9   In much of the literature called folklore, it is possible to read manifestations of the popular wisdom of inhabiting place (the home plot, the landscape, the quality of being a local). Think, for example, of the marvelous works of the poet and musician from northern Argentina, Atahualpa Yupanqui.

10 From the inspired farewell text by Subcomandante Marcos, "Entre la luz y la sombra," translated as "Between Light and Shadow," May 27, 2014. See http://enlacezapatista.ezln.org.mx/2014/05/27/between-light-and-shadow.

Chapter 2: From Below, on the Left, and with the Earth

Thanks to Pablo Gentili and Fernanda Saforcada for inviting me to give this talk at the VII Conference of CLACSO (Medellín, November 10–14, 2015). Thanks also for the comments given to me on the first version of the essay by Patricia Botero, Charo Mina Rojas, Betty Ruth Lozano, Carlos Rosero, Manuel Rozental, Eduardo Gudynas, Laura Gutiérrez, Xochitl Leyva, Gustavo Esteva, Enrique Leff, and Héctor Alimonda. I have slightly revised the text for this book.

1   Emir Sader, "La crisis del pensamiento crítico latinoamericano" [The crisis of Latin American critical thought], América Latina en Movimiento, April 11, 2015, http://www.alainet.org/es/articulo/173375.

2   I think the song and video "Latinoamérica" by the Puerto Rican band Calle 13 display the multiplicity of worlds, of ways of knowing, and of practices that makes up our continent.

3   The notion of communities in resistance is developed in the books of collective research and action edited by Patricia Botero (2015) and by Botero and Palermo (2013).

4   This essay omits citations of particular authors, with a few exceptions. An extensive bibliography about these topics can be found in Escobar 2010, 2014b, 2018.

5 A useful review and critical appraisal of the high and low points of LACT can be found in the book by the Colombian philosopher Santiago Castro Gómez (1996).

6 I will not deal in this essay with the question of whether these three currents constitute a "new Left," or whether the pro-autonomy and Earth currents should be seen as distinct from the Left. In the latter case, the "right–left" political spectrum would be breaking, giving way to a wide variety of options—not as "third ways" but as genuine manifestations of new forms of seeing political practice. Nor will I pause to analyze the distinctions between "progressivism" and "the Left" (see the recent work by Eduardo Gudynas on this topic).

7 I am thinking of the beautiful paintings and engravings by the Colombian Maoist (MOIR) artist Clemencia Lucena, now little remembered but among the most eloquent documents of the period, done in a powerful Latin American neorealist style. Of course, we could recall Antonio Berni, the Mexican muralists, or Guayasamín, among a great many more artists on the left (without even mentioning theater, literature, or music).

8 As the Mexican ecologist Víctor Toledo put it so well, speaking of environmental struggles, "Latin America is at the boiling point" (IV Congreso Latinoamericano de Etnobiología, Popayán, September 28–October 2, 2015). A global map of environmental struggles and protests is kept by the Atlas of Environmental Justice, maintained by ICTA at the Universitat Autonoma de Barcelona. See http://ejatlas .org. A good look at the atlas might lead you to conclude that the worlds are indeed boiling, because we are destroying the Earth.

9 See the recent works by Gudynas, Svampa, Zibechi, and Acosta, among others, on these topics.

10 The phrase "building autonomy" is written underneath the "Ten Principles of Good Government" posted at the entrances to some autonomous Zapatista communities. See http://www.cgtchiapas.org/denuncias-juntas-buen-gobierno -denuncias/jbg-morelia-denuncia-ataque-orcao-con-arma-fuego-bases.

11 Autonomism is a phenomenon of movements and collectives. Its political-theoretical expressions are to be found in these collectives, including many movements of indigenous, Afro-descendant, and peasant movements. It is being conceptualized in diverse ways by a growing number of intellectuals and activists, among whom we should mention Gustavo Esteva, Raquel Gutiérrez Aguilar, Xochitl Leyva, Raúl Zibechi, Manuel Rozental, Vilma Almendra, Silvia Rivera Cusicanqui, Patricia Botero, John Holloway, Carlos Walter Porto-Gonçalves, the Colectivo Situaciones, Maristella Svampa, Luis Tapia, and the Aymara intellectuals Pablo Mamani, Julieta Paredes, Felix Patzi, and Simón Yampara, among others. Many of these actors converged on the First International Congress of Communality in Puebla, Mexico, organized by Raquel Gutiérrez Aguilar and her colleagues. See https://www.youtube.com/watch?v=HPZkfNiKZ6w. An important related trend can be found in the intercultural and decolonizing focuses put forth by the doctoral degree program in Latin American cultural studies at the Universidad Andina Simón Bolívar in Quito, directed by Catherine Walsh. There is also a large group of women and men thinking about autonomy and communality

centered in the city of Popayán, Colombia, who continuously exchange ideas with Nasa, Misak, peasant, and Afro-descendant community leaders and intellectuals in the Northern Cauca, particularly in the master's program in interdisciplinary development studies (a bastion of autonomous, communal, and decolonizing thought) and in the biannual Tramas y Mingas por el Buen Vivir (Networks and Working Parties on Good Living), including Olver Quijano, Javier Tobar, Lorena Obando, Adolfo Albán Achinte, Olga Lucía Sanabria, and Carlos Corredor. See https://tramasymingasparaelbuenvivir.wordpress.com/2015/06/24/tramas-y-mingas-para-el-buen-vivir-2015.

12 See the Escuela Matrística (Matriztic School) founded by Maturana and Ximena Dávila Yáñez in Santiago de Chile, http://matriztica.cl/.

13 Open letter from Francia Márquez, leader of La Toma, April 24, 2015.

14 Consejo Regional Indígena del Cauca (CRIC) 2008, quoted in Quijano 2012, 209.

15 Cabildo Indígena de Guambía 1980, quoted in Quijano 2012, 257.

16 Cabildo, Taitas y Comisión de Trabajo del Pueblo Guambiano 1994, quoted in Quijano 2012, 263.

17 Ricardo Aguilar Agramont, *Animal Político* blog, "Eduardo Gudynas: La derecha y la izquierda no entienden a la naturaleza," *La Razón,* August 23, 2015, http://www.la-razon.com/suplementos/animal_politico/Eduardo-Gudynas-izquierda-entienden-naturaleza_0_2330167108.html.

18 In the Global North, for example, the notion of degrowth points to the need to live differently, beyond the idea of "consuming less." Some theorists and activists speak of "Wests," or "alternative, non dominant modernities" within Europe itself. This important notion, however, should not keep us from considering the historical impacts of dominant modernities and of Europe as a whole (the modern/colonial world-system).

19 The quotation is from Berry 1999, 3.

20 Tramas y Mingas para el Buen Vivir, Popayán, October 21–22, 2015.

21 On the symposium in Chiapas (Encuentro "Pensamiento Crítico Frente a la Hidra Capitalista"), see for example the brief reviews at http://seminarioscideci.org/video-entrevistas-seminario-pensamiento-critico-frente-a-la-hidra-capitalista-semillero-ezln. For the events in Popayán, see https://tramasymingasparael buenvivir.wordpress.com/2015/06/24/tramas-y-mingas-para-el-buen-vivir-2015.

Chapter 3: The Earth~Form of Life

Epigraph: Banner title from the video documenting the brutal police repression of one Nasa march to recover the land of an hacienda, May 10, 2017: https://www.youtube.com/watch?v=q7wBLXDnDRU&feature=youtu.be.

Epigraph: Song by the Nasa musical youth group Fxiw: https://www.youtube.com/watch?v=oHCoZ3WQXcs; https://www.facebook.com/247381632124387/videos/372149839647565/.

1 The Nasa quotes cited in this chapter come from the following sources: booklets produced by ACIN on the process of Liberation of Mother Earth, as well as multiple texts on its webpage, from 2005 onward, https://nasaacin.org/; "Libertad

para la Madre Tierra," May 28, 2005, https://liberaciondelamadretierra.org/en/libertad-para-la-madre-tierra/; "El desafío que nos convoca," May 28, 2010, http://www.nasaacin.org/el-desafio-no-da-espera; "Lo que vamos aprendiendo con la liberación de Uma Kiwe," January 19, 2016, http://pueblosencamino.org/?p=2176; "Lo que vamos aprendiendo con la Liberación de la Madre Tierra," Noviembre del 2015, https://liberaciondelamadretierra.org/en/lo-que-vamos-aprendiendo-con-la-liberacion-de-la-madre-tierra/; Vilma Almendra, "La paz de la Mama Kiwe en libertad, de la mujer sin amarras ni silencios," August 2, 2012, http://pueblosencamino.org/?p=150. See also "Libertad y alegría con Uma Kiwe"; "Palabra del Proceso de Liberacion de la Madre Tierra." I should note that ACIN's website is often taken down or sabotaged by unknown actors.

2 Special thanks to Manuel Rozental and Vilma Almendra for helping me understand over the years the nature and context of the Nasa struggle and Nasa thought. I am grateful to Mauricio Dorado for sending me the most recent text on the process of Mother Earth liberation (December 17, 2016). I also thank Luis Carlos Arboleda, Carmen Cecilia Muñoz, Gilberto Loaiza, and Alfonso Rubio for inviting me to prepare this text for the inaugural conference for the doctorate in the cultural history of Colombia at the Universidad del Valle, Cali, November 1, 2016; and to Leopoldo Múnera for inviting me to present it again at the Colloquium on Multiple Ways of Knowing, Universidad Nacional de Colombia, Bogotá, October 18–21, 2016.

3 The background of the Nasa struggle goes all the way back to the Conquest, of course. As they put it: "One day in 1535 the Conquest arrived. One night we went to sleep Nasa and woke up Indians. . . . Ever since then we have had no peace or rest." For a recent account of the history of the struggle and its current situation, see "Libertad y alegría con Uma Kiwe."

4 "El desafío que nos convoca," May 28, 2010, http://www.nasaacin.org/el-desafio-no-da-espera.

5 Vilma Almendra, "La paz de la Mama Kiwe en libertad, de la mujer sin amarras ni silencios," August 2, 2012, http://pueblosencamino.org/?p=150. See also Almendra 2017.

6 Written underneath the "Ten Principles of Good Government" posted at the entrances to some autonomous Zapatista communities. See http://www.cgtchiapas.org/denuncias-juntas-buen-gobierno-denuncias/jbg-morelia-denuncia-ataque-orcao-con-arma-fuego-bases.

7 "Libertad y alegría con Uma Kiwe," 9.

8 "Libertad y alegría con Uma Kiwe," 10.

Chapter 4: *Sentipensar* with the Earth

1 The most important works in this regard are Santos 2002, 2007, and 2014.

2 In what follows, I use a number of ES formulations from various sources; I have amended them slightly in some cases, which is why I do not include them as exact quotes. This section is *not* intended as a comprehensive or systematic presentation

of ES; rather, I highlight a few of its principles that will allow me to underscore the ontological implications of the framework.

3 Santos describes the gap between Western theory and subaltern experience as the phantasmal relation between theory and practice. He makes clear that at its most fundamental, this distance is also an ontological distance involving "ontological conceptions of being and living [that] are quite distinct from Western individualism" (2012, 50). These conceptions are what we call "relational ontologies." In a similar vein, Santos takes a clear stand for what he calls "rearguard theories," that is, the political-theoretical work that goes on in the transformative work of social movements. I could not agree more (see, e.g., Escobar 2008 for a similar claim).

4 The Yurumanguí is one of five rivers that flow into the bay of Buenaventura in the Pacific Ocean, with a population of about six thousand people, largely Afrodescendants. In 1999, thanks to active local organizing, the communities succeeded in securing the collective title to about 52,000 hectares (82 percent of the river basin). Armed conflict, the pressure from illegal crops, and mega development projects in the Buenaventura area, however, have militated against the effective control of the territory by locals. Nevertheless, the collective title implied a significant step in the defense of their commons and the basis for autonomous territories and livelihoods.

5 Statement by Francia Marquez of the Community Council of La Toma, taken from the documentary *La Toma*, by Paula Mendoza, accessed May 20, 2013, http://www.youtube.com/watch?v=BrgVcdnwUoM. Most of this brief section on La Toma comes from meetings in which I have participated with La Toma leaders in 2009, 2012, and 2014, as well as campaigns to stop illegal mining in this ancestral territory and the March to Bogotá of November 2014.

6 From the documentary by Mendoza cited earlier.

7 I borrow the term *futurality* from the Australian designer Tony Fry (2012).

8 How to understand the situation in Ferguson, Missouri; Detroit, Michigan; and Buenaventura in the Colombian Pacific; or in so many ethnic minority quarters in the big capitals of the Global North, other than as ontological (often ontological-military) occupations?

9 See, e.g., the powerful and incredibly inspiring work of the Nishnaabeg scholar, artist, and activist Leanne Betasamosake Simpson (2017); see also the excellent collection of writings on the Idle No More movement (Kino-nda-niimi Collective 2014). Many of the articles, stories, and poems can be read on an ontological register.

10 On the economics of happiness and Helena Norberg-Hodge's four-decade-long pioneering work on local economies, see https://www.localfutures.org.

11 Statement by Marcos Yule, Nasa *gobernador*, at the conference "Política Rural: Retos, Riesgos y Perspectivas," Bogotá, October 28–30, 2013. These ideas resonate with the extension of the Ubuntu principle ("I exist because you exist") to the entire realm of the living.

12 Berry developed a well-worked-out statement on the Anthropocene *avant la lettre*. As he put it in *The Dream of the Earth*, "We are acting on a geological and biological order of magnitude. . . . The anthropogenic shock that is overwhelming the earth is of an order of magnitude beyond anything previously known in human historical and cultural development. As we have indicated, only those geological and biological changes of the past that have taken hundreds of millions of years for their accomplishment can be referred to as having any comparable order of magnitude" (1988, 206, 211). One can read his proposal of the Ecozoic era as a purposive response to the Anthropocene.

13 From the newspaper *El Espectador* (Bogotá), July 9, 2012.

Chapter 5: Notes on Intellectual Colonialism and the Dilemmas of Latin American Social Theory

This chapter appeared (in a slightly different form) in a special dossier of the journal *Cuestiones de Sociología* edited by Maristella Svampa, with contributions by Silvia Rivera Cusicanqui, José M. Domingues, Arturo Escobar, and Enrique Leff. See "Debates sobre el colonialismo intelectual y los dilemas de la teoría social latinoamericana," *Cuestiones de Sociología* 14 (2016): 1–32. My thanks to Maristella for inviting me to contribute. http://www.cuestionessociologia.fahce.unlp.edu.ar /article/view/CSn14a09/7368.

1 This was the first question in the call for contributions sent by Maristella Svampa.

2 This was the second question in the call for contributions sent by Maristella Svampa.

3 As Teilhard de Chardin or Maturana and Varela might have said.

4 For a description of the sources of pro-autonomy and communalitarian thought, see chapter 2.

5 This is a brief statement of a complex web of research and trends in fields as disparate as phenomenology, complexity sciences, cognitive sciences, ecology, and postdualist, neomaterialist, and postconstructivist critical theory in general. It is worth noting, however, that Buddhism and the ancient cosmologies of many peoples have explored, and lived, the principle of the inevitable interconnection of everything that exists, the unity of everything alive, including the notion of a living universe in which even so-called inanimate beings have a certain form of consciousness. For a discussion of this concept, see Escobar 2014b, 2018.

6 I am referring to the work of Latin American thinkers such as María Lugones, Rita Segato, Silvia Rivera Cusicanqui, Betty Ruth Lozano, Sylvia Marcos, Aida Hernández, Aura Cumes, Julieta Paredes, Irma Alicia Velásquez Nimatuj, Diana M. Gómez, Xochitl Leyva, Moira Millán, Yuderkis Espinosa, Karina Ochoa, Brenny Mendoza, Karina Bidaseca, Ochy Curiel, Patricia Botero, Juliana Flórez, Natalia Quiroga, Mara Viveros, and Francesca Gargallo, among others; in Europe, but with relevance to Latin America, Claudia von Werlhof, Veronika Bennholdt-Thompsen, Barbara Duden, and Silvia Federici; and in Australia, Ariel Salleh, Wendy Harcourt, Katherine Gibson, and Val Plumwood. An entire multigenera-

tional group of researchers and activists is developing perspectives on the intersection of depatriarchalization and decolonization; many of them are represented in the volume *Tejiendo de otro modo: Feminismos, epistemología y apuestas decoloniales en Abya Yala* (Espinosa, Gómez, and Ochoa 2014). See also Bidaseca and Vázquez Laba 2011. The perspective of matriztic culture, developed by Humberto Maturana and Gerda Verden-Zöller from the concept of the "biology of love," could be linked to some of the critical perspectives on patriarchy in this current (Escobar 2018).

7 There is a major difference between dualist and dual conceptions (e.g., of gender). In dualist views, "men" and "women" exist independently; in dual conceptions, they are categories that coemerge in reciprocity with each other, so that one cannot exist without the other. Some writers relate dual gender to relational ontologies and vernacular practices.

8 See, from the Chiapas group, Kohler et al. 2010; Leyva 2018; from the Manizales group, P. Botero 2015; Botero and Itatí Palermo 2013. Among the collective works that have recently emerged from the UASB doctoral program, see Torres 2012; Walsh 2013, 2017; from the CIESAS group, see Hernández 2016; Sieder 2017; Sierra, Hernández, and Sieder 2013. Finally, from the Popayán group, see Albán 2013; Obando 2016; Quijano 2012; Tobar 2014.

9 From the call for contributions sent by Maristella Svampa.

Chapter 6: Postdevelopment @ 25

Epigraph: From the song "Latinoamérica," by the Puerto Rican group Calle 13, https://www.youtube.com/watch?v=DkFJE8ZdeG8.

Epigraph: From the song "El discurso del progreso" (The discourse of progress), by Juan Vásquez, from the Caquetá region in Colombia. This song tells of the value that place (the *terruño*, homeland or territory) holds for people, and of the importance of defending it, as is occurring in many parts of the world. In Colombia, the rise of *consultas populares* (local referendums) against large-scale mining operations is the clearest political expression of this attachment to place, which is precisely what development and "progress" destroy.

1 The chapter was originally written at the invitation of Aram Ziai of the University of Kassel, in Germany, for the journal *Third World Quarterly*. Thanks to Tatiana Gutiérrez, Andrea Neira, and Eduardo Restrepo for inviting me to publish it in Spanish in *Revista Polisemia*, put out by UniMinuto (Bogotá), no. 22 (August 2017). For a more recent volume on postdevelopment, see Kothari et al. 2019.

2 "The pathology of relatedness has already become less dangerous than the pathology of unrelatedness" (Nandy 1987, 51); ecologically at least, this seems an incontrovertible statement.

3 This idea has found a lucid expression in the domain of insurrectionary politics: "The biggest problem we face is a philosophical one: understanding that this civilization is *already dead.* . . . [Its end] has been clinically established for a century" (Invisible Committee 2015, 29). For this group, it is the West that is the catastrophe—nobody is out to "destroy the West"; it is destroying itself.

4 Wolfgang Dietrich/Wolfgang Sützl, "A Call for Many Peaces," http://www
   .friedensburg.at/uploads/files/wp7_97.pdf.
5 For a brief analysis of Habitat III, see chapter 8.

Chapter 7: Cosmo/Visions of the Colombian Pacific Coast Region and Their Socioenvironmental Implications

1 The following text was originally prepared for the forum "Pacific Vision: Sustainable Territory," organized by *Revista Semana*, the most widely read Colombian
   weekly magazine, the World Wildlife Fund (WWF), and the United Nations Development Program (UNDP), which took place in Bogotá on May 18, 2016. Thanks
   to *Revista Semana*, especially to Marcela Prieto, general director of forums, and to
   Camilo Martínez, project director, for inviting me to participate.
2 As this is not an academic text, I will skip the bibliographic references, with few
   exceptions. Suffice it to say here that the various positions summarized (regarding
   the civilizational crisis, the transitions, the analysis of cosmovisions or ontologies,
   the critique of development, and the pro-autonomy and territorial-ethnic movements) are all well substantiated in a variety of academic and social-movement
   literatures. For a list of these references and a development of these topics, see Escobar 2008, 2014b, 2018.
3 Humberto Maturana and Gerda Verden-Zöller underscore the relationship between patriarchy, the notion of progress, and the culture of hierarchy and control. "The most basic thrill in our patriarchal culture in relation to the notion
   of progress," they argue, "comes from the desire for appropriation or authority,
   mixed up with the conversations [cultures] of hierarchy, growth, control, and subordination" (1993, 95; see chapter 1). Or, to lean on Benjamin's well-known reading
   of Paul Klee's painting *Angelus Novus*, "This storm"—the storm that propels humanity into the future, while the pile of debris left in its wake grows skyward—
   "is what we call progress" (1968, 257).
4 In this connection, see the research on the positive impact of granting collective
   property titles in the Pacific, carried out by Ximena Peña, Juan Camilo Cárdenas, María Alejandra Vélez, and Natalia Perdomo, and presented by Juan Camilo
   Cárdenas at the same Foro Semana about the region: https://papers.ssrn.com/sol3
   /papers.cfm?abstract_id=2932883.
5 These are the words of Álvaro Arroyo at the workshop "Otra economía posible
   para otros mundos posibles" (Another possible economy for other possible worlds),
   organized by the Proceso de Comunidades Negras (PCN), Buga, July 17–21, 2014,
   and cofacilitated by Marilyn Machado (PCN) and myself.
6 There has been a lot of discussion in South America about Buen Vivir as an alternative *to* development, not another form of development but a strategy for getting
   away from all the key notions underlying development, such as growth, dependence on experts and large investments, individualism, and modernity itself. Although both Ecuador and Bolivia have enshrined Buen Vivir as the aim of public
   policy in their current constitutions, little of this has happened in practice. Nevertheless, many grassroots groups insist on Buen Vivir as the goal of their collec-

tive action, as a counterproposal to "development" (Escobar 2014b and chapters 4 and 6 in this book).

7 The sociologist Saskia Sassen (2014) identifies what she calls the logic of the expulsion of people, places, local economies, and the biosphere as a historically unprecedented force in global capitalism, whether it involves the United States, Russia, or China. Extractivism is one of the key forms of expulsion. It appears to me that expulsion and what I call here occupation are parallel and frequently coordinated logics.

8 Betty Ruth Lozano, message sent to the email list of the Grupo de Académicos e Intelectuales en Defensa del Pacifico Colombiano (Group of Academics and Intellectuals in Defense of the Colombian Pacific, GAIDEPAC), July 26, 2017. See also Lozano 2016 and the declaration of the International Forum on Feminicides in Ethnicized and Racialized Groups: Murders of Women and Global Accumulation, Buenaventura, April 25–28, 2016, organized by Betty Ruth Lozano and others: http://forofeminicidios2016.blogspot.com.co.

9 So-called casas de pique—houses in which bodies of murder victims are dismembered and disposed of so as to leave no trail—have become sadly familiar in Buenaventura. This practice has been well documented by human rights organizations. It is no coincidence that these houses apparently popped up just as the large-scale development projects for the port were being rolled out, including plans for evicting many inhabitants from their self-made housing in the low-tide zones.

10 Could anything be more anachronistic for talking about the public policy of a country than the "locomotives of development," a metaphor straight out of the nineteenth century, which constitutes the basis of President Juan Manuel Santos's development plans (2010–18)?

11 ILO Convention 169, the Indigenous and Tribal Peoples Convention of 1989, is an international agreement of the International Labor Organization guaranteeing the rights of indigenous peoples, ratified by almost every country in Latin America and a handful of countries elsewhere in the world. The Afro-Colombian leader Zulia Mena and the indigenous leader Aída Suárez referred in their presentations at the Foro to the need to stop the imposition of development strategies designed by outsiders and for these to give way to forms of development based on communities' own visions and categories. Similarly, Carlos Rosero emphasized the principle of self-directed development agreed to by the Proceso de Comunidades Negras (PCN) since the 1990s for the Region-Territory (control, compensation, integrality, sustainability, self-determination).

12 To avoid repetition, I have left out here a section from the Spanish original that discusses the application of an autonomous-communal codesign strategy for the Pacific, which is similar to the transition autonomous design principles listed in chapter 8 for the Cauca River valley region.

13 Otro Pazífico Posible is the name of an international campaign to defend the Pacific coast region, launched in 2010 by the Grupo de Académicos e Intelectuales en Defensa del Pacifico Colombiano (Group of Academics and Intellectuals

in Defense of the Colombian Pacific, GAIDEPAC), in cooperation with various territorial-ethnic groups from the region, particularly the Proceso de Comunidades Negras (PCN). (Note that because *Pazífico* is spelled with a *z* instead of a *c*, it includes the Spanish word *paz*, which means "peace.") I participate actively in leading this campaign.

14 Idea expressed in his presentation at the same Foro Semana of May 18, 2016. (Bocachico, *Prochilodus magdalenae*, is a freshwater fish found in the rivers of Colombia's Pacific coast.)

15 My thanks to the philosopher Lina Álvarez Villarreal for introducing me to Eboussi Boulaga's work.

16 I am thinking, for example, of the organization Manos Visibles, led by Paula Moreno, an intelligent effort to respond to the sheer marginalization and racism prevailing in Colombian society, but to whose participants we nevertheless must ask these questions, with all the respect they unquestionably deserve. See http://www.manosvisibles.org.

Chapter 8: Beyond "Regional Development"

Epigraph: The song lyrics in the epigraph come from the Valle del Cauca singer Yuri Buenaventura's "Están quemando la caña" (They are burning the sugar cane), on his album *Yo Soy* (Mercury Records, 2000).

1 The Australian anthropologist Michael Taussig wrote a book in 1975 under the pseudonym Mateo Mina (Mina 1975), in which he examined the making of a major free black peasantry after the abolition of slavery in 1851 in a large portion of the Cauca River valley, based on the black model of "traditional" polyculture-based farming on small parcels. This whole process started to break down after the takeoff of large-scale sugarcane cultivation in the first decades of the twentieth century and its consolidation after the 1950s. This important social process is corroborated by the environmental histories of the region (e.g., Mota and Perafán 2010). The important and classic social history of the region by the Universidad del Valle scholar Germán Colmenares (1979) is a must for researchers interested in the area.

2 There are two Spanish-language editions of this book, both under the title *Autonomía y diseño: La realización de lo comunal*, the first published in Colombia in 2016 (Editorial Universidad del Cauca) and the second in Argentina in 2017 (Editorial Tinta Limón). Both are freely available on the internet under a Creative Commons license.

3 My thanks to David López and Douglas Laing for some of the information in this section.

4 According to the excellent study by the anthropologist Arlene Dávila (2015), Latin America, including Colombia, is the world region where globalized-style shopping malls are growing the fastest, a fact that obviously affects a broad range of cultural practices (now more centered on consumption), social structures, and identity processes.

5 In a recent proposal (Escobar 2014b, 2015), I suggest that the process could take off over an initial period of ten years. See the theoretical rationale appended to the project. In this section, "Cauca Valley" refers to the geographical valley (particularly the segment from the Salvajina Dam in Northern Cauca to the northern tip, past the city of Cartago), and not to the administrative jurisdiction (department of Valle del Cauca).

6 Manzini (2015, 89) stresses the importance of the "creative community" in the initial phase in collaborative design experiences.

7 The concept of "lab" is used widely in the design field. While it should be subjected to scrutiny, it is often conceived as an open-ended and action-oriented space, where experiments and alternatives can be imagined and tried out. In the autonomous transition design framework, it has a self-directed, collective character.

8 Manzini's (2015) discussion of design for social innovation is highly useful for thinking about many of these aspects, and so is the entire Transition Design framework spearheaded by Terry Irwin and Gideon Kossoff at Carnegie Mellon School of Design (see, e.g., Irwin 2018). The school's website has a wealth of materials on this framework; see https://design.cmu.edu/tags/transition-design.

9 This was the title of a four-day workshop designed and organized by the PCN that took place in Buga, north of Cali, in July 2013, with the participation of seventy PCN activists from Northern Cauca and the southern Pacific region, as well as a handful of academics, including me. The aim was to discuss the idea that other economies are possible and to give examples of autonomous economic projects in the communities. The workshop was funded by a small grant from the Paul K. Feyerabend Foundation (see http://pkfeyerabend.org/en).

10 For an expanded version of this section, including the work of Harold Martínez, see Escobar 2019.

11 See the "Manifesto de Quito," in Borja and Carrión 2017. This program features seven specific principles to guide a new urbanism—including, in their first principle, "Who makes our cities?," the postulate that "cities are made by people, but they get taken over by the cartel of landowners, developers, and builders," to which we can add governments and the financial sector (312).

12 Koolhaas spares no words in his critique of Junkspace: "Junkspace is political. It depends on the central removal of the critical faculty in the name of comfort and pleasure [and also security, it might be added]. . . . Comfort is the new Justice. Entire miniature states now adopt Junkspace as political program, establish regimes of engineered disorientation, instigate a politics of systematic disarray. . . . *The cosmetic is the new cosmic*" (2002, 183, 190; my italics).

13 Throughout this work, Martínez Espinal explains and clarifies his conceptual framework, which interweaves theories of self-organization, complexity, and emergence; autopoiesis (Maturana and Varela); new orientations in physics and mathematics (quantum physics, complex and nonlinear systems); the Gaia theory; and phenomenology (Heidegger). He introduces concepts that would be

useful in design, such as "wellness, comfort, and playfulness" (*salubridad, comodidad y ludicidad*) as the basic conditions for reconsidering the function of residing that looks at conserving as well as transforming the inhabited place. On Martínez Espinal's large body of work, see the excellent study by the Universidad del Valle architects Verónica Iglesias García and Hilda Graciela Ortíz Moya (2016).

14 See the excellent exhibit on forensic architecture at the Barcelona Museum of Contemporary Art (MACBA), April 28–October 15, 2017: http://www.macba.cat /en/exhibition-forensic-architecture. The exhibit includes a module on the effects of aerial fumigation with glyphosate on the Colombian Pacific rain forest for the supposed purpose of eradicating coca-growing operations.

15 From "lo que vamos aprendiendo con la Liberación de la Madre Tierra," Noviembre del 2015, https://liberaciondelamadretierra.org/en/lo-que-vamos -aprendiendo-con-la-liberacion-de-la-madre-tierra/.

REFERENCES

Acosta, Alberto. 2010. *El Buen Vivir en el camino del post-desarrollo: Una lectura desde la Constitución de Montecristi.* Quito: Fundación Friedrich Eber.

Acosta, Alberto, and Esperanza Martínez, eds. 2009. *El Buen Vivir: Una vía para el desarrollo.* Quito: Abya Yala.

Alayza, Alejandra, and Eduardo Gudynas, eds. 2011. *Transiciones, post-extractivismo y alternativas al extractivismo en el Perú.* Lima: RedGE.

Albán Achinte, Adolfo. 2013. *Más allá de la razón hay un mundo de colores.* Santiago de Cuba: Editorial Oriente.

Almendra, Vilma. 2017. "Una mirada al pensamiento crítico desde el hacer comunitario." In *Pensamiento crítico, cosmovisiones, y epistemologías otras, para enfrentar la guerra capitalista y construir autonomía,* ed. J. Regalado, 61–78. Guadalajara: Universidad de Guadalajara.

Alvarez, Sonia, Evelina Dagnino, and Arturo Escobar, eds. 1998. *Cultures of Politics, Politics of Culture: Re-visioning Latin American Social Movements.* Boulder, CO: Westview Press.

Amin, Ash, and Nigel Thrift. 2017. *Seeing like a City.* Cambridge: Polity Press.

Anzaldúa, Gloria, and Analouise Keating, eds. 2002. *This Bridge We Call Home: Radical Visions for Transformation.* New York: Routledge.

Bachelard, Gaston. 1969. *The Poetics of Space.* Boston: Beacon.

Bélanger, Pierre. 2015. *Going Live: From States to Systems.* New York: Princeton Architectural Press.

Benjamin, Walter. 1968. *Illuminations.* New York: Schocken Books.

Berry, Thomas. 2013. "The Determining Features of the Ecozoic Era." *Ecozoic* 3:4–6.

Berry, Thomas. 1999. *The Great Work: Our Way into the Future.* New York: Bell Tower.

Berry, Thomas. 1998. *The Dream of the Earth.* San Francisco: Sierra Club Books.

Berry, Thomas. 1988. *Evening Thoughts: Reflecting on Earth as Sacred Community.* San Francisco: Sierra Club Books.

Bidaseca, Karina, and Vanesa Vázquez Laba, eds. 2011. *Feminismos y poscolonialidad: Descolonizando el feminismo desde y en América Latina.* Buenos Aires: Ediciones Godot.

Blaser, Mario. 2013. "Ontological Conflicts and the Stories of Peoples in Spite of Europe: Towards a Conversation on Political Ontology." *Current Anthropology* 54 (5): 547–68.

Blaser, Mario. 2010. *Storytelling Globalization from the Chaco and Beyond.* Durham, NC: Duke University Press.

Blaser, Mario. 2009. "The Political Ontology of a Sustainable Hunting Program." *American Anthropologist* III (I): 10–20.

Blaser, Mario, Marisol de la Cadena, and Arturo Escobar. 2014. "Introduction: The Anthropocene and the One-World." Unpublished manuscript.

Bogues, Anthony. 2003. *Black Heretics, Black Prophets: Radical Political Intellectuals.* New York: Routledge.

Bollier, David. 2014. *Think like a Commoner: A Short Introduction to the Life of the Commons.* Gabriola Island, BC: New Society.

Bollier, David, and Silke Helfrich, eds. 2012. *The Wealth of the Commons: A World beyond Market and the State.* Amherst, MA: Levellers Press.

Borja, Jordi, and Fernando Carrión. 2017. "Introducción: Ciudades resistentes, ciudades posibles." In *Ciudades resistentes, ciudades posibles*, ed. J. Borja, F. Carrión, and M. Corti, 17–58. Barcelona: Editorial OOC.

Botero, Andrea. 2013. *Expanding Design Space(s): Design in Communal Endeavours.* Helsinki: Aalto ARTS Books.

Botero, Patricia, ed. 2015. *Resistencias: Relatos del sentipensamiento que caminan la palabra.* Manizales: Universidad de Manizales. https://www.academia.edu/19657178/Libro_Resistencias_version_digital

Botero, Patricia, and Alicia Itatí Palermo, eds. 2013. *La utopía no está adelante: Generaciones, resistencias, e institucionalidad emergentes.* Buenos Aires: CLACSO/CINDE, 2013. https://aasociologia.files.wordpress.com/2013/03/la-utopi_a-no-esta_-adelante-isbn-para-impresion.pdf.

Cabildo Indígena de Guambía. 2007. "Misak Ley: Por la defensa del derecho mayor, patrimonio del pueblo misak." Unpublished manuscript. Territorio Wuampia-Silvia.

Cabildo, Taitas y Comisión de Trabajo del Pueblo Guambiano. 1994. *Plan de vida del Pueblo Guambiano.* Territorio Guambiano-Silvia, Cauca: Cabildo del Pueblo Guambiano.

Campo, María Mercedes, y Otras negras . . . y feministas! 2018. "Los feminismos, si son tales, tienen la tarea de ir a las raíces de las opresiones." Presented at the conference "Corpus Africana: Danser et Penser L'Afrique et ses Diasporas." Toulouse, October 25–November 9.

Castro Gómez, Santiago. 1996. *Crítica de la razón latinoamericana.* Barcelona: Puvill Libros.

Cayley, David. 2005. *The Rivers North of the Future: The Testament of Ivan Illich.* Toronto: House of Anansi Press.

Chandler, Nahum. 2014. *The Problem of the Negro as a Problem for Thought.* New York: Fordham University Press.

Colmenares, Germán. 1979. *Historia económica y social de Colombia.* Vol. 2, *Popayán: Una sociedad esclavista, 1680-1800.* Bogotá: La Carreta.

Comisión Sexta del EZLN. 2016. *El pensamiento crítico frente a la hidra capitalista I.* Mexico City: Ediciones Mexicanas.

Consejo Regional Indígena del Cauca (CRIC). 2008. *Plan de vida regional de los pueblos indígenas del Cauca reconstruir el pasado para vivir el presente y reafirmar el futuro.* Popayán: CRIC.

Coraggio, José Luis, and Jean-Louis Laville, eds. 2014. *Reinventar la izquierda en el siglo XXI: Hacia un diálogo norte-sur.* Buenos Aires: Universidad de General Sarmiento.

Dalai Lama. 1994. *A Flash of Lightning in the Dark of Night: A Guide to the Bodhisattva's Way of Life*. Boston: Shambhala.

Dávila, Arlene. 2015. *El Mall: The Spatial and Class Politics of Shopping Malls in Latin America*. Berkeley: University of California Press.

Davis, Fania, and Angela Davis. 2016. "The Radical World of Healing: Fania and Angela Davis on a New Kind of Civil Rights Activism." *Yes!* February 18, 2016. http://www.yesmagazine.org/issues/life-after-oil/the-radical-work-of-healing-fania-and-angela-davis-on-a-new-kind-of-civil-rights-activism-20160218.

de la Cadena, Marisol. 2015. *Earth Beings: Ecologies of Practice across Andean Worlds*. Durham, NC: Duke University Press.

de la Cadena, Marisol. 2010. "Indigenous Cosmopolitics in the Andes: Conceptual Reflections beyond Politics." *Cultural Anthropology* 25 (2): 334–70.

de la Cadena, Marisol, and Mario Blaser, eds. 2018. *A World of Many Worlds*. Durham, NC: Duke University Press.

Deleuze, Gilles. 1988. *Foucault*. London: Athlone.

Deleuze, Gilles, and Félix Guattari. 1987. *Mil mesetas: Capitalismo y esquizofrenia*. Valencia: Pre-Textos.

Eboussi Boulaga, Fabien. 2014. *Muntu in Crisis: African Authenticity and Philosophy*. Trenton, NJ: Africa World Press.

Eisenstein, Charles. 2018. "Earth Spirituality." In *The Post-Development Dictionary*, ed. Ashish Kothari, Ariel Salleh, Arturo Escobar, Federico Demaria, and Alberto Acosta. London: Zed Books.

Escobar, Arturo. 2019. "Habitability and Design: Radical Interdependence and the Re-earthing of Cities." *Geoforum* 101: 132–40.

Escobar, Arturo. 2018. *Designs for the Pluriverse: Radical Interdependence, Autonomy, and the Making of Worlds*. Durham, NC: Duke University Press. (Published in Spanish as *Autonomía y diseño: La realización de lo comunal* [Popayán: Editorial Universidad del Cauca, 2016].)

Escobar, Arturo. 2015. *"Transiciones*: A Space for Research and Design for Transitions to the Pluriverse." *Design Philosophy Papers* 13 (1): 13–23.

Escobar, Arturo. 2014a. "Response to Knudsen's 'Is Escobar's *Territories of Difference* Good Political Ecology?'" *Social Analysis* 58 (2): 97–104.

Escobar, Arturo. 2014b. *Sentipensar con la Tierra: Nuevas lecturas sobre desarrollo, territorialidad, y diferencia*. Medellín: UNAULA.

Escobar, Arturo. 2011. *Encountering Development: The Making and Unmaking of the Third World*. 2nd ed. Princeton, NJ: Princeton University Press.

Escobar, Arturo. 2010. "Latin America at a Crossroads: Alternative Modernizations, Postliberalism, or Postdevelopment?" *Cultural Studies* (24) 1: 1–65.

Escobar, Arturo. 2008. *Territories of Difference: Place, Movements, Life*, Redes. Durham, NC: Duke University Press.

Espinosa, Yuderkis, Diana Gómez, and Karina Ochoa, eds. 2014. *Tejiendo de otro modo: Feminismos, epistemología y apuestas decoloniales en Abya Yala*. Popayán: Universidad del Cauca.

Esteva, Gustavo. 2015. "Para sentipensar la comunalidad." *Bajo el Volcán* 16 (23): 171–86.

Esteva, Gustavo. 2009. "What Is Development?" Unpublished manuscript, Universidad de la Tierra, Oaxaca.

Esteva, Gustavo. 2005. "Celebration of Zapatismo." *Humboldt Journal of Social Relations* 29 (1): 127–67.

Esteva, Gustavo, Salvatore Babones, and Philipp Babcicky. 2013. *The Future of Development: A Radical Manifesto.* Chicago: Policy Press.

Fals Borda, Orlando. 1984. *Resistencia en el San Jorge.* Bogotá: Carlos Valencia Editores.

Fals Borda, Orlando. 1970. *Ciencia propia y colonialismo intelectual.* Mexico City: Editorial Nuestro Tiempo.

Fehér, Ferenc, Agnes Heller, and Gyorgy Markus. 1986. *Dictatorship over Needs.* Oxford: Blackwell.

Foerster, Heinz von. 1991. "Ethics and Second-Order Cybernetics." Opening address for the International Conference "Systems and Family Therapy: Ethics, Epistemology, New Methods," Paris, France, October 4, 1990. http://ada.evergreen.edu/~arunc/texts/cybernetics/heinz/ethics.pdf.

Foucault, Michel. 1983. "Preface." In *Anti-Oedipus: Capitalism and Schizophrenia,* by Gilles Deleuze and Félix Guattari, xi–xiv. Minneapolis: University of Minnesota Press.

Foucault, Michel. 1973. *The Birth of the Clinic: An Archaeology of Medical Perception.* New York: Pantheon Books.

Foucault, Michel. 1972. *The Archaeology of Knowledge.* New York: Pantheon Books.

Foucault, Michel. 1970. *The Order of Things: An Archaeology of the Human Sciences.* New York: Pantheon Books.

Freire, Paulo. 1970. *Pedagogy of the Oppressed.* New York: Herder and Herder.

Fry, Tony. 2012. *Becoming Human by Design.* London: Berg.

Gago, Verónica. 2015. *La razón neoliberal.* Buenos Aires: Tinta Limón.

Gibson-Graham, J. K. 2002. "Beyond Global vs. Local: Economic Politics outside the Binary Frame." In *Geographies of Power: Placing Scale,* ed. A. Herod and M. Wright, 25–60. Oxford: Blackwell.

Gordon, Avery. 2018. *The Hawthorn Archive: Letters from the Utopian Margin.* New York: Fordham University Press.

Grossberg, Lawrence. 2019. "Cultural Studies in Search of a Method, or Looking for Conjunctural Analysis." *New Formations* 38: 39-68.

Grossberg, Lawrence. 2018. *Under the Cover of Chaos: Trump and the Battle for the American Right.* London: Pluto Press.

Grossberg, Lawrence. 2010. *Cultural Studies in the Future Tense.* Durham, NC: Duke University Press.

Gudynas, Eduardo. 2015. *Extractivismos: Economía, ecología y política de un modo de entender el desarrollo y la naturaleza.* Cochabamba: CEDIB/CLAES.

Gudynas, Eduardo. 2014. *Derechos de la naturaleza: Ética biocéntrica y políticas ambientales.* Lima: PDTG/RedGE/CLAES.

Gudynas, Eduardo. 2011. "Más allá del nuevo extractivismo: Transiciones sostenibles y alternativas al desarrollo." In *El desarrollo en cuestión: Reflexiones desde América Latina,* ed. Ivonne Farah and Fernanda Wanderley, 379–410. La Paz, Bolivia:

CIDES UMSA. http://www.gudynas.com/publicaciones/GudynasExtractivismo
TransicionesCidesII.pdf.

Gudynas, Eduardo, and Alberto Acosta. 2011. "La renovación de la crítica al desarrollo y el buen vivir como alternativa." *Utopía y Praxis Latinoamericana* 16 (53): 71–83. http://www.gudynas.com/publicaciones/GudynasAcostaCriticaDesarrollo
BVivirUtopia11.pdf.

Gutiérrez Aguilar, Raquel. 2017. *Horizontes comunitarios-populares.* Madrid: Traficantes de Sueños.

Gutiérrez Aguilar, Raquel. 2013. "Pistas reflexivas para orientarnos en una turbulenta época de peligro." In *Palabras para tejernos, resistir y transformar en la época que estamos viviendo,* 31–56. Oaxaca: Pez en el Árbol.

Gutiérrez Aguilar, Raquel. 2008. *Los ritmos del Pachakuti.* Buenos Aires: Tinta Limón.

Gutiérrez Borrero, Alfredo. 2015a. "El sur del diseño y el diseño del sur." In *Actas del Coloquio Internacional Epistemologías del Sur,* 745–59. Coimbra: Proyecto Alice.

Gutiérrez Borrero, Alfredo. 2015b. "Resurgimientos: Sures como diseños y diseños otros." *Revista Nómadas* 43: 113–29.

Gutiérrez Escobar, Laura. 2017. "Seed Sovereignty Struggles in an Embera-Chamí Indigenous Community in Colombia." *Alternautas,* Special Issue: *Agribusiness, (Neo) Extractivism and Food Sovereignty: Latin America at a Crossroads,* 4 (2): 27–45.

Hartman, Saidiya. 2019. *Wayward Lives, Beautiful Experiments: Intimate Histories of Social Upheaval.* New York: W. W. Norton & Company.

Hernández, Aida Rosalva. 2016. *Multiple Injustices: Indigenous Law, Women, and Political Struggle in Latin America.* Tucson: University of Arizona Press.

hooks, bell. 2000. *All about Love: New Visions.* New York: HarperCollins.

Iglesias García, Verónica, and Hilda Graciela Ortíz Moya. 2016. *Naturaleza y espacio: La arquitectura de Harold Martínez Espinal.* Cali: Editorial Universidad del Valle.

Ingold, Tim. 2011. *Being Alive: Essays on Movement, Knowledge, and Description.* New York: Routledge.

Ingold, Tim. 2000. *The Perception of the Environment.* London: Routledge.

Invisible Committee. 2015. *To Our Friends.* Cambridge, MA: MIT Press.

Irwin, Terry. 2018. "The Emerging Transition Design Approach." Design Research Society Conference, DRS2018, Limerick, Ireland, June 25–28. https://www.academia.edu/36984858/DRS_2018_The_Emerging_Transition_Design_Approach.

Kino-nda-niimi Collective. 2014. *The Winter We Danced: Voices from the Past, the Future, and the Idle No More Movement.* Winnipeg: ARP Books.

Klein, Naomi. 2014. *This Changes Everything: Capitalism vs. the Climate.* New York: Simon and Schuster.

Kohler, Axel, Xochitl Leyva, Xuno López Intzin, Damián Martínez, Rie Watanabe, Juan Chawuk, José A. Jimenez, Floriano E. Hernández, Mariano Estrada, and Pedro A. Ico Bautista. 2010. *Sjalel Kibeltik, Sts'isjel ja Kechtiki: Tejiendo nuestras raíces.* San Cristóbal de las Casas: CIESAS.

Kongtrul, Jagmon. 2005. *The Great Path of Awakening.* Boston: Shambhala.

Koolhaas, Rem. 2002. "Junkspace." *October* 100: 175–90.

Koolhaas, Rem. 1995. "Whatever Happened to Urbanism?" *Design Quarterly* 164: 28–31.

Kothari, Ashish, Ariel Salleh, Arturo Escobar, Federico Demaria, and Alberto Acosta, eds. 2019. *Pluriverse: A Post-Development Dictionary.* Delhi: Tulika Books/ AuthorsUpFront.

Kyabgon, Traleg. 2001. *The Essence of Buddhism.* Boston: Shambhala.

Larsen, Soren, and Jay Johnson. 2017. *Being Together in Place: Indigenous Coexistence in a More than Human World.* Minneapolis: University of Minnesota Press.

Latouche, Serge. 2009. *Farewell to Growth.* London: Polity Press.

Law, John. 2011. "What's Wrong with a One-World World." Presented to the Center for the Humanities, Wesleyan University, September 19. Published by *Heterogeneities*, September 25, 2011. http://www.heterogeneities.net/publications/Law2011 WhatsWrongWithAOneWorldWorld.pdf.

Law, John. 2004. *After Method: Mess in Social Science Research.* London: Routledge.

Leff, Enrique. 2015. *La apuesta por la vida.* Mexico City: Siglo XXI.

Leyva, Xochitl, ed. 2018. *Prácticas otras de conocimiento(s): Entre crisis, entre guerras.* 3 vols. San Cristóbal de las Casas: Cooperativa Editorial Retos.

Lisifrey, Ararat, Luis A. Vargas, Eduar Mina, Axel Rojas, Ana María Solarte, Gildardo Vanegas, and Anibal Vega. 2013. *La Toma: Historias de territorio, resistencia y autonomía en la cuenca del Alto Cauca.* Bogotá: Universidad Javeriana and Consejo Comunitario de La Toma.

Lorde, Audre. 1984. "The Master's Tools Will Never Dismantle the Master's House." In *Sister Outsider: Essays and Speeches,* by Audre Lorde, 110–14. Berkeley, CA: Crossing Press.

Lozano, Betty Ruth. 2017. "Pedagogías para la vida, la alegría y la re-existencia: Pedagogías de mujeresnegras que curan y vinculan." In *Pedagogías decoloniales: Prácticas insurgentes de resistir, (re)existir y (re)vivir,* vol. 2, ed. Catherine Walsh, 273–90. Quito: Abya Yala.

Lozano, Betty Ruth. 2016. "Violencias contra las mujeres negras: Neo conquista y neo colonización de territorios y cuerpos en la región del Pacífico colombiano." *Revista La Manzana de la Discordia* (11) 1: 7–17.

Lozano, Betty Ruth. 2014. "El feminismo no puede ser uno porque las mujeres somos diversas: Aportes a un feminismo negro decolonial desde la experiencia de las mujeres negras del Pacífico colombiano." In *Tejiendo de otro modo: Feminismos, epistemología y apuestas decoloniales en Abya Yala,* ed. Yuderkys Espinosa Miñoso, Diana Gómez Correal, and Karina Ochoa Muñoz, 335–52. Popayán: Editorial Universidad del Cauca.

Lugones, María. 2010a. "The Coloniality of Gender." In *Globalization and the Decolonial Option,* ed. Walter Mignolo and Arturo Escobar, 369–90. London: Routledge.

Lugones, María. 2010b. "Toward a Decolonial Feminism." *Hypatia* 25 (4): 742–60.

Machado, Marilyn. 2017. "Territorios de resistencia: Minería, ancestralidad y esperanzas." In *Paz para quién? Defensa del territorio y minería en Colombia,* ed. Lina M. Gonzales and Alejandra Duran, 236–58. Barcelona: Editorial Descontrol.

Maldonado-Torres, Nelson. 2008. *Against War: Views from the Underside of Modernity.* Durham, NC: Duke University Press.

Manzini, Ezio. 2015. *Design, When Everybody Designs.* Cambridge, MA: MIT Press.

Martínez Espinal, Harold. 2016. *Del hábito, al hábitat y al habitar.* Cali: Editorial Universidad del Valle.

Massuh, Gabriela, ed. 2012. *Renunciar al bien común: Extractivismo y (pos)desarrollo en América Latina.* Buenos Aires: Mardulce.

Maturana, Humberto. 1997. *Metadesign.* Santiago: Instituto de Terapia Cognitiva. https://www.pangaro.com/hciiseminar2019/Maturana_Metadesign.pdf.

Maturana, Humberto, and Francisco Varela. 1987. *The Tree of Knowledge: The Biological Roots of Human Understanding.* Berkeley, CA: Shambhala.

Maturana, Humberto, and Francisco Varela. 1980. *Autopoiesis and Cognition: The Realization of the Living.* Boston: Reidel.

Maturana, Humberto, and Gerda Verden-Zöller. 2008. *The Origin of Humanness in the Biology of Love.* Charlottesville, VA: Imprint Academic.

Mbembe, Achille. 2017. *Critique of Black Reason.* Durham, NC: Duke University Press.

Maturana, Humberto, and Gerda Verden-Zöller. 1993. *Amor y juego: Fundamentos olvidados de lo humano, desde el patriarcado a la democracia.* Santiago: J. C. Sáez Editor.

Mignolo, Walter. 2000. *Local Histories/Global Designs.* Princeton, NJ: Princeton University Press.

Mignolo, Walter, and Catherine Walsh. 2018. *On Decoloniality: Concepts, Analytics, Praxis.* Durham, NC: Duke University Press.

Mina, Mateo. 1975. *Esclavitud y libertad en el valle del rio Cauca.* Bogotá: La Rosca.

Mingyur Rinpoche, Yongey. 2007. *The Joy of Living.* New York: Harmony Books.

Mota, Nancy, and Aceneth Perafán. 2010. *Historia ambiental del Valle del Cauca.* Cali: Editorial Universidad del Valle.

Moten, Fred. 2018. *Stolen Life: Consent Not to Be a Single Being.* Durham, NC: Duke University Press.

Nandy, Ashis. 1987. *Traditions, Tyrannies, and Utopias: Essays in the Politics of Awareness.* Delhi: Oxford University Press.

Nhat Hanh, Thich. 2008. *The World We Have.* Berkeley, CA: Parallax Books.

Nonini, Donald, ed. 2007. *The Global Idea of the Commons.* New York: Berghahn Books.

Obando, Nancy Lorena. 2016. *Pensando y educando desde el corazón de la montaña: La historia de un intelectual indígena Misak, Avelino Dagua Hurtado.* Popayán: Editorial Universidad del Cauca.

Ogden, Laura. 2011. *Swamplife: People, Gators, and Mangroves Entangled in the Everglades.* Minneapolis: University of Minnesota Press.

Oslender, Ulrich. 2008. *Comunidades negras y espacio en el Pacífico colombiano: Hacia un giro geográfico en el estudio de los movimientos sociales.* Bogotá: ICANH.

Palacios, Elba Mercedes. 2019. "Sentipensar la paz en Colombia: Oyendo las re-existentes voces Pacíficas de mujeres negras afrodescendientes." *Revista Memorias* 38: 131–161.

Paredes Pinda, Adriana. 2014. "Historia y cultura Mapuche." Talk and poetry reading, Institute for the Study of the Americas, University of North Carolina, Chapel Hill, October 31.

Quijano, Olver. 2012. *Ecosimías: Visiones y prácticas de diferencia económico/cultural en contextos de multiplicidad.* Popayán: Editorial Universidad del Cauca.

Randers, Jorgen. 2012. *2052: A Global Forecast for the Next Forty Years.* White River Junction, VT: Chelsea Green.

Restrepo, Eduardo. 1996. "Los tuqueros negros del Pacífico sur colombiano." In *Renacientes del Guandal*, ed. Eduardo Restrepo and Jorge I. del Valle, 243–350. Bogotá: Universidad Nacional/Biopacífico.

Restrepo, Eduardo, and Arturo Escobar. 2005. "Otras antropologías y antropologías de otro modo: Elementos para una red de antropologías del mundo." In *Más allá del Tercer Mundo: Globalización y diferencia*, ed. Arturo Escobar, 231–56. Bogotá: ICANH.

Ribeiro, Gustavo Lins, and Arturo Escobar, eds. 2006. *World Anthropologies: Disciplinary Transformations in Contexts of Power.* Oxford: Berg.

Rist, Gilbert. 1997. *The History of Development: From Western Origins to Global Faith.* London: Zed Books.

Rivera Cusicanqui, Silvia. 2014. *Hambre de huelga: Ch'ixinakax Utxiwa y otros textos.* Querétaro, Mexico: La Mirada Salvaje.

Rozental, Manuel. 2017a. "¿Guerra? ¿Cuál guerra?" In *Pensamiento crítico, cosmovisiones, y epistemologías otras, para enfrentar la guerra capitalista y construir autonomía*, ed. J. Regalado, 93–124. Guadalajara: Universidad de Guadalajara.

Rozental, Manuel. 2017b. "Reconocer y enfrentar la tentación y la transición totalitaria para tomar la decisión de vivir." *Pueblos en Camino*, July 28, 2017. http://pueblosencamino.org/?p=4414.

Sachs, Wolfgang, ed. 1992. *The Development Dictionary: A Guide to Knowledge as Power.* London: Zed Books.

Salazar Bondy, Augusto. 1968. *¿Existe una filosofía de nuestra América?* Mexico City: Siglo XXI.

Santos, Boaventura de Sousa. 2014. *Epistemologies of the South: Justice against Epistemicide.* Boulder, CO: Paradigm Publishers.

Santos, Boaventura de Sousa. 2012. "Public Sphere and Epistemologies of the South." *Africa Development* 37 (1): 43–67.

Santos, Boaventura de Sousa. 2007. *The Rise of the Global Left: The World Social Forum and Beyond.* London: Zed Books.

Santos, Boaventura de Sousa. 2002. *Towards a New Legal Common Sense.* London: Butterworth.

Sassen, Saskia. 2014. *Expulsions: Brutality and Complexity in the Global Economy.* Cambridge, MA: Harvard University Press.

Scott, Felicity. 2016. *Outlaw Territories: Environments of Insecurity / Architectures of Counterinsurgency.* New York: Zone Books.

Segato, Rita. 2016. *La guerra contra las mujeres.* Madrid: Traficantes de Sueños.

Segato, Rita. 2015. *La crítica de la colonialidad en ocho ensayos.* Buenos Aires: Prometeo Libros.

Sexton, Jared. 2016. "Afro-pessimism: The Unclear Word." *Rhizomes* (electronic journal), no. 29. https://doi.org/10.20415/rhiz/029.e02.

Sharma, Kriti. 2015. *Interdependence: Biology and Beyond*. New York: Fordham University Press.

Sieder, Rachel, ed. 2017. *Demanding Justice and Security: Indigenous Women and Legal Pluralities in Latin America*. New Brunswick, NJ: Rutgers University Press.

Sierra, María Teresa, R. Aída Hernández, and Rachel Sieder, eds. 2013. *Justicias indígenas y estado: Violencias contemporáneas*. Mexico City: FLACSO.

Silva, Denise Ferreira da. 2007. *Toward a Global Idea of Race*. Minneapolis: University of Minnesota Press.

Simone, AbdouMaliq, and Edgar Pieterse. 2017. *New Urban Worlds: Inhabiting Dissonant Times*. Cambridge: Polity Press.

Simpson, Leanne Betasamosake. 2017. *As We Have Always Done: Indigenous Freedom through Radical Resistance*. Minneapolis: University of Minnesota Press.

Solé, Ricard, and Brian Goodwin. 2000. *Signs of Life: How Complexity Pervades Biology*. New York: Basic Books.

Taussig, Michael. 1980. *The Devil and Commodity Fetishism in South America*. Chapel Hill: University of North Carolina Press.

Thrangu Rinpoche, Khenchen. 2003. *Je Gampopa's The Jewel Ornament of Liberation*. Crestone, CO: Namo Buddha Publications.

Tobar, Bernardo Javier. 2014. *La fiesta, una obligación: Artesanos intelectuales en la imaginación de otros mundos*. Popayán: Editorial Universidad del Cauca.

Torres, Víctor Hugo. 2012. *Miradas alternativas desde la diferencia y las subalternidades*. Quito: Abya Yala, 2012.

Ulloa, Astrid. 2012. "Los territorios indígenas en Colombia: De escenarios de apropiación transnacional a territorialidades alternativas." *Scripta Nova* 16 (65). https://www.researchgate.net/publication/305681376_Los_territorios_indigenas_en _Colombia_de_escenarios_de_apropiacion_transnacional_a_territorialidades _alternativas.

Ulloa, Astrid. 2011. "The Politics of Autonomy of Indigenous Peoples of the Sierra Nevada de Santa Marta, Colombia: A Process of Relational Indigenous Autonomy." *Latin American and Caribbean Ethnic Studies* 6 (1): 79–107.

Ulloa, Astrid. 2010. "Reconfiguraciones conceptuales, políticas y territoriales en las demandas de autonomía de los pueblos indígenas en Colombia." *Tabula Rasa* 13: 73–92.

Varela, Francisco. 1999. *Ethical Know-How: Action, Wisdom, and Cognition*. Stanford, CA: Stanford University Press.

Varela, Francisco, Evan Thompson, and Eleanor Rosch. 1991. *The Embodied Mind: Cognitive Science and Human Experience*. Cambridge, MA: MIT Press.

Vía Campesina. 2009. "Small Scale Sustainable Farmers Are Cooling Down the Earth." https://viacampesina.org/en/small-scale-sustainable-farmers-are -cooling-down-the-earth/.

von Werlhof, Claudia. 2019. "Matriarchal Alternatives." In *Pluriverse: The Post-Development Dictionary*, ed. Ashish Kothari, Ariel Salleh, Arturo Escobar,

Federico Demaria, and Alberto Acosta, 253–55. Delhi: Tulika Press/Authors UpFront.

von Werlhof, Claudia. 2015. *Madre Tierra o muerte! Reflexiones para una teoría crítica del patriarcado.* Oaxaca: El Rebozo.

von Werlhof, Claudia. 2011. *The Future of Modern Civilization and the Struggle for a "Deep" Alternative.* Frankfurt am Main: Peter Lang.

Walsh, Catherine, ed. 2017. *Pedagogías decoloniales: Prácticas insurgentes de resistir, (re)existir, y (re)vivir.* Vol. 2. Quito: Abya Yala.

Walsh, Catherine, ed. 2013. *Pedagogías decoloniales: Prácticas insurgentes de resistir, (re)existir, y (re)vivir.* Vol. 1. Quito: Abya Yala.

Ward, Jesmyn. 2013. *Men We Reaped: A Memoir.* New York: Bloomsbury.

Warren, Calvin L. 2018. *Ontological Terror: Blackness, Nihilism, and Emancipation.* Durham, NC: Duke University Press.

Warren, Calvin L. 2017. "Black Mysticism: Fred Moten's Phenomenology of (Black) Spirit." *Zeitschrift für Anglistik und Amerikanistik* 65 (2): 219–30.

Weitzman, Eyal. 2017. *Forensic Architecture.* New York: Zone Books.

Weitzner, Viviane. 2017. "Pueblos ancestrales ante la economía cruda y el derecho crudo: Minería, derecho y violencia en Colombia." Doctoral thesis, CIESAS, Mexico City.

Willis, Anne-Marie. 2006. "Ontological Designing: Laying the Ground." *Design Philosophy Papers* 4 (2): 69–92.

Winograd, Terry, and Fernando Flores. 1986. *Understanding Computers and Cognition.* Norwood, NJ: Ablex.

Zea, Leopoldo. 1969. *Filosofía Americana como filosofía sin más.* Mexico City: Siglo XXI.

Italicized page numbers indicate illustrations.

consumerism, 21, 130, 139, 149; individualism and, 38, 105, 117; modernity and, 38, 62, 104, 106; shopping malls and, 146, 151, 152, 172n4; Thich Nhat Hanh on, 113–14

corazonar ("hearting"), 94

Corporación Autónoma Regional del Cauca, 138, 144

cosmovisions, 14, 21, 41, 59; communal, 124–28, 131–35; definition of, 121–22; dialogue of, 120–21, 130, 134; nondualist, 76

critical thought, 31–35, 90–91

"critical traditionalism," 113

cultural studies, xi, 36, 93, 164n11

cybernetics, 7, 22–23

Dalai Lama, 19, 29, 163n6

Dávila, Arlene, 172n4

Dávila, Ximena, 162n4 (chap. 1)

Davis, Angela, xxvii

Davis, Fania, xxvii

decolonization, 30, 36, 84, 133; depatriarchalization and, 93, 169n6; feminism and, xxxii–xxxiii, 9, 92, 162n3; of knowledge, 38; perspectives of, 64. *See also* colonialism

de la Cadena, Marisol, xiii, 24

Deleuze, Gilles, 22, 57, 118; on Foucault, 50–52, 65

depatriarchalization, 30, 93, 128, 169n6

dependency theory, 9, 36, 85

Descartes, René. *See* dualist ontology

development studies, 100, 103, 165n11. *See also* sustainable development

Dewey, John, 22

Dietrich, Wolfgang, 116

Dinas Zape, Luis Enrique, 137

discourse analysis, 8, 49, 50

Dorado, Mauricio, 126

"dreamagination" (*disoñación*), 43–44

drug trafficking, 127, 132

dualist ontology, 23–29, 75, 88, 122–23; Buddhism versus, 18–21; Cartesian, 3–4, 15, 28, 90, 92, 116; cybernetics

and, 22; gender and, 93, 169n7. *See also* ontologies

Duque, Iván, 161n2 (prologue)

Earth~form of life, 8–9, 46–49, 56–64

Earth spiritualities, 14, 20, 21

Earth thought, 33–35, 40–43, 91

Eboussi Boulaga, Fabien, xxvi–xxvii, 133

ecofeminism, 20

Ecozoic era, 43, 57, 77, 79–80, 168n12

Ecuador, 10, 20, 138, 151; Buen Vivir in constitution of, 170n6; development in, 122, 123; leftists of, 37, 38

Einstein, Albert, 5–6, 116, 124

environmentalism, 36, 124–25, 169n2; Earth thought and, 91; episteme of, 56–63; "green economies" and, 6, 63, 104, 125, 129; Marxist, 36; species extinction and, 121; transition discourses of, 77; World Bank and, 5. *See also* climate change

environmental justice, 42, 45, 107, 164n8

epistemes, 36, 49–56, 53; colonial, 88–90; definitions of, 52, 85–86; ecological, 56–63; of modernity, 36, 46–56, 54, 64, 85–90, 87

Epistemologies of the South (ES): Buen Vivir and, 78; ontological dimension of, 69–70; pluriverse and, 69, 76; political ontology and, 80–81; for social transformation, 67–68

Esteva, Gustavo, 10, 44, 98–119

Eurocentrism, 9, 54, 68, 69

Fals Borda, Orlando, 34–35, 85, 161n1 (prologue)

Fanon, Frantz, xxv, 88

Federici, Silvia, 162n3, 168n6

femicide, 124, 127–29, 171n9

feminisms, 20, 36, 84–85, 128; decolonial, xxxii–xxxiii, 9, 92, 162n3; gender fluidity and, 93, 169n7; Marxist, 86

Flores, Fernando, 140–41

Foerster, Heinz von, 22

"forensic architectures," 156

Foucault, Michel, 8, 9, 49–56, *53*, 85–86; biopolitics of, 49, 155; Borges and, 64; Deleuze on, 50–52, 65; on posthuman, 95–96
Freire, Paulo, 34–35, 85
French Revolution, 122
Fry, Tony, 77, 167n7
"futurality," 73, 167n7
FXIW (Nasa musical youth group), 46

Gago, Verónica, 105
Gaia theory, 57, 62, 173n13
Galeano, Eduardo, 152
Galeano, Subcomandante, 29, 159n6
Geddes, Patrick, 156
gender fluidity, 93, 169n7
genetically modified organisms (GMOs), 41, 58
Gibson-Graham, J. K., xx
Glissant, Édouard, 160n11
globalization, 78–79, 110, 127; colonialism and, 15; definition of, 122; Eurocentric, 9; extractivism and, 38–39; global studies and, 75; One-World World and, 60–61, 73–74. *See also* capitalism; neoliberalism
Global Tapestry of Alternatives (GTA), 159n5
global warming. *See* climate change
"Goldman Sachs" approach, 100
gold mining, 42, 59, 73, 81–82, 149
Goodwin, Brian, 23
Gordon, Avery, xxviii
Gordon, Lewis, 160n11
Gramsci, Antonio, xi
Great Transition Initiative (GTI), 77
"green economies," 6, 63, 104, 125, 129. *See also* environmentalism
Grossberg, Lawrence, xi, xxxii
Grupo de Académicos e Intelectuales en Defensa del Pacífico Colombiano (GAIDEPAC), 171n8, 171n13
Guattari, Félix, 22, 118
Gudynas, Eduardo, 43
Guevara, Ernesto "Che," 35
Gutiérrez Aguilar, Raquel, xxi, xxxvi

"habitability," 153–54
Hale, Charles, x
Hall, Stuart, xi, 36
Harcourt, Wendy, 162n3, 168n6
Hartman, Saidiya, xxvii–xxviii, 160n13
Harvard University, 162n4 (intro.)
Heidegger, Martin, 154, 173n13
Heller, Agnes, 108
Henry, Paget, 160n11
heteropatriarchy, 18, *87*, 92, 115, 121; capitalism and, 38, 64, 69, 95. *See also* patriarchy
Hobbes, Thomas, 116
homophobia, xv, 86, 93, 111–12, 169n7
hooks, bell, xxvii
Hopkins, Rob, 77

Idle No More movement, 167n9
Iglesias García, Verónica, 174n13
Illich, Ivan, 98, 101, 103–4, 107–9
Indigenous and Tribal Peoples Convention, xviii
Ingold, Tim, 26, 72
Inter-American Development Bank, 128
interbeing, 19, 21, 162n5
interculturality, 11, 33, 36, 68; autonomism and, 38, 164n11; strategies for, 129–30
interdependence, 7, 24, 30, 92, 125; Buddhist view of, 19–21, 162n5, 168n5; denial of, 18; radical, 4–5, 14–16, 40
International Colloquium of Multiple Knowledges and Social and Political Sciences (Bogotá, Colombia, 2016), 8
International Colloquium on Epistemologies of the South (Coimbra, Portugal, 2014), 9
International Forum on Feminicides of Racialized and Ethnicized People (Buenaventura, Colombia, 2016), xxxii–xxxiii, 127–28, 161n14, 171n8
International Labour Organization (ILO), 129, 135, 171n11
Irwin, Terry, 77, 173n8

James, William, 22
Johnson, Jay, xvii
justice, 117, 152; cognitive, 38, 42, 68; environmental, 42, 45, 107, 164n8; social, 37, 42, 68, 78, 107

Kankuamo people, 16
Klee, Paul, 170n3
Klein, Naomi, xi
knowledge, 35, 38, 67–69; coloniality of, 85, 95; "positive unconscious" of, 52–53; reflexive, 53
"knowledges otherwise," 10
Kogui people, 16, 59, 162n2
Koolhaas, Rem, 152–53, 173n12
Kossoff, Gideon, 77, 173n8

Larsen, Soren, xvii
Latin American critical thought (LACT), 31–35, 90–91
La Toma (Colombia), 126–27; mining in, 42, 59, 73, 81–82
Latouche, Serge, 108
Law, John, 14–15
Leff, Enrique, 62
Left thought, 8, 35–40, 43, 91
Leyva, Xochitl, 93, 164n11, 168n6
Liberation of Mother Earth, 30, 43–49, 114–15; by Nasa, 4, 8–9, 58–59, 66, 137
liberation theology, 36, 43, 85
Life Plans (Planes de Vida), 42, 48; Buen Vivir and, 129; of Misak people, 58
logic, 64; communal, 77; of expulsion, 170n7; rhizome, 71
Lorde, Audre, xviii
Lozano, Betty Ruth, 20, 127–28, 168n6
Lugones, María, 54, 87, 162n3, 168n6

Machado, Marilyn, 120, 170n5 (chap. 7)
Macy, Joanna, 77
Maldonado-Torres, Nelson, 160nn11–12
Malthus, Thomas, 56, 108
Manos Visibles (organization), 172n16
Manzini, Ezio, 173n8

Mao Zedong, 36
Mapuche people, 34, 91
Marcos, Subcomandante, 111, 163n10
Marcos, Sylvia, 162n3
Marley, Bob, xxii–xxiii
Maroons, xxix–xxx, 34, 120
Márquez, Francia, 59, 167n5
Martí, José, 34
Martínez Espinal, Harold, 153–55, 173n13
matriarchal societies, 7, 14, 17–18, 21, 41, 93, 162n3
matriztic cultures, 14, 17–18, 41, 93, 162n4 (chap. 1), 169n6
Matriztic School, 162n4 (chap. 1), 165n12
Maturana, Humberto, 2, 14, 162n4 (chap. 1); on autopoiesis, 55; on "biology of love," 41, 163n8; on patriarchal culture, 17–18, 170n3; Varela and, 22–23
Mbembe, Achille, xxvi, xxx
Mena, Zulia, 171n11
Mexico, 10, 93, 127; development in, 102; muralists of, 164n7; neoliberal policies in, 79; peasant protest movements in, 38. See also Zapatistas
Mies, Maria, 162n3
mingas (collective work groups), 33, 38, 137; para el Buen Vivir, 44, 94; de pensamiento, 8
Mingyur Rinpoche, Yongey, 162n6
Misak people, 40, 42, 58
modern/colonial episteme, 88–90, 92, 124, 165n18
modern/colonial world-system, xii, xxii, 54, 75, 85, 87
modernity, 54, 69; anthropocentrism of, 53; capitalist, 39, 76; consumerist, 38, 62, 104, 106; cosmovision of, 122–24; "death" of, 113; dualisms of, 23–29, 122–23; episteme of, 36, 46–56, 54, 64, 85–90, 87; exiting from, 43–45; logic of, 64; nondominant forms of, 76; as onto-epistemic configuration, 49–56, 53, 54; pathologies of, 125; politics of, xv–xxii
Moisés, Subcomandante, 109

Molano, Alfredo, 81
Moraga, Cherríe, xxvii
Morales, Evo, xxxvi, 39
Moreno, Paula, 172n16
Moten, Fred, xxiv, 160n13
Mother Earth, 57, 90; Uma Kiwe and, 48, 65–66, 157. See also Liberation of Mother Earth; Pachamama
Movement of Afro-descendant Women, 82–83
Muntu philosophy, 15–16, 40, 76, 133

Nagarjuna (Buddhist teacher), 19
Nandy, Ashis, 113, 125
Nasa people, xvii, 4, 57–66; communal world of, 90, 126–27; "cosmoaction" of, 58–60
nature, rights of, 37, 42–43, 78, 92, 130, 143
neoliberalism, 16, 88, 122. See also globalization
new spiritualities, 20, 33
Newton, Isaac, 116
new urbanism, 151–53, 173n11
Nicolas of Cusa, 68
nondualistic philosophy: Buddhism as, 18–21; cybernetics and, 22
Norberg-Hodge, Helena, 167n10
Ñuke mapu. See Mother Earth

oil palm. See palm oil production
One-World World (oww), 14, 15, 38–39; environmental crisis and, 27; globalization and, 60–61, 73–74; monoculture and, 72, 74; pluriverse and, 26, 75–76
ontological turn, xxv, 23–29, 75–76
ontologies, 36; matriztic, 14, 17–18; political, xv–xvii, xxx–xxxiii, 74–75, 78, 80–81; relational, 71–72, 167n3; of separation, 14, 122–23
Organización Nacional Indígena de Colombia (ONIC), 47
Ortíz Moya, Hilda Graciela, 174n13
Oxfam (NGO), xvi, 107

Pachamama, 34, 56, 88; Earth thought and, 91; Muntu philosophy of, 40. See also Mother Earth
Pacific Region-Territory (Colombia), 120–35
Pacific Vision: Sustainable Territory forum (Bogotá, 2016), 10–11, 121, 170n1
Palacios, Elba Mercedes, xxix
palm oil production, 60, 74, 82, 123, 127; for agrofuels, 68, 72, 79
Paredes, Julieta, 168n6
Paredes Pinda, Adriana, 66
participatory action research, 35
Pascal, Blaise, 68
patriarchy, 17–18, 124, 170n3; depatriarchalization of, 30, 93, 128, 169n6; matriarchal societies and, 7, 14, 21, 41, 93, 162n3; violence against women and, 127–28; world-system of, 54. See also heteropatriarchy
Patterson, Orlando, 160n13
"Peacific," 10, 128, 131, 171n13
"pedagogy of cruelty," 18
Peña, Ximena, 170n4 (chap. 7)
pensamiento autonómico. See pro-autonomy thought
pensamiento crítico, 8, 163n1, 165n21
pensamiento de la Tierra. See Earth thought
pensamiento otro (another way of thinking), 34
Perdomo, Natalia, 170n4 (chap. 7)
Peru, 38, 79
pluriverse, xv–xxii, 26–29, 43, 130–31; definition of, 26; Epistemologies of the South and, 69, 76; flourishing of, 30; interdependence of, 7; One-World World versus, 26, 75–76; principles of, 62; transitions to, xvi, 76–80, 128–35
political ontology, xv–xvii, xxx–xxxiii, 74–75, 78, 80–81
postdevelopment, 10, 20, 33, 51, 95, 97–119; rights of nature and, 92; transitions to, 77–78

www.ingramcontent.com/pod-product-compliance
Lightning Source LLC
Chambersburg PA
CBHW031056280326
41928CB00049B/769